Selling Sin

The Marketing of Socially Unacceptable Products

Second Edition

D. KIRK DAVIDSON

PRAEGER

Westport, Connecticut
London

Library of Congress Cataloging-in-Publication Data

Davidson, D. Kirk.
    Selling sin : the marketing of socially unacceptable products / D. Kirk Davidson. —
    2nd ed.
      p. cm.
    Includes bibliographical references and index.
    ISBN 1–56720–612–3 (alk. paper) — ISBN 1–56720–645–X (pbk. : alk. paper)
      1. Marketing—Social aspects.   2. Marketing—Moral and ethical aspects.   3.
Cigarettes—Marketing.   4. Alcoholic beverages—Marketing.   5. Gambling—
Marketing.   6. Firearms—Marketing.   7. Pornography—Marketing.   I. Title.
HF5415.122.D38   2003
658.8—dc21   2003045786

British Library Cataloguing in Publication Data is available.

Library of Congress Catalog Card Number: 2003045786
ISBN: 1–56720–612–3
      1–56720–645–X (pbk.)

First published in 2003

Praeger Publishers, 88 Post Road West, Westport, CT 06881
An imprint of Greenwood Publishing Group, Inc.
www.praeger.com

Printed in the United States of America

Every reasonable effort has been made to trace the owners of copyright materials in this
book, but in some instances this has proven impossible. The author and publisher will be
glad to receive information leading to more complete acknowledgments in subsequent
printings of the book, and in the meantime extend their apologies for any omissions.

Contents

Illustrations

Figures

Tables

Preface

Since the first edition of this book was published in 1996, there have been several quite important developments in the five industries under study. Reporting on these developments has been the first order of business in this revision.

TOBACCO

In 1996, the legal environment began shifting against the cigarette manufacturers, and there ensued a fascinating, protracted case study in the interactive relationship between business and society. A number of informal meetings were held between the companies and representatives of various tobacco-control organizations. In brief, the anti-tobacco advocates wanted much stricter controls on cigarette marketing, funds to finance anti-smoking public service messages, and FDA regulatory authorization. The companies, more than anything else, wanted protection from potentially ruinous punitive damage awards. The hope on both sides was that a tentative agreement could be handed over to Congress to be codified into law.

Agreement was never reached. Some of the tobacco-control representatives were unwilling to put any limits on the potential liability awards, and Congress resented the whole notion that it would not be involved from the beginning in the negotiations.

Once this deal had fallen through, the tobacco companies quickly reached a different agreement in 1998 with the attorneys general of forty-six states and the District of Columbia, settling the ongoing suits to reimburse the states for past health-care expenditures. It took very little time for the companies to agree to pay more than $200 billion over twenty-five years, believing that price increases could provide the necessary money, and the states were very eager to get their hands on this new revenue source.

The years between 1998 and 2003 continued to be difficult for the tobacco business. For the first time the companies suffered serious defeats in various liability lawsuits leading to billion-dollar penalties and fines, while at the same time their popular and profitable premium brands came under severe competitive pressure from discount cigarettes.

ALCOHOLIC BEVERAGES

There have been two significant developments affecting the alcoholic beverage industries. First, the distilled spirits makers, after four or five decades of voluntarily limiting their advertising only to print media, began taking initial steps toward ending that policy. Spot television ads for distilled spirits began to appear in local markets; before long they were appearing also on cable channels. It looked like a major breakthrough when NBC agreed to join with Smirnoff vodka, a product of Diageo, in a carefully orchestrated ad campaign, but the network withdrew at the last minute under serious pressure from Congress and anti-alcohol advocacy groups.

The second development has been the introduction of a new category of malt beverages, often citrus-flavored, and often carrying brand names of the spirits makers—Bacardi Silver, for example. These have been criticized for two reasons. They appear to be aimed at minors because they tend to hide the acquired taste of beer and are more akin to lemon-flavored colas. Also, these products have allowed the spirits makers, Bacardi, in this example, to get their brand names on prime-time network television, promoting these malt-based products.

FIREARMS

In the firearms industry, it was a case of the dog that didn't bark. In spite of the tragic shooting at Columbine High School in Littleton, Colorado, that left fourteen students and a teacher dead, and in spite of gun control groups' efforts to use the tragedy to reinvigorate their efforts, almost nothing happened in the way of increased regulation on the buying, selling, owning, or registration of guns.

GAMBLING

Additional states have added lotteries since 1996, more riverboat casinos have been launched, and more Native American tribes have been granted approval to open gambling operations within their respective states. Beyond that, the development of the Internet has led to the mush-rooming of online gambling operations. These are either patently illegal or are situated outside the borders of the United States and designed to function just within the restrictions of the law and beneath the radar screen of federal authorities.

PORNOGRAPHY

While there may not be much the purveyors of pornography can do to add to the "product," they have been persistent in encroaching on main-stream entertainment media. They have also been very quick and very entrepreneurial in adapting their delivery of adult material to the Internet. For several reasons, this is an ideal medium for pornography, whether soft-core or hard-core: It goes directly to the consumer and bypasses to a large degree the attention of social regulators, it can be enjoyed in the privacy of the viewer's home, and both the buyer and seller can remain anonymous.

But as the French say: *plus ça change, plus c'est la même chose.* In spite of these dramatic changes in the landscape surrounding the marketing of socially unacceptable products, the fundamental tenets and conclusions in the first edition of *Selling Sin* remain solid. Whenever there is a signifi-cant segment of the population that views a company's products as so-cially unacceptable—when society denies legitimacy to that company or industry—the marketers of those products must operate under severe constraints. As spelled out in 1996 and restated in this edition, these mar-keters cannot encourage nonusers to become customers, they do not have access to the same media opportunities as those who are deemed legiti-mate, they must wage serious public relations battles with advocacy groups that are often relentless and powerful, and they are under constant scru-tiny as to how they price and distribute their products. Some things, it appears, never change.

CHAPTER 1

Introduction

Marketing is always an exciting business, and with any degree of success it can be great fun as well. Forget the dry textbook definitions of marketing as "facilitating exchanges." In fact, designing creative products and packages, choosing the perfect markets, selecting a price that will sell the product and yield some profit, and putting together an attention-grabbing promotion strategy—whether for automobiles or toothpaste, milling machines or insurance policies—are all challenging and exciting activities.

The marketing of most products and services takes place within a positive, or at least a neutral, environment. A new personal digital assistant with instant e-mail and Internet connections, a more soothing cough syrup with fewer adverse side effects, even a tasty salad dressing with a lower fat content—all can be exciting to launch and are greeted in the market with a hospitable, perhaps enthusiastic, welcome. Even those products that see only limited success as well as those that have reached their mature stage and so are no longer new and exciting meet with general approval or, at the very least, *no widespread disapproval*.

However, there are several categories of products for which the marketing environment is actually hostile. Hostility in this instance does not stem from the consumers of the products. Quite the contrary, the buyers, and of course the sellers too, are satisfied with the products and enter quite willingly, often enthusiastically, into the exchange transaction. The hostility stems from the fact that some portion of our society, large enough in numbers or in importance to make their views significant, considers these products to be unacceptable.

Although they may be heavily regulated, these products are perfectly legal. Nevertheless, certain segments of the public find them offensive, inappropriate, or harmful for a variety of reasons. And so the marketer faces a quite different environment: outright antagonism. In addition to the predictable and normal marketing challenges and risks such as competitive pressures, changing economic conditions, unexplained consumer whims, incomplete data, and so forth, now the marketer must try to overcome some considerable degree of social and often political or regulatory opposition.

This book examines the marketing problems and challenges of five such product categories: cigarettes, alcoholic beverages, firearms, gambling, and pornography. This list is not meant to be all-inclusive; violent video games, and more recently, fast-food hamburgers join the list. The reader is invited to make additions. Each of these five categories is quite different in many respects, but they have some things in common. They are all consumer products,[1] they are all subject to a high degree of controversy in this first decade of the twenty-first century, and they certainly illustrate the very special problems marketers experience in promoting and selling products that are regarded by some as socially unacceptable.

COMMON ELEMENTS

There are additional similarities among these product categories that need to be recognized.

Legitimacy

One important issue for all five of these product groups, and for the firms that produce and market them, is legitimacy. As the term is used in social science and business literatures, legitimacy means a congruence between the operations of a firm, including the marketing of its products, and the values of the society in which the firm conducts its business.[2] To speak of socially unacceptable products is to say that they have lost to some degree their legitimacy. There is some negative reaction to these products, they are suspect, and in some measure they run against the grain of society's standards.

Each of the five product categories has its own unique problems in terms of legitimacy. Some of the products, as subsequent chapters will explore in greater detail, have followed a cyclical pattern over time—first losing, then regaining, and then losing again their social acceptance. The legitimacy of some products seems to be on a straight downward trend, while for others the trend has turned up.

One sign of lost legitimacy is apparent when society decides to levy a tax on the product; we read and talk about "sin taxes" on tobacco products, alcoholic beverages, and gambling. In the chaotic California gubernatorial recall election of 2003, one of the candidates, Lt. Governor Cruz Bustamante, proposed solving the state's multi-billion-dollar budget deficit by raising the state's already high taxes on cigarettes and alcohol.

Another sign of lost legitimacy is when advocacy groups mount critical attacks on the industry or company in question. Sometimes, however, other businesses will try to distance themselves. For example, motorcycle manufacturer Harley-Davidson recently sued to break an agreement it made a few years ago, in which its name was licensed to be used as a cigarette brand. A growing number of Kimberly-Clark shareholders are pushing each year through shareholder resolutions for that company to stop supplying paper and sheets of reprocessed tobacco to cigarette manufacturers. Manville Corporation sued to break its contract to supply Reynolds Tobacco with glass fibers.[3] In March 2002, H&R Block, this country's largest tax preparation firm, backed away from a controversial relationship with the National Rifle Association when anti-gun advocacy groups got wind of the arrangement and brought pressure to bear on the company through the media.[4]

Other signs of legitimacy lost:

- Pecos Bill, a popular, crusty cartoon character often seen on the Disney Channel, no longer rolls, lights, and smokes cigarettes. Disney has excised these scenes from the cartoons.
- Irish Americans no longer appreciate their characterization as excessive drinkers. They criticized Coors for its promotion of Killian's Irish Red and Budweiser for a St. Patrick's Day commercial featuring *Sports Illustrated* cover model Kathy Ireland.

In every case, it is absolutely critical that the marketers of these products understand what legitimacy means, why it has been lost, and how society either grants legitimacy or takes it away. Only if they grasp these changing patterns in the society around them can they hope to build effective and successful marketing strategies.

Legal Problems

Closely related to the issue of legitimacy is the fact that each of these industries must deal with legal challenges to a far greater extent than most other industries. This is not surprising, given what we have just reviewed regarding the absence of widespread public approval. When a segment of the population becomes concerned about an issue—underage drinking, the potential of a gambling casino opening nearby, the health problems associated with passive cigarette smoke—it is typical for that group of citizens to form one or more advocacy groups as a way to work more actively for their cause. If they are unable to gain complete satisfaction from the firm or the industry involved—which is most often the case—then inevitably they will seek redress either in the courts or through the legislative process. In either case, the industry is soon embroiled in legal wrangling.

The five industries under review in this book are certainly good examples. Litigation against the tobacco companies in recent years has escalated almost beyond imagination, and the industry has been forced to deal with adverse legislative proposals in virtually every state and scores of communities, not to mention at the federal level of government. All three segments of the alcoholic beverage industry are constantly targeted by proposed legislative restrictions. Casino gambling is closely regulated, and taxed, wherever it exists. There are persistent calls for tighter regulations on the distribution and sale of firearms. And pornography, whether in the form of prostitution, adult book stores, or smutty magazines, is always struggling to stay just on the right side of the law. Now the pervasiveness of pornography on the Internet has given birth to an entirely new complex of legal problems.

Rites of Passage

It is instructive to note that all of our five product categories are part of the rites of passage in our society from adolescence to adulthood. This is officially recognized by government regulations setting minimum age restrictions on the purchase or consumption of all five products. One must be eighteen or older to buy cigarettes legally, to buy a rifle or shotgun, to be admitted to a movie that is rated NC-17, and, in theory, to access certain pornographic sites on the Internet. An individual must be at least twenty-one to buy alcoholic beverages, to gamble, or to purchase a handgun. As a society we recognize that these products all represent some risk to our physical, emotional, or psychological health, and we decree that they are adult products and activities. Even though there is a wide divergence in conformance to the law—some parents are more concerned than others whether their teenagers (and even their preteen children) begin to smoke or to drink alcohol—there is nevertheless general agreement that these products and activities are not for children. For young people, therefore, all five products are perceived as part of the growing-up process; a teenager or preteen is likely to think: "When I begin to smoke or drink or when I have a gun of my own, then I will have taken another step toward the exciting and enticing world of being an adult."

These perceptions have special importance because they tempt marketers to pander to adolescent yearnings in product design and promotion tactics. They are also significant because critics of all five product categories are especially sensitive to marketers' attempts to focus on or target children.

Paranoia

Another common element among these five industries is a certain level of paranoia. This should not come as a surprise. Because there is criticism directed at each of these industries from various advocacy groups, managers of the companies involved are often leery of answering questions or granting interviews. A few examples:

- Reynolds Tobacco's cigarette ads are seen by millions of people every day, but the company refused to grant permission to reprint any of its ads in this book, citing company policy as a reason. When I asked the rationale for this policy, a company spokeswoman responded that Reynolds would not be able to insure that only adults saw the reprints. When she was asked how Reynolds could be certain that only adults looked at its thousands of billboards around the country-side and its print ads in magazines like *Sports Illustrated*, for example, the spokeswoman had no coherent answer.

- When I requested an updated financial statement from the National Rifle Association (NRA) by phone, they insisted that since I was not a member, the request would have to be submitted in writing. The financial statement was ultimately sent.

- In a later call to the NRA for this second edition, a spokesperson wanted to be certain that I was "not a reporter" before she gave me information on the organization's position on gun control issues that, it turned out, was already on the NRA Web site.

- When I called a store that sells pornographic magazines and videos, and explained to the manager that I was doing research on the industry, he ended the conversation abruptly and hung up the phone.

Are these five products really sinful, as suggested by the book's title? Are they wicked or evil? Perhaps to the disappointment of the reader it is not the purpose of this book to build a case for the evil or virtue, the faults or merits of any of these product categories. It is sufficient that certain groups in our society believe that these products are unacceptable and inappropriate, and that these groups are large enough or carry enough weight to influence the environment in which the products are marketed.

This book does not engage in or explore to any significant extent the public policy debate that swirls around each of these product categories. Such debate has a long history, dating back to biblical times in the case of some products, and it cuts deep into the social fabric of the United States. Scarcely a day goes by that one cannot find some mention in the popular press of the controversies associated with at least one of these five products. Should the advertising of cigarettes be limited or banned entirely? Should the alcoholic content of beverages be included on their labels? What about interactive gambling via home computers? To what extent shall we accept pornography under the Free Speech Amendment? Does the Constitution *really* guarantee the right of individual citizens to bear arms, and would gun registration abridge that right?

These are challenging, gripping issues that inspire heated arguments, sometimes informed, often simply emotional, from a wide spectrum in our society today. There is a steady flow of books and academic journal articles on these and a myriad of related public policy questions from numerous disciplines: politicians and political scientists, economists, psychologists, sociologists, ethicists, and business managers as well. But public policy is not the purpose here.

This book does not attempt to measure the degree of "sin" involved in each of the five products. Here, too, there is wide variance in our society. For some individuals and advocacy groups, cigarettes are the most harmful of the five products, and so the marketing of cigarettes should be severely restricted. For others, gambling strikes at the moral fiber of our society and, therefore, should be eliminated.

It is interesting that newspapers readily accept advertising for cigarettes, chewing tobacco, beer, wine, hard liquor, and lottery tickets, but are only half as likely to accept ads for X-rated movies or adult book stores.[5] For the purposes of this book, however, it is sufficient that all five products have their critics, and that this level of criticism is important enough to influence the ways in which the products are marketed or should be marketed.

This book has a more modest agenda: to examine how the marketing of these five product categories is challenged, changed, and otherwise made more difficult by their problematic status—their questionable legitimacy—in our society today.

There is a need to set other limits for the subject matter of this book: in time and in geography. The economic, social, and political focus is the United States at the beginning of the twenty-first century. All of our product categories, with the possible exception of firearms, have gone through cycles of public approval and disapproval, and some modest attention is devoted to describing and explaining these cycles. But such historical reviews are ancillary to our primary purpose of exploring the marketing challenges inherent in these suspect products.

Likewise, other countries and cultures for a combination of religious, political, economic, and historic reasons hold different opinions regarding these five subject categories. For any one of the five, it is easy enough to name a country, or perhaps a region, that is more accepting of that product than are we in the United States, and conversely there are countries that hold a more restrictive view. We make no effort here to explore a cross-cultural comparison.

A GENERAL CRITICISM OF MARKETING

Under the best of circumstances, and even when directed at the most benign of products, the concept of marketing carries with it some uncomfortably heavy baggage. There are economists who argue that marketing is for the most part a waste of money and other resources, that it adds no inherent value to the product. Certain psychologists criticize advertising, claiming that it can influence consumers to buy things they neither need nor even want. Marxists see marketing as a capitalist tool to exploit lower income classes for the sake of enhancing the profits of owners and managers. Sociologists and theologians complain that marketing promotes base values such as materialism.

Marketers can and do defend themselves and their profession vigorously from all of these assaults. The point is, however, that there is a muted strain of discord, dissatisfaction, and tension attached to all marketing activities. When these activities are applied to a product category that is problematic itself, for example, cigarettes or "cop-killer" bullets, the usual marketing tactics are especially problematic.

The only widely accepted measurement of marketing success is the extent to which sales increase over some baseline period or over some target or budgeted goal. Success may be measured in unit sales or dollar sales, or it may be measured at some other level of the income statement, for example, gross margin, contribution, or even net profit. But it is growth, improvement, or increase that is the name of the game for marketers and the yardstick for measuring their success.

There is some dissonance here between the business world and the world of academe. The marketing academic community does not embrace this emphasis on continuous growth; in fact, it is the source of some embarrassment. Marketing scholars would prefer to think in terms of creating *value*, establishing *relationships* with customers, or as noted above, *facilitating exchanges.* Such textbook niceties are either totally lost in the day-to-day world of marketing or well hidden in the competitive battles for market share and product success. If increases in sales over last month or last year are the true measure of success, then it is not surprising that marketers focus their considerable skills, their art, and their science on maximizing sales. In the mainstream of product marketing, from aspirin tablets to automobiles, this is generally expected, accepted, and even encouraged by those who see a growing and healthy economy as a result.

CONSTRAINTS ON MARKETING

But what does all this mean for our socially unacceptable product categories? It is a thesis of this book that for such products as cigarettes, alcoholic beverages, firearms, gambling, and pornography, marketers cannot simply seek to maximize sales and profits as they do with soap and shoes. By definition, socially unacceptable products have some organized opposition, and these opposing groups are constantly looking for ways, whether through laws and regulations or through social constraints, to *limit* sales and growth of the products in question. Thus, the challenge for marketers in these industries is made dramatically more complex: They must still produce increases in sales and profitability to satisfy their companies and their companies' stockholders, but at the same time they must try to appease their critics. Sales growth and profitability are widely approved in the marketing of most products. For these five suspect categories, however, they are not universally acceptable goals.

There are at least three other situations in which marketers are constrained from making an all-out effort to maximize sales, and it is important to draw distinctions between these three and the subject of this book, which is the marketing of socially unacceptable products.

"Demarketing"

Philip Kotler and Sidney Levy[6] coined the phrase "demarketing" in 1971 to describe a number of circumstances, such as a temporary shortage of supply, wherein marketers would need to control or shape rather than stimulate demand for a product. Under such circumstances, the role of the marketer is to allocate the available supply of the product among various classes of customers, old and new, large and small, in such a way as to establish or maintain a competitive advantage in the firm's market.

It is readily apparent how this set of circumstances differs from the subject at hand. Shortage of supply is hardly a problem with these socially unacceptable product categories, and so managing or controlling demand to correspond to a limited supply is not the issue.

Green Marketing

A second set of conditions in which marketers must rein in their natural go-for-broke instincts can be classified as a form of "green marketing."[7] As late as the 1960s, for example, it was common for electric utility companies to promote the sale of electric blankets as Christmas presents or to advertise electric dishwashers with the tag line, "Don't be a dishwasher, buy one!" The utility would not profit directly from the sale of either blankets or dishwashers, of course; but the purpose was plain enough—to promote the use and sale of electric power.

Today, after the trauma of two oil embargoes and four decades of education and warnings about the environmental damage done by excessive energy usage, such advertising by utilities is unthinkable. In fact, electric utility companies now routinely advertise messages to their customers on how to *reduce* energy usage. How extraordinary, that marketers should employ the tools and tactics of their trade to actually dampen, rather than stimulate, demand for their product and in fact decrease the amount of product that they sell.

Embarrassing Products

The third situation is one in which discussion of the specific product causes some embarrassment in our society. In this category are products like condoms, feminine hygiene items, and over-the-counter preparations for acne or hemorrhoids. The problem here is not social disapproval, but that we are reluctant to discuss these products freely, and since marketing is all about communication or discussion, this poses a challenge for marketers.

All the constraints exercised by marketers in these three situations are self-imposed limits, but they are quite different from the subject matter of this book. Here, as already noted, we examine certain specific industries in which, because of significant *social disapproval,* marketers must exercise, or ought to exercise, some restraint in the formulation of their strategies and their tactical implementation.

CHAPTER ORGANIZATION

Each of the next five chapters examines, in turn, the industries and/or product categories selected: tobacco, alcoholic beverages, firearms, gambling, and pornography. It is important to gain some sense of the nature of the product and the structure of each industry—how large the industry is, how concentrated or fragmented, how many firms are involved, and some analysis of the nature of competition among the leading firms. It is especially important to explore the origins and nature of the opposition to the products of each industry; in other words, who or what groups disapprove and how strong and widespread the opposition is.

Chapters 7–13 slice through the subject matter in a different direction. They deal with standard marketing textbook topics: selecting target markets, the design of products and packages, promotion strategies, pricing and distribution decisions, public relations, and governmental affairs. Within each of these topics we look at our categories to see how a hostile social, and sometimes political, environment affects the marketing of the product. Chapter 11 is devoted entirely to exploring the use of the Internet by our subject industries.

Chapter 14 draws together our findings and formulates a set of recommendations on the marketing of products under conditions of social disapproval. We have focused on the five categories explored in this book, but they are not the only ones to struggle with the concept of legitimacy. There are others that could be examined today; there undoubtedly will be still others tomorrow. The conclusions and recommendations in the final chapter, however, and the marketing principles that underlie them go beyond these specific problem areas and have widespread applicability across industries and across time.

The research and writing of both editions of this book have taken place over the past ten years. During that period, the controversy over cigarettes and their marketing has been especially intense. For that reason, there is more material in the book on cigarettes than on the other industries. This should not be construed to mean that the lessons to be learned from marketing cigarettes are more important or valuable than those from marketing the other four products.

We are exploring social issues and their impact on, and importance for, marketers. This is a rapidly changing subject. Between the time of writing and publication there will certainly be new developments. For example, in this cyberspace age, there are ongoing efforts to purge the Internet of pornography (or at least limit its availability to children) and to restrict the sale of cigarettes and outlaw gambling via that medium. The resulting regulations or legislation, if any, could be of enormous importance to the industries and companies involved. That this book represents only a snapshot, and therefore an incomplete picture, of a very dynamic process is a necessary limitation the author understands and accepts.

NOTES

1. Technically, gambling and some aspects of pornography are more properly described as services. However, for the sake of brevity and readability, we use the generic term "products."

2. The subject of legitimacy is covered by, among others, Talcott Parsons, "Suggestions for a Sociological Approach to the Theory of Organizations," *Administrative Sciences Quarterly* 1 (1956): 63–85; Charles Summer, *Strategic Behavior in Business and Government* (Boston, MA: Little, Brown and Company, 1980); and Edwin M. Epstein and Dow Votaw, eds., *Rationality, Legitimacy, Responsibility* (Santa Monica, CA: Goodyear Publishing Company, Inc., 1978). For specific coverage of legitimacy and the tobacco industry, see D. Kirk Davidson, "Legitimacy: How Important Is It for Tobacco Strategies?" in *Contemporary Issues in the Business Environment*, ed. Dean Ludwig and Karen Paul. (Lewiston, NY: The Edwin Mellen Press, 1992).

3. Suein L. Hwang and Yumiko Ono, "Companies Crush Out Ties to Cigarettes," *Wall Street Journal*, April 4, 1995, B1; and "Kimberly-Clark Corp. Holders Vote Briskly on Smoking Issue," *Wall Street Journal*, April 21, 1995, B8.

4. From a letter dated March 8, 2002, to the Brady Center to Prevent Gun Violence from H&R Block, and from a press release dated March 12, 2002, from the Brady Center in conjunction with the Million Mom March.

5. Kathleen T. Lacher and Herbert J. Rotfeld, "Newspaper Policies on the Potential Merging of Advertising and News Content," *Journal of Public Policy and Marketing* 13, no. 2 (Fall, 1994): 285.

6. Philip Kotler and Sidney J. Levy, "Demarketing, Yes, Demarketing," *Harvard Business Review*, November–December 1971.

7. Green marketing, also referred to as environmental marketing, can mean different things to different people. At best, it is an attempt by marketers to be sensitive to, and to minimize, environmental damage caused or exacerbated by the marketing process. At worst, it is a mere exploitation of society's environmental interests as a way to sell newly designed or formulated products.

CHAPTER 2

Tobacco: Past and Present

Tobacco is big business. In 2002, some 565 billion cigarettes rolled off the production lines of factories in the United States,[1] generating approximately $35 billion in revenue for the manufacturers. Most sales were made through 625,000 retail outlets, although the business churned out by the country's several hundred thousand cigarette vending machines amounted to 3–5 percent of the total. A review of selected production and consumption figures for recent years is shown in table 2.1.

Although this is unquestionably big business, tobacco no longer enjoys the same standing it once did, either in this country's overall economic picture or in its social fabric; these production and sales figures mask a complex and confusing business picture. U.S. cigarette production peaked in 1996 at 755 billion units, and so the 2002 figure represents a sharp

Table 2.1
U.S. Tobacco Production and Consumption (billions of cigarettes except for per capita figures), 1970–2002

Cigarettes	2002	1992	1981	1970
Produced	565	712	n/a	n/a
Exported	127	206	n/a	n/a
Consumed	420	500	640	536
Per Capita Consumption *	1,775	2,680	3,818	3,969

*For U.S. residents age eighteen and older.
Source: Federal Trade Commission, Cigarette Report for 2001. Issued: 2003. Alcohol and Tobacco Tax and Trade Bureau, http://www.ttb.gov. Issued Sept. 9, 2003.

decline of more than 25 percent in just six years. Cigarette consumption continued its slow but steady decline of 1–2 percent per year, although on a per capita basis the decline has been slightly more pronounced. During the years 1997–2001 cigarette prices (even excluding taxes) increased so rapidly that the major manufacturers were able to more than offset the decline in units and continued to set revenue records. Beginning in 2002, however, this pattern came to an abrupt end. Severe competition limited price increases, and for the first time cigarette producers watched overall revenues on their domestic sales actually decline. The reasons behind this confusing picture are explored in the chapters that follow.

TOBACCO INDUSTRY STRUCTURE

When the federal government prevailed against the old American Tobacco Company in its antitrust suit of 1911, the resulting breakup left the industry in the hands of the so-called Big Six tobacco firms. Liggett & Myers, Philip Morris, P. Lorillard, Reynolds Tobacco, Brown & Williamson, and a much-reduced American Tobacco jockeyed for position and market share in an active, if not fierce, competitive environment. Over the following forty to fifty years as the population grew and cigarette smoking gained in popularity, the tobacco industry, dominated by these Big Six firms, comprised an important segment of the U.S. economy along with steel, autos, utilities, and the other common mainstay industries. Because of heavy consumer promotion in newspapers, magazines, and on billboards these companies, and especially their brands, became household names. A few of the brands, such as Camel and Philip Morris, have remained on the market for decades; others, such as Raleigh, Old Gold, and Spud have long ago faded from the American scene.

Recent Structural Changes

In these early years of the twenty-first century, the structure of the tobacco industry has changed significantly. First, mergers and acquisitions have played their part in this industry as in so many others. Brown & Williamson was purchased in 1927 by the British and American Tobacco Company (BAT), itself a joint venture formed in 1902 by American Tobacco and Imperial Tobacco of Great Britain. In 1968, the Loew's Corporation, an operator of hotels and movie theaters, acquired Lorillard. BAT, through Brown & Williamson, acquired American Tobacco, which had been an operating division of American Brands, Inc. Currently, R. J. Reynolds and Brown & Williamson have agreed to a merger.

Philip Morris now dominates the U.S. industry with a market share of just under 50 percent. Its success has come at the expense of all its competitors. Reynolds Tobacco's share has fallen below 22 percent, Brown & Williamson's share is under 11 percent, Lorillard is at 9.4 percent, Liggett

Table 2.2
Market Shares (%) of Major Cigarette Manufacturers, 1950–2003

	2003	1990	1980	1970	1960	1950
Philip Morris	50	40	31	15	10	11
Reynolds Tobacco	22	30	32	32	32	27
American Tobacco	n/a	7	12	19	25	32
Brown & Williamson	11	10	13	16	10	5
Lorillard	9	8	9	9	11	5
Liggett & Myers	3	3	2	n/a	n/a	19

Source: Vanessa O'Connell of the *Wall Street Journal,* telephone conversation with author, September 22, 2003, and various unpublished papers.

at 2.8 percent, and a growing number of smaller producers account for roughly 6 percent.[2] These companies' market share figures for selected dates over the past thirty years are shown in table 2.2.

The second dimension of change in the tobacco industry is that the major competitors are no longer simply cigarette manufacturers. When it became apparent with the publication of the surgeon general's 1964 report, *Smoking and Health,*[3] that the health issue and the linkage between smoking and cancer were serious long-term problems for the industry, the largest firms set out upon a calculated strategy to diminish the importance of tobacco in their operations. Company officials were concerned not only about the appearance of producing and selling a product that was coming under criticism and attack; they worried also about the eventual effects on their firms' sales and profits. Their strategy was developed along two parallel tracks, both of which were designed to deemphasize the tobacco part of their businesses. First, the cosmetic or public relations part of their problem was addressed by subtle name changes. Reynolds Tobacco became RJR, and American Tobacco became American Brands. Philip Morris Tobacco was renamed Philip Morris Industries, and in April 2002, the company renamed itself Altria. Critics immediately blamed the company for trying to conceal its most profitable business, but the company argued that it was simply recognizing the fact that its business had evolved beyond that of a purely tobacco company.[4] Henceforth, brand names would be used by the companies to sell cigarettes, while corporate names would be kept on a higher plane, so to speak, where they were less likely to be sullied by the direct association with tobacco, cigarettes, and smoking.

The strategy's second track involved merging with or acquiring companies, usually consumer product firms, in totally different industries to diminish the importance of tobacco. Philip Morris acquired Miller Brewing and later General Foods, Kraft, and Jacob Suchard, the European chocolate and confectionery company. Reynolds merged with Nabisco although in 2000, under the pressure of declining share in its tobacco busi-

ness and the need for cash, it sold Nabisco to Philip Morris and returned
to being primarily a tobacco company. American Brands diversified into
distilled spirits, life insurance, golf clubs, hardware, and office products.
Liggett became part of the Brooke Group, and Lorillard, as noted, became
a part of Loew's. The irony of this aspect of the companies' strategy has
been that while the sale of tobacco products has significantly declined as
a percentage of each firm's total sales (R.J. Reynolds excepted), cigarette
manufacturing and marketing has become increasingly profitable so that
each company's *profits* are still heavily dependent on tobacco.[5]

Although dollar sales of tobacco products set a record in 2000, the tobacco industry no longer has the distinction and prominence it had in the
1950s. By 1984, it had been melded into the "Food, Beverages, & Tobacco"
group by Standard & Poor's *Industry Surveys*, and in a *Business Week* review of industry prospects for 1995, tobacco was not even mentioned.[6]

Cigars, Pipe Tobacco, and Snuff

Over the decades leading up to World War II, due largely to the wide-
scale introduction of more efficient cigarette-making machinery that rapidly increased the supply and lowered prices, cigarette smoking became
the dominant form of tobacco use. Cigars, pipe tobacco, snuff, and chewing tobacco together account for less than 5 percent of tobacco use today.

As the smoking of cigarettes became more popular because it was more
convenient and more economical, cigar smoking declined dramatically. In
1920, the adult male in the United States smoked an average of 269 cigars,
but by 1993 that figure had dropped to only 26.[7] Cigar manufacturers and
distributors have searched for a strategy that would allow them to hang
on to their dwindling $100–200 million business. Marketers now are trying
to create, or perhaps re-create, an aura of prestige by positioning cigars
as the smoke for the wealthy, the famous, and the socially prominent.
Pictures of a dapper Winston Churchill with a long cigar clamped firmly
in his teeth as well as images of more recent cigar-smoking celebrities such
as George Burns and Dave Letterman are used in cigar advertising. Distributors and retailers have teamed with expensive hotels to host special
dinners at which customers are encouraged to enjoy a fine cigar or two
right at the table, rather than being banished to the outdoor sidewalk.
Premium cigar smokers even have their own slick magazine, *Cigar Aficio-
nado*, which boasts a readership of more than one hundred thousand and
counts Rolex watches, Cartier jewelers, and Cadillac automobiles among
its advertisers.

Marketers of snuff and chewing tobacco have also felt compelled to
change their product's image and their target customer, but certainly have
not tried to move toward the upscale market. Thirty years ago, snuff customers typically were older men in rural areas. Currently, the target cus-

tomer is a young male looking for a macho, slightly hip image. This targeting switch has paid off; snuff has the distinction of being the only segment of the tobacco industry in the United States that has continued to grow. This also means big business and big profits for the United States Tobacco Co. division of UST Inc., which controls at least two-thirds of this country's $1.1 billion snuff market.

Smokeless tobacco also has its own specific health concerns to deal with: principally cancer of the lips, mouth, and tongue, as well as receding gums and other oral problems. It must deal also with social proscriptions—the inevitable spitting that accompanies the use of snuff and chewing tobacco may be acceptable in the baseball dugout but almost nowhere else; and so it seems unlikely that snuff could ever seek a more affluent, prestige market.

Because cigarettes now dominate the tobacco industry's sales, we focus for the most part on the problems surrounding cigarette marketing.

THE TOBACCO TRADE

The concern about tobacco as a socially unacceptable product has focused attention almost entirely on the cigarette manufacturers. Largely ignored have been the hundreds of thousands of retail establishments that actually sell the product to consumers. This final link in the marketing distribution channel and the decision making of the retailer in this set of issues deserves attention.

The majority, roughly 55 percent, of all cigarettes are now sold by convenience stores. Supermarkets account for approximately 13 percent, and cigarette discount stores for perhaps 12 percent. The remaining share of the retail cigarette market is split among a wide variety of small food stores, liquor stores, and miscellaneous outlets.

Cigarettes are a very significant revenue- and profit-generating category for most of these retail groups. For the typical convenience store, a surprising 36 percent of its in-store sales come from tobacco products,[8] up from 26 percent in 1993. There are other positive attributes of this product category for retailers: margins and turnover are both relatively high, there is no concern about markdowns or spoilage, and perhaps most important of all, the category requires very little floor or shelf space, which means that sales and gross profits per square foot of store area or per linear foot of shelf space are very high.

Because cigarette advertising is almost exclusively the purview of the manufacturers and because this is the most visible and easily criticized of marketing activities, cigarette retailers have been spared the harsh spotlight of advocacy attention. When confronted with the question, "Should the store consider giving up the sale of cigarettes, given what we now know about their effects on health?" retailers will most often respond that they are simply meeting the wants and needs of their customers, and that the customers themselves should wrestle with the health concerns and whether or not to smoke. Only one or two retailers, responding to a survey conducted by this author, were honest enough to admit that they feared the loss of business that might result if they gave up this significant product category.[9]

Retailers' actions, however, belie their words. The argument made by retailers that they sell cigarettes only because their customers demand them loses its persuasiveness when one considers the number of stores that have developed their own private label brands. For retailers, a move into private-label merchandise is a tried-and-true tactic for expanding the sales potential and maximizing the profit potential from a given product category. Typically, the margins for retailers on private-label merchandise are considerably higher than on nationally advertised brands.[10] This is a far cry, however, from merely satisfying customer expectations. It is one thing to offer Marlboro, Winston, Camel, and the other highly advertised major brands for sale to customers who come into a store expecting to find them; it is quite another to also offer Cavalier, Plain Wrap, Scotch Buy, Jacks, and other private labels and generics because of the handsome profit potential.

SOCIAL CHANGES

The change in tobacco's role in the U.S. economy has been significant over the past fifty or sixty years, but it pales in comparison to the change in *social* perception regarding smoking. Go back in time a generation or two, and the contrast between the social acceptance of smoking, then and now, is extraordinary. Consider several examples:

- Tune in to an old movie on late-night television, vintage 1940s or early 1950s, and one of the most jolting surprises is that the *heroes* all smoke. Not just the tough guys like Humphrey Bogart; even the suave sophisticates like Fred Astaire and William Powell used a cigarette as an important prop—lighting it, holding it, and smoking it in a way that affirmed their worldliness and social position. The same was true of the female stars. In contemporary films, however, when an actor or actress lights a cigarette, it is almost a guaranteed signal that he or she is either an outright villain or at least morally suspect.

- During World War II, the military distributed free cigarettes to the troops on the battlefronts as a standard part of their K ration meals. Film clips from the war showed soldiers in the field, even hospital orderlies, offering lighted cigarettes to their wounded companions, and we were touched by these caring, tender gestures. But in 1990, the Department of Defense was forced to *apologize* for its mistake in distributing millions of cigarettes donated by Philip Morris and Reynolds Tobacco to U.S. forces in the Persian Gulf, admitting that this was contrary to the department's policy of discouraging smoking.

- In a 1933 issue of *Fortune* magazine, Mrs. Hamilton Fish, Jr., a *doyenne* of New York's social elite, appeared in an advertisement for Camel cigarettes. The copy of the ad tells us that Camels occupied a place at Mrs. Fish's table along with her museum-quality American amber glass and her memorable asparagus and eggs Hollandaise. Mrs. Fish is then quoted as saying, "My debutante daughter really taught me to smoke. . . . When my two younger children grow up and start to smoke, Camels will probably be their cigarette, too."

So many aspects of this ad would simply be out of the question now: the association of smoking with social prominence, the anticipation and approval of one's children becoming smokers, and certainly the juxtaposition of a pack of cigarettes and a gourmet meal on a table set with fine china and glassware.

The demographics of the smoking population represent another change in how smoking fits into early twenty-first-century U.S. society. The average age of smokers has been dropping steadily as older smokers die or give up the habit and teenagers take it up. Traditionally, men have smoked in greater numbers than women, but the figures have been shifting as the percentage of men who have quit smoking has exceeded the percentage of women who have stopped. In 1965, roughly 52 percent of men smoked, compared to 34 percent of women. But by the close of the twentieth century, the overall smoking rate had dropped to around 25–26 percent, almost equally divided between men and women.

It appears that education has also played a part in whether or not a person gives up smoking. Those with the most education, that is, with college or postgraduate degrees, are more likely to have given up smoking than those who have not completed high school, and that likelihood declines steadily with each drop in level of education. Not surprisingly, since years of education and household income are related, those with higher incomes have quit smoking in larger numbers, relatively speaking, than those with lower household incomes, and once again, there is a stair-step drop at each stage as incomes decline.

NATURE OF TOBACCO COMPETITION

During most of the last forty years, competition among the manufacturers and marketers of cigarettes has been hard fought. Because per capita consumption of cigarettes in the United States has been cut almost in half between 1963 and 2000 and total consumption has been declining by roughly 3 percent per year since 1980, maintaining sales levels, especially unit sales levels, has been a signal achievement. In such a mature and, of late, declining industry, the battle for market share is intense. But the prize is enormous. Every one-tenth of a percentage point of market share gained or lost represents $40–50 million of extraordinarily profitable revenue.

Heavy promotion of brand names and new product introductions have been the preferred strategies of cigarette marketers for the past several decades. Significant, and uncharacteristic for such a mature industry, has been the absence of serious price competition, at least until the 1990s. All of the major U.S. cigarette marketers were content to limit their jousting to the advertising arena (new images, different messages, more effective blend of media) and to introducing new brand names as well as line extensions (longer lengths, lower tar, different packaging, new filter technologies). Prices actually rose during this period by an average 10 percent per year, which, along with increasing productivity in the factories and low tobacco leaf prices, were more than enough to offset declines in unit consumption and in fact record steady gains in the already hefty cigarette margins and profits. This scenario of growing profitability in a declining industry is unusual and served to take some of the edge off the otherwise sharp level of competition.

Rise of Discount Brands

Until recently, cigarette makers did not compete to any meaningful degree on the basis of price. Nationally advertised "premium" brands dominated the market. Some writers attribute this to the level of brand loyalty in cigarettes, the highest level for any major consumer product category (figure 2.1). Other reasons suggested are the relatively low price of the item and the fact that because smoking is an addictive habit, smokers are less interested in shopping around for the best price.

The first significant private-label effort in the cigarette industry was

Figure 2.1
Brand Loyalty by Product Category

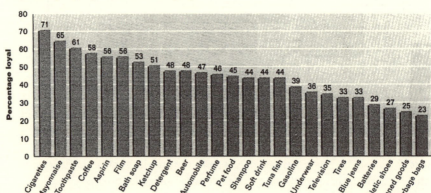

Source: Wall Street Journal.

initiated in 1979 by Liggett and Myers in collaboration with Topco, a major tobacco distributor. These generic cigarettes gained some success with supermarket chains that sold them under their own labels at 40¢ to 70¢ less than the premium brand prices. Five years later, Reynolds introduced Doral, its own branded generic label, selling for 25¢ to 40¢ below premium prices, to fill in the gap. Other cigarette manufacturers began responding by introducing their own lower priced brands, and then in 1988, yet another category was created with the introduction of Pyramid cigarettes, the first subgeneric label, selling at a discount of 70¢ to 90¢ under premium prices. However, in spite of this proliferation of brands below the premium price level, by 1990 their total still accounted for only 16.7 percent of industry dollar sales.[11]

By that year, however, a number of forces coalesced to change the situation:

- Premium cigarettes had continued to increase their prices faster than the rate of inflation. The average price of all brands skyrocketed from less than 50¢ per pack in 1975 to $1.55 in 1990, and by 1993, the price on the leading brands had broken through the psychological barrier of $2 per pack. By 2002, the retail price of major brands had doubled again to nearly $4 per pack, pushed upward by increased taxes and the costs of dealing with tobacco's legal challenges.
- Cigarette excise tax increases in many states had contributed to the upward pressure on prices.
- The number of smokers in the United States continued to shrink.
- An economic recession made everyone, even smokers, more conscious of looking for ways to save money.
- Private-label merchandise was enjoying increasing success in other consumer product categories from soft drinks to detergents.
- Wide margins and handsome profits at the manufacturing end opened the door to potential price cutters.
- So much of the expense structure of the premium brands was being spent on marketing and promotion that big cuts in these categories allowed for major price reductions.
- At the heart of the matter, there is very little, if any, difference in quality between premium and discount cigarettes; in other words, the premium brands added very little value. Once a smoker switched to a less-expensive label, there was little reason to switch back to the high-priced brand.

With all of these forces at work, sales of discount brand cigarettes accelerated dramatically between 1990 and 1993 when they reached roughly 30 percent of industry dollar volume and a full 36 percent of unit volume.[12]

Marlboro Monday

A healthy portion of the increase in private label and generic cigarette sales had come at the expense of Philip Morris's Marlboro brand, by far the dominant cigarette brand in the United States. Since taking over as chairman and CEO of Philip Morris in August 1991, Michael Miles had watched helplessly as his company's perennial cash machine and life-blood, Marlboro cigarettes, lost market share steadily from almost 26 per-cent to just over 22 percent a year and a half later. This meant a decline of 366 million packs just from 1991 to 1992; at an estimated profit of 55¢ per pack, this was a serious loss. It wasn't the only problem for Miles, the first non-tobacco man to head Philip Morris. Some of the company's most prominent food brands had also fallen on hard times: Maxwell House ground coffee was off 16.6 percent, Kraft cheese slices were down 8.6 percent, and Kool-Aid had declined 3.8 percent. For a company that had grown accustomed to double-digit growth, these were unacceptable fig-ures, and stockholders had already seen the value of their holdings drop by 20 percent.[13]

By the spring of 1993, the pressure on Miles reached the point where he was forced to take desperate action. On Friday, April 2, Philip Morris announced it would cut the price of its Marlboro brand by 20 percent, thus narrowing by about 40¢ the spread between the retail price of its premium brand and the private labels.

This was desperate action indeed. The company subsequently an-nounced a series of worker layoffs and other expense reductions that would partially offset the drop in revenue and margin expected as a result of the price cut. At the same time, the company actually increased its advertising budget in an attempt to regain the lost market share points.[14] Philip Morris executives estimated the result of these actions would re-duce the company's pretax profits by 40 percent, or $2 billion. On the Monday following the announcement, Philip Morris shares dropped 23 percent, a paper loss of nearly $13 billion in just one day.

Predictably, in such a tightly knit industry, Marlboro's competitors were quick to follow the leader's price cut, and so stocks of the other tobacco manufacturers—RJR, American Brands, Brooke Group (Liggett), and Loew's (Lorillard)—were dumped as well. Nor did the effects stop with the tobacco industry. Investors worried that the same combination of forces could affect leading brands in other consumer product categories. Would the price spread between Coca-Cola, Heinz, and Hershey products and their private-label competition need to be narrowed? The worry and confusion sent those stocks and other leading consumer goods producers down as well. All told, on "Marlboro Monday" the Dow Jones average suffered a 68½-point drop, close to 20 percent, largely attributable to Miles's decision.

The action at Philip Morris and its aftereffects are of interest to man-agement scholars as well as to marketers. On the day the price cut was announced, the company put the best possible face on its action by pre-dicting that eventually Marlboro would regain its lost market share and that higher sales and profits for the company would be the result. Philip Morris did, in fact, suffer through a full four quarters of terrible earnings reports. This, along with confusion and dissension in the company's executive suite as to whether or not the firm's tobacco and food divisions should be split, led to Miles's sudden resignation in June 1994, and his replacement by William Murray and Geoffrey Bible, two solid tobacco executives. In retrospect, Miles's sacking seems especially ironic in that his decisions and predictions seem to have been good ones; a little more than a year after Marlboro Monday, the brand had actually regained and even surpassed its previous market share high, and Philip Morris's sales and profits were once again on the rise.

A PATTERN OF CHANGE FOR TOBACCO

Even more than for most industries, a changing environment has become the norm for the tobacco companies: change in industry structure, in the nature of competition within the industry, in the demographic makeup of the market for cigarettes, and an extraordinary, dramatic shift in society's perception of smoking, from embrace to rejection. Perhaps this last change should not be so surprising. For more than three hundred years tobacco use has followed a roller-coaster course through periods of strong disapproval, always to emerge with improved social standing. As early as 1604, King James I of England uttered the oft-quoted condemnation of smoking as a "custome loathsome to the eye, hatefull to the Nose, harmfull to the brain, dangerous to the Lungs," reason enough, he hoped, to justify his onerous tobacco taxation plan.

An anti-smoking movement flourished in the United States around the end of the nineteenth century, and by 1909, twelve states had enacted restrictive legislation. However, World War I brought an end to that particular cycle of disapproval. Until that time, cigarette smoking had been a custom or habit primarily of the wealthy. The dynamics of men from all walks of life serving together in the armed forces helped to increase the popularity of cigarettes at all income levels.[15]

Not until the middle of the twentieth century did society's views on smoking begin another downward cycle, a slide that has yet to run its course. This time, the trigger mechanism was scientific evidence regarding the effects of smoking on health.

There has always been a health concern. As noted, King James hated the habit although his beliefs were unsupported, as far as we know, by any scientific data available at the time. Chronic smokers throughout the centuries have suffered from a hacking cough and raspy throat among other symptoms. In the late 1940s, comedian Phil Harris popularized a humorous song that told of an inveterate smoker who, after puffing himself to death, kept Saint Peter waiting at the Golden Gate while he finished one last cigarette.

Cigarette advertising from 1930 through 1950 dealt with this common perception in a number of ways. In countless magazine ads during this period Reynolds Tobacco assured readers that "More doctors smoke Camels than any other brand." Chesterfield cigarettes from Liggett and Myers, one of the top-selling brands of that period, enlisted singers Bing Crosby and Perry Como to endorse its cigarettes, implying that Chesterfields couldn't possibly be harmful to the throat if the most popular singers of the day smoked them. And the same ad in which Mrs. Hamilton Fish, Jr. assured *Fortune* readers that the flavor of Camels was "so smooth and rich and they are very mild," went on to promise, "And even if you smoke a great deal, Camels never get on your nerves."

The smoker's cough and other related ailments of the throat, nose, sinuses, and lungs were common enough symptoms, but it was not until 1953, when researchers at the Sloan-Kettering Cancer Institute linked the incidence of lung cancer with smoking, that the health effects of tobacco use gained solid scientific backing. Then it was another eleven years before U.S. Surgeon General Luther L. Terry placed the weight of the federal government squarely on the side of the health advocates, officially recognizing in his landmark 1964 report that "cigarette smoking is a health hazard of sufficient importance in the United States to warrant appropriate remedial action."[16] Over the ensuing four decades, the health issue has snowballed and developed a momentum of its own. In 1993, the Environmental Protection Agency gave the movement another huge push forward when it officially recognized secondhand tobacco smoke as a cause of cancer in nonsmokers.[17]

No longer is the tobacco-and-health issue just the subject of catchy tunes. Throughout the 1990s the issue brought together a powerful army of opponents who, while often divided in their choice of tactics, all shared the long-run goal of limiting the sale—and therefore the marketing—of cigarettes.

THE OPPOSITION

Once the surgeon general's report, ranking smoking as a national health concern, appeared in 1964, an entirely new set of anti-smoking forces was set in motion and has continued to gather momentum. These forces fall into three categories.

First, the major health organizations in the United States—the American Medical Association, the American Cancer Society, the American Heart Association, and the American Lung Association—all endorsed the surgeon general's conclusions, thereby adding scientifically and socially respected weight to the anti-tobacco movement. Each of the groups has organized its individual programs and task forces to promote better health through smoking cessation. Probably the most widely publicized has been the Cancer Society's "Great American Smokeout Day," an annual, one-day promotional blitz encouraging smokers to give up smoking for at least the day to prove to themselves that they can do it, with the hope that their abstinence will continue.

The second prong of this three-pronged anti-smoking movement has been the emergence of a plethora of advocacy groups. Some adopted catchy acronyms such as ASH (Action on Smoking and Health), formed in 1968 and one of the most pugnacious in pushing anti-smoking efforts through litigation; GASP (Georgians against Smoking Pollution); DOC (Doctors Ought to Care); and STAT (Stop Teenage Addiction to Tobacco). Others, such as the Advocacy Institute and the Coalition on Smoking OR Health, itself an advocacy arm of the Cancer, Heart, and Lung organizations, have proven to be highly effective in disseminating information and generating grass-roots involvement.

The Infant Formula Action Coalition (INFACT), the same advocacy group that gained worldwide attention by organizing and promoting the Nestle boycott in response to the infant milk formula controversy of the early 1980s, announced in April 1994, "a major international boycott" against Philip Morris's non-tobacco products such as Velveeta cheese, Jell-O, Post cereals, and Miller Lite beer.[18] INFACT stated it was protesting the company's marketing of cigarettes to children and young people around the world, and threatened a boycott of RJR Nabisco's food products as well.

Advocates have been active at the local level also. Members of The Lost Chords, a group of former smokers within the American Cancer Society who have had a laryngectomy as a result of cancer of the larynx and who now speak through handheld voice transmitters, visited teenagers' classrooms to preach their anti-smoking message and present a very visible sign of the effects of smoking.

The Tobacco Divestment Project, formed in 1990, has urged colleges and universities to purge cigarette manufacturers from their investment portfolios. Harvard University and the City University of New York agreed to do so. The activist organization is applying the same pressure on the pension holdings of hospital and insurance companies, arguing that these industries especially represent a conflict of interest when they ally themselves in any way with tobacco.

Especially effective has been the Campaign for Tobacco-Free Kids, which under the leadership of William Novelli and Matthew Myers, focused attention on what has become the tobacco industry's Achilles' heel—the marketing of cigarettes to teenagers and preteens and the frightening statistics of teenage addiction to tobacco.

The growth and success of advocacy groups had a snowballing and self-reinforcing effect during the 1970s and 1980s. As the number and size of the groups continued to grow, their influence has been more widely felt, more smokers have abandoned the habit, this success has made anti-smoking activity more attractive and fun, scientific data has emerged on new health problems related to tobacco use, more government regulations have appeared, and so on.

Government Regulation and Influence

The third prong in this trident of forces in opposition to the tobacco industry has been government itself, in all of its many forms and at all of its many levels. Quite naturally, the federal government has been the locus of most of the attention and most of the controversy.

The Surgeon General's Office

Luther Terry, as surgeon general in 1964, may have given his name and the imprimatur of his office to the now-famous report of that year, and may have been the first and highest-ranking federal official to so directly criticize smoking, but he was certainly not the last. C. Everett Koop, who held the surgeon general's post from 1981 through 1989, was a tireless battler against the effects of smoking on health, in spite of being a member of the generally pro-tobacco Reagan administration. While in office, he became a very high-profile tobacco critic, his white-bearded face becoming almost a symbol of the anti-smoking movement, and he helped lay the groundwork for much of the work done by other agencies. Since leaving public office, Koop has continued his battle as a private citizen. His successors in the office have maintained the anti-smoking stance, although with somewhat less passion and effect.

Bureau of Alcohol, Tobacco, and Firearms (BATF)

In 1951, the responsibility for collecting tobacco excise taxes was assigned to the Alcohol Tax Unit of the Treasury Department, which assumed even more duties over the succeeding years and took on its current name, the Bureau of Alcohol, Tobacco, and Firearms (BATF) in 1972. The bureau collected approximately $7.8 billion in tobacco taxes in 2002, and its enforcement activities are aimed primarily at the prevention of smuggling and of the sale of black market (i.e., untaxed) cigarettes. Its function in the industry-government complex is certainly important, but not particularly controversial, since it is less involved in policymaking.

Federal Trade Commission (FTC)

The FTC's role with the tobacco industry has been to monitor cigarette advertising and other marketing tactics and to enforce compliance with the laws and regulations related to marketing, including price competition. As anti-smoking criticism has gained momentum over the past two decades and because much of it has been directed at the companies' advertising campaigns, as we shall explore in a later chapter, the FTC has played an increasingly important role.

Tax Policy

Although the cigarette companies complain at every opportunity about the stifling effects of the combined federal and state excise taxes, it is relatively modest compared to that of most other industrialized countries. In 1994, Canada experimented with a $2.50 per pack tax, high at the time, in an effort to reduce smoking, but this had to be dramatically rolled back to reduce the smuggling of cigarettes from the United States into Canada. Most Western European countries also have higher tobacco tax rates.

The controversy over the level of federal taxes on cigarettes grew intense during the 1994 debate over health-care policy in the United States. President Clinton's first proposal included a federal tax of $2 per pack to help pay for expanded medical care, and in the process to cut down on the consumption of cigarettes. Predictably, the lobbying efforts of the tobacco industry pulled out all the stops to quash even the idea of such a major increase. Other affected industries rallied to the cause; the convenience store association predicted massive layoffs because of reduced sales if taxes were to go that high. With each subsequent version of the administration's health plan, the tax rate proposal was reduced, and the entire argument became moot when health-care reform failed completely. Nevertheless, this is another source of pressure from the federal government on the industry. As one of the "sin" taxes, with new health issues appearing regularly, and with fewer smokers each passing year, many politicians find this tobacco excise tax an easy one to support.

State excise taxes vary widely. To no one's surprise, the chief tobacco growing states have the lowest excise tax rates on cigarettes; in 2003, Virginia's rate was still only 2.5¢ per pack, Kentucky's 3¢, and North Carolina's 5¢. At the other end of the scale, by that same date, New Jersey had increased its excise tax to $2.05 per pack, and fourteen other states plus the District of Columbia all had imposed excise taxes on cigarettes of $1 a pack or more.[19] A New York City excise tax of $1.50 brings the price of a pack of cigarettes there to $7 or more. Outside New York, however, local tobacco taxes are relatively minor; they account for only about 1.5 percent of the total tobacco excise taxes collected.

Environmental Protection Agency (EPA)

Unlike a number of other federal agencies, the EPA does not have a long history of involvement in the complex of issues surrounding tobacco,

smoking, and cigarettes. But in January 1993, the agency became an over-
night major player in the conflict when it issued its long-delayed report
identifying environmental tobacco smoke (ETS), better known as secondhand tobacco smoke, as a "Class A" carcinogen in the same league with
asbestos, arsenic, and benzene, and the cause of some three thousand lung
cancer deaths in the United States per year.

The report has stirred controversy both within and outside the agency.
In 1986, when Surgeon General Koop named "passive" smoking as a cause
of lung cancer in nonsmokers, the EPA had been developing its data and
conclusions throughout the years of the first Bush administration. The
final report was withheld due to internal concerns that the statistical evidence was too thin to support the findings. As the Clinton team was about
to assume control, outgoing EPA administrator William Reilly released
the report. To no one's surprise, the tobacco industry cried "Foul!" and
has waged a relentless campaign against the findings ever since. The main
area of criticism cited by tobacco executives and some others as well is
that "normal" statistical rules were not followed. For example, the results
of several studies were blended together to arrive at the widely publicized
figures on lung cancer deaths, and the traditional standard of 95 percent
certainty was allegedly relaxed to 90 percent.

Occupational Safety and Health Administration (OSHA)

The EPA report on the dangers of secondhand tobacco smoke brought
OSHA and the Labor Department into the controversy more forcefully
than before to eliminate smoking as a workplace hazard. This set loose a
succession of proposals for banning smoking in an estimated six to ten
million of the nation's workplaces. No longer would smoking be prohibited just on the shop floors of factories but in all office buildings as well.
No longer would segregated smoking areas be permitted, because OSHA
pointed out that the smoke from such areas was recirculated into the rest
of the building. Smoking would be prohibited in the entire building unless an area or room had its own distinct ventilation system, which was
financially out of the question in most circumstances. This led to the now-
familiar clusters of smokers, subject of cartoons and documentaries, gathered near the entrances to office buildings sometimes braving the snow
or rain. The tobacco industry fought back for a few years with advertising
and public relations campaigns that claimed the proposals were too strict
and inclusive—for example, that individuals would not even be allowed
to smoke at home if they used their homes as their offices. However, these
industry efforts have been abandoned as the non-smoking public has welcomed the smoke-free work environments and as smokers have accepted,
albeit with some reluctance, their banishment to restricted smoking areas.

The EPA report and subsequent OSHA initiatives helped set off a flurry of additional bans on smoking. Smoking would no longer be permitted in most military facilities, nor in most federal office buildings. California, Maryland, Vermont, Washington, and other states pushed for tough regulations extending the smoking ban. Texas now prohibits smoking even in the state's prison facilities, affecting one hundred thousand inmates and fifty thousand employees, even though doing so will cut roughly $1 million from the prison commissaries' sales. The action, taken by the Texas Board of Criminal Justice, was motivated in part by concern for the prisoners' health and also to rein in the health-care costs that smoking imposes on the state's prison system. At least sixteen other states have also banned prison smoking.

Many of the nation's cities also jumped on the smoking ban bandwagon. On his way out of office in 1993, Mayor Tom Bradley of Los Angeles signed an ordinance prohibiting smoking in the city's 7,000 restaurants. Shortly thereafter in New York City, incoming Mayor Rudolph Giuliani endorsed a proposal that would make his city one of the toughest in the country on smoking restrictions, banning smoking even in such outdoor settings as Yankee Stadium, certain Central Park concerts, and the playground areas of day-care centers.[20]

The private sector has not been left behind. One out of every three firms had banned smoking by 1990, and 60 percent of companies imposed some restrictions.[21] McDonald's prohibits smoking in all its company-owned restaurants and urges its franchisees to do likewise. Wendy's, Arby's, Taco Bell, and Dairy Queen moved in the same direction. U.S. airlines were initially skittish for competitive reasons about imposing unilateral bans on smoking, fearing that their passengers would simply switch to another carrier, although they have gladly followed government restrictions affecting the entire industry. The Civil Aeronautics Board required nonsmoking sections as early as 1973, and Congress banned smoking on all domestic flights of six hours or less in 1990. However, Delta took a more aggressive approach; it announced in full-page ads that as of January 1, 1995, it would prohibit smoking on all of its flights worldwide, trumpeting the fact that it would be the only U.S. airline to do so. Delta thus became the first major airline to realize that a totally smoke-free environment could become a competitive advantage, indicating the dramatic shift in societal perceptions and nonacceptance of smoking in the United States.

Food and Drug Administration (FDA)

Given what we now know about the relationship between smoking and health, it is something of a paradox that tobacco is specifically exempted from the FDA's regulatory powers. Legend has it that when the agency was established in 1906, crucial support from tobacco state legislators was gained only when tobacco was removed from the official list of drugs in the U.S. Pharmacopoeia.[22] In recent years, however, the agency has been thrust into the controversy because of the growing concern about nicotine and its use as an addictive drug. Also, under the aggressive leadership of Dr. David Kessler, the FDA uncovered evidence, from its own research and from work done by the tobacco companies themselves, that nicotine is in fact addictive and that the cigarette makers have "manipulated" the amount of nicotine that goes into each brand of cigarette.

This has put the agency in something of a bind. Under Kessler, and with the support of advocacy groups and anti-tobacco members of Congress, the FDA sought to exercise control over the content and the marketing of cigarettes. But if it proves that nicotine is in fact addictive, then it would have no other recourse under current law than to ban the sale of cigarettes so long as they contained nicotine. However, with the problems surrounding the prohibition of alcoholic beverages in the 1920s very much in mind and with the number of smokers in the United States still exceeding fifty million, the FDA does not want even to consider a general ban on smoking.

Lawsuits and the Master Settlement Agreement

Throughout the early 1990s, various state, county, and local governments put pressure on the tobacco industry by increasing taxes and restricting the areas where smoking was permitted. The industry found it increasingly difficult to fight so many "brushfire" battles far away from the halls of Congress in Washington, where its long history of political contributions guaranteed it at least a certain understanding and sympathetic treatment. The results during those years:

- Idaho and Michigan increased their excise taxes on cigarettes.
- Utah eliminated smoking in workplaces, including restaurants.
- Vermont considered a bill to ban the use of cartoon characters (e.g., Joe Camel) in advertising for addictive products like cigarettes.
- Pitkin County, Colorado, eliminated smoking from all workplaces, including bars and restaurants.
- Erie County, New York, banned tobacco advertising in Rich Stadium, home of the Buffalo Bills professional football team.
- The Licking County Health Department in Ohio restricted smoking in all public places and workplaces.
- East Brunswick, New Jersey, banned cigarette vending machines.
- Andover, Massachusetts, prohibited smoking in all workplaces and restaurants.
- Foster City, Healdsburg, Long Beach, Pinole, Salinas, Santa Clara, Tracy, and Vallejo, all in California, adopted ordinances protecting nonsmokers in workplaces and/or restaurants.

The pressure on the industry increased by a quantum leap, however, when in 1994, Mississippi's attorney general, Michael Moore, teamed up with plaintiff's lawyer, Richard Scruggs, to devise a new legal assault on the cigarette companies. The new strategy: rather than focus on the harm done to individual smokers, Mississippi sued the tobacco companies to recover the billions of dollars spent by the state in extra health-care costs caused by cigarette smoking. The ambitious attorneys general from a number of other states quickly followed suit. Suddenly the companies were faced with the frightening prospect of defending themselves against the resources of state governments. When subpoenaed documents revealed examples of collusion among the companies to suppress information about the harmful effects of smoking, they signed in 1998 what has come to be known as the Master Settlement Agreement (MSA) with forty-six states and the District of Columbia. Under the settlement, the cigarette companies would pay $206 billion to the states over a period of twenty-five years and in addition agreed to a number of advertising restrictions, including a ban on the use of cartoon characters, a ban on using their brands on promotional merchandise such as T-shirts, and limitations on the sponsorship of sporting events.

What an extraordinary situation! Has there ever been such an embattled industry—facing the combined opposition of citizen advocacy groups, respected national health organizations, and a wide assortment of governmental agencies at all levels? Can any industry under such pressure hope to survive? Even before the new wave of lawsuits and the Master Settlement Agreement, *Business Week* on its July 4, 1994, cover asked the question directly, "Tobacco: Does It Have a Future?"

The cigarette manufacturers might all have ceased to exist before now save for two factors. Smoking is, after all, an addictive habit. Some one-third of the smokers in the United States try to quit in any given year, and fewer than 10 percent succeed. This gives the product unusual staying power in the marketplace.

Second, the production and sale of cigarettes is *enormously* profitable. For the year 2002, Philip Morris earned an extraordinary 26.5 percent operating profit on its domestic tobacco sales. This was actually an improvement over the previous years in spite of mounting price competition from discount cigarette brands, the tangle of lawsuits and expensive settlements, declining numbers of smokers, a weakened position in Congress and in the halls of state legislatures, and the unrelenting pressure from respected and sometimes strident advocacy groups. Such an income stream and cash flow from this controversial product category provide both the resources and certainly the incentive for the companies to stay the course in spite of the opposition.

WILL THE PENDULUM SWING BACK?

In these early years of the new century, it is hard to imagine that tobacco could ever return to the prominence and respectability—or the legitimacy—that it once commanded as one of the foundations of the U.S. economy. Advocacy groups are no less adamant about protecting the health of the public—especially the health of the nation's children—from the dangers of smoking. And the MSA certainly did not put an end to the industry's legal problems. That agreement merely resolved tobacco's disputes with most of the states. Individual civil suits continued. While many of these were unsuccessful because juries decided that the individual smokers had been properly warned about the risks of smoking, a handful of trials on the West Coast proved a dangerous exception. In Oregon and California, juries in five lawsuits had awarded plaintiffs several billion dollars in compensatory and punitive damages.[23] Each of these success stories would prompt attorneys to find other likely plaintiffs, and if enough of these suits were to survive the appeals process, the financial viability of these once proud and dominant companies could well be jeopardized. Indeed Reynolds, long saddled with a burdensome debt structure, was forced to sell its profitable international cigarette business to Japan Tobacco and, as noted above, is planning a merger with Brown & Williamson. Even mighty Philip Morris/Altria, in spite of its highly profitable operations, claimed that it could not afford to post the $12 billion bond required by an Illinois judge while the company appealed an adverse ruling in a lawsuit over the marketing of its "light" cigarettes. Altria threatened to declare bankruptcy, and the bond was reduced to $6 billion.[24] Regardless of the outcome of specific suits still being litigated or appealed, neither Altria nor the other tobacco companies could count on the absolute invulnerability they had enjoyed for decades.

Nor could they count on steadily rising profits. In the second quarter of 2003, Altria's profits declined slightly, while the net income for Brown & Williamson and Reynolds fell by 27 percent and 67 percent, respectively. for the latter company this prompted a cut of 40 percent of its workforce. All three companies were suffering severe price competition. Gone, at least from the surface, was the aura of arrogance and power that had been the hallmark of these companies and of the entire industry.

But it is far too early for the opponents of tobacco to declare victory. Smoking rates are no longer declining as fast as a few years ago. There are indications that teenagers, and now preteens, are experimenting and taking up the smoking habit just as readily as the cohorts that preceded them. Smoking among ten- to eighteen-year-olds is still perceived as a way to gain instant maturity and status. The manufacturers are stepping up their efforts to produce a less harmful product, which, if the companies were successful, could alleviate much of the social antagonism and pressure in some future decade. Most important, however, is that any product as profitable as cigarettes with a devoted (or addicted) market of fifty million consumers generates its own rationale and staying power. Tobacco has experienced turbulent times in the past and has managed not just to survive but actually thrive.

NOTES

1. U.S. Department of Agriculture, www.ers.usda.gov/briefing/tobacco/tables.htm.

2. From a telephone conversation with Vanessa O'Connell of the *Wall Street Journal*, September 22, 2003.

3. U.S. Department of Health, Education, and Welfare, *Smoking and Health, Report of the Advisory Committee to the Surgeon General of the Public Health Service*, Washington, DC: Government Printing Office, 1964.

4. Gordon Fairclough, "Not Just Smokes: Philip Morris Renames Itself 'Altria Group,'" *Wall Street Journal*, November 16, 2001, A3.

5. A further irony is that the combination of tobacco with other businesses is now seen as detrimental to shareholder value, and Philip Morris has been urged by some shareholders to split off its tobacco operations.

6. *Business Week*, January 9, 1995, 72.

7. Tim Triplett, "Interest in Premium Cigars Rises despite Anti-Smoking Crusade," *Marketing News*, March 14, 1994, 14.

8. NACS, *2000 State of the Industry* (Alexandria, VA: National Association of Convenience Stores, 2001).

9. D. Kirk Davidson, "Camels, Coffee, and Cauliflower: An Application of Stakeholder Theory" (paper presented to the Academy of Management, Dallas, TX, August 14–16, 1994).

10. One convenience store chain reported, for example, that it purchased private-label cigarettes from the manufacturer at less than half the cost of major brands and realized 50 percent more gross margin dollars per carton on its own brand compared to Marlboro, Camel, and the other nationally advertised brands. With the introduction of private-label cigarettes and the volume generated at the lower retail prices, the chain was able to triple the gross margin dollars produced by this product category. In addition, foot traffic more than doubled in the stores, which presumably led to increased sales of other merchandise as well.

11. Raymond M. Jones, "Strategic Management in a Hostile Environment" (doctoral dissertation, University of Maryland, 1993), 64.

12. Eben Shapiro, "Price Cut on Marlboro Upsets Rosy Notions about Tobacco Profits," *Wall Street Journal*, April 5, 1993, A1.

13. Laura Zinn and Sunita Wadekar Bhargava, "Even Philip Morris Feels the Pull of Gravity," *Business Week*, February 15, 1993, 60. Also, Shapiro, "Price Cut on Marlboro."

14. Kevin Goldman, "Philip Morris to Put Its Ad Money Where Its Price Cuts Are," *Wall Street Journal*, April 6, 1993, B3.

15. This was the same period of time, sometimes referred to as the first wave of regulation, when the tobacco industry, or more specifically the American To-

bacco Company, was hit with antitrust charges and split into several competing companies.

16. U.S. Department of Health, Education, and Welfare, *Smoking and Health*.

17. The health concerns introduced in the 1950s and 1960s generated the second wave of tobacco regulation, and the effects of secondhand smoke have created the so-called third wave.

18. "Activist Group Is Planning Boycotts of Tobacco Firms," *Wall Street Journal*, April 13, 1994, B9.

19. The state budgetary problems had become so severe by 2003 that even the tobacco-growing states were considering increasing their tobacco excise taxes as a way to ease their financial problems.

20. Steven Lee Myers, "Tough New Limits on Smoking Sought for New York City," *New York Times*, March 17, 1994, A1. Richard Turner, "Smoking Ban Signed by Mayor in Los Angeles," *Wall Street Journal*, June 25, 1993, B-5A. See also Kara Swisher, "The Puff Is Rebuffed," *Washington Post*, March 26, 1994, G1.

21. Fred Williams, "Firms' Rules Put Smokers Under Fire," *USA Today*, May 1, 1990, B1. *Wall Street Journal*, July 10, 1990, A1.

22. Maurine B. Neuberger, *Smoke Screen: Tobacco and the Public Welfare* (Englewood Cliffs, NJ: Prentice-Hall, Inc., 1963), 50.

23. Gordon Fairclough, "Philip Morris Loss in Oregon Court Is Fifth Straight West Coast Setback," *Wall Street Journal*, March 25, 2002, B8.

24. This talk of bankruptcy posed a serious threat to all forty-six states and the District of Columbia that were parties to the Master Settlement Agreement. Ever since the MSA was signed in 1998 the states had become dependent on the billions of dollars flowing into their coffers from the tobacco industry, much of it from Altria. Had Altria declared bankruptcy, this flow would have been cut in half. As a result, the states found themselves in the awkward position of arguing for more favorable treatment for Altria, their longtime foe in courts, to preserve the flow of MSA funds.

CHAPTER 3

The Alcoholic Beverage Industries

The joys and woes of alcoholic beverages have been a part of the history of mankind from our earliest days. In what surely must be the very first example of alcohol's detrimental effects, we are told in Genesis 9:20–21 that Noah, once his ark found land on Mount Ararat and the waters had receded, became a "husbandman, and he planted a vineyard: And he drank of the wine, and was drunken; and he was uncovered in his tent." Two of his sons, Shem and Japheth, were thoughtful enough to cover their father with a garment, but they were circumspect and kept their faces "backward, and they saw not their father's nakedness."

Much later, wine gained what would seem to be an unequivocal seal of approval when it became the subject of Jesus' very first miracle at the wedding in Cana. Not long after, Saint Paul advised both Timothy and Titus that holiness requires that men and women be "not given to much wine," although he did prescribe the use of "a little wine for thy stomach's sake and thine often infirmities." This mild inconsistency is explained in notes as follows: "While the Biblical references to the use of wine are, on the whole, contradictory, it is certainly true to say that its abuse is condemned universally both in the Old and New Testaments."[1]

No literary character better captures this ambivalence toward alcohol—its pleasures and its harmful consequences—than Shakespeare's Falstaff, who was at once lovable, wise, and loyal, yet at the same time could be gross and self-destructive when under the influence, as he often was, of strong drink.

In the nineteenth century, contradiction and controversy still swirled around the use of alcoholic beverages. In Europe, an English translation of the ancient Persian poet Omar Khayyam included wine in the most idyllic of settings, "A book of verses underneath the bough, a jug of wine, a loaf of bread, and thou," while the Frenchman Brillat-Savarin unwittingly coined one of the industry's earliest advertising slogans when he wrote, "A meal without wine is like a day without sunshine."

In the United States, however, a different picture of alcoholic beverages was emerging, and controversy was apparent from the very beginning. James Oglethorpe banned the sale of distilled spirits from the state of Georgia, although this early restriction lasted only nine years. In the nineteenth century Neal Dow, sometimes called the "Father of Prohibition," was a tireless campaigner against the sale and consumption of alcohol and succeeded in his home state in pushing through "The Maine Law," at the time the most stringent statute against the sale of sprits anywhere in the world. Dow was indefatigable on the subject. Wounded and taken prisoner by the Confederates during the Civil War, he managed to antagonize both his captors and his fellow Union prisoners with his tirades on the evils of alcohol. Dow continued his crusade after the war. He was instrumental in founding the Prohibition Party in 1869 and was the party's candidate in the presidential election of 1880, but he received less than 1 percent of the country's votes.[2]

In spite of such isolated efforts, consumption of rum, whiskey, brandy, gin, hard cider, wine, and beer grew rapidly as distilling and brewing techniques improved. Later in the nineteenth century a powerful movement gathered momentum with its sole purpose being the prohibition of all alcoholic beverages in this "nation of drunkards."[3] This movement was largely inspired and promoted by religious-related organizations: the Women's Christian Temperance Union, the Anti-Saloon League (sometimes referred to as the Church in Action against the Saloon), the Good Templars, and others.

A passionate "lecturer on sociology and temperance" at Syracuse University in 1917 described the situation as follows:

God has no earthly enemy so inveterate as King Alcohol. No such assaults have been made on the Church as those waged by the saloon. There never was a more clearly defined issue between right and wrong than in the conflict between the Church and the saloon during this modern temperance revolution. . . . The saloon breeds disease, disorder, misery, crime; the Church brings order, health, happiness and virtue. The Church represents the idea of God the best, the saloon the idea of the devil the worst in the world. The saloons are the breeding place of all kinds of vice and crime. In them the thieves, the gamblers, the murderers, the gunmen, the ballot-box stuffers, grafters, purchasers of law, the debauched and the ruined find their education and protection, and from them go out to prey upon society.[4]

After such a diatribe, can there be any doubts as to the social unacceptability of alcoholic beverages and the places that serve them?

It was convenient for those opposed to drinking alcohol in any form to speak of "the liquor trust," but this phrase had little basis in fact and was used more to capitalize on the antitrust sentiment of the times. In fact, one reason for the growth of the Anti-Saloon League and the acceptance of its teachings was that the distillers and brewers were battling among themselves. Consumers' tastes and preferences were changing and moving away from spirits more toward the purchase of beer. Rather than joining forces with the spirits companies, the brewers chose instead to draw a sharp distinction between the two, position beer as the drink of moderation, and look to market forces to regulate the former.

The years leading up to and during World War I added emotional fuel to the fires of rhetoric. By the end of 1916, nineteen states had abolished the sale of alcoholic beverages. In the spring of the following year, Germany resumed all-out submarine warfare against American shipping, and the United States was forced to enter the war. Now, mobilization became the country's major concern. Prohibitionists pushed their cause as part of the national concern to conserve resources. Distillers and brewers argued that their products provided comfort for frightened soldiers and weary factory workers. The "drys" had the better argument, and in December 1917, Congress submitted the Eighteenth Amendment, prohibiting the sale of alcoholic beverages, to the states for ratification. Just a year and a month later, Nebraska became the thirty-sixth state to vote its approval, and America's "Noble Experiment" was scheduled to begin a year later.[5]

William Jennings Bryan, three-time presidential candidate and noted orator of the early twentieth century, proclaimed that two of the most important victories in human history occurred in the very same week of November 1918: the defeat of the German "Hun" forces signified by the signing of the Armistice, and the destruction of the other Hun—the liquor traffic.[6]

Morality and religious conviction were not the only forces that pushed and promoted the Prohibition movement. "Wets" and "drys" were separated by politics (Democrats vs. Republicans), regions (eastern states vs. western), occupation (industrial vs. agrarian), and class (lower income ethnic groups vs. middle-class WASPs). And as the United States was drawn into World War I, a strong anti-German sentiment infused the movement as well. Prohibition was perceived as a way to destroy the successful German family brewing industry centered in Milwaukee and St. Louis.

Prohibition certainly was an experiment in governmental control of social behavior—although its "nobility" has long been questioned. Prohibition did not stamp out all "drinking," but it did reduce consumption of alcohol by an estimated 50 percent in spite of only halfhearted enforcement. Cities recorded fewer deaths from alcohol, and arrests for drunkenness did decline. Prohibition was a spectacular failure, however, in one of its goals: reducing crime. Instead, it created a new, very profitable illegal industry in which both small "moonshiners" and large, well-organized gangs such as Al Capone's could flourish.

Ironically, Prohibition pushed the pendulum back in favor of stronger drink. In the years leading up to World War I, beer consumption had grown rather rapidly at the expense of whiskey and other spirits. But during the Prohibition years, since the sale of all alcoholic beverages was illegal, those who risked breaking the law were more likely to produce and peddle whiskey, which, gallon for gallon, would yield a much higher profit.

Economic change spoiled whatever hope there was for this social experiment. In 1933, the Depression swept the Democrats back into overwhelming control of the federal government, and repeal of the Eighteenth Amendment was one of their earliest accomplishments. Repeal, via the Twenty-First Amendment, took even less time than passage had taken. On December 5, 1933, Utah, that bastion of morality and religious devotion, cast the final vote to kill Prohibition.

It is important to this study that Prohibition is widely acknowledged to have been a failure. What we as a society remember about the experiment is the crime that it spawned, not its contributions to public health. We remember the speakeasies and bathtub gin, not the significant reduction in the amount of alcohol consumed. We are left with the strong sense that this type of social behavior, the consumption of socially unacceptable products, cannot be simply legislated away. Other forms of social control must be employed instead: "sin" taxes, moral suasion, education, and the support of not just religious groups but of a broader range of social advocates.

Since Prohibition, the percentage of adults in the United States who report drinking alcoholic beverages has fluctuated between 55 and 72 percent. This rate has proved impervious to the usual influence of economic swings. In fact, the Gallup Poll, which tracks these statistics, suggests that difficult economic times will sometimes lead to an increase in the drinking rate.[7]

THE BEER INDUSTRY

Beer also has a long and distinguished history. Especially in climates that were inhospitable to grapes, various ancient civilizations fermented grains for the brewing of beer, used in some instances for medical treatments or as a food product, but most often as a social beverage. Twenty-third century B.C. Chinese manuscripts refer to *kiu*, an ancestor of today's beer, and the pictographs on Babylonian and Sumerian tablets portray beer being brewed.

In Colonial America, beer was a staple product, although it was brewed for the most part at home, and it was very mild by today's standards, containing only about 1 percent alcohol. George Washington took some pride in his abilities as a home brewer at Mount Vernon. Thomas Jefferson, along with his seemingly endless other interests, collected a small library on brewing at Monticello, where he also produced his own beer. They, along with Samuel Adams, James Madison, and other leading figures, considered beer the beverage of temperance and excluded brewing property from taxation.

A true beer *industry* began to evolve as waves of German immigrants came to the United States beginning in the 1840s, bringing with them their taste for beer and their knowledge of brewing. A new fermentation process produced a lighter "lager" brew, which began to improve beer's popularity. And by the turn of the century, new technology such as refrigerated railroad cars made it possible for brewers like Adolphus Busch and Frederick Pabst to market and ship their beer across the country.

Such nationwide marketing was the exception rather than the rule at that time, however. Local distribution was much more common, and at the peak of German immigration there were more than twenty-two hundred commercial breweries operating in the United States. Competition inevitably began to take its toll; those brewers who gambled on the new lager product and found ways to market their beer across a wider area gained a competitive advantage. By 1914, at the outbreak of World War I, the number of brewers had decreased to around 1,400.[8]

When Prohibition finally ended in 1933, only 164 breweries had managed to survive. Production increased steadily over the next fifteen years, even during World War II. But at the end of that war, as the nation settled into a new era of peace and economic growth, another wave of consolidation hit the beer industry, this one brought about by changes in marketing strategies. In this postwar period, a few brands—notably Budweiser, Schlitz, Pabst, and Miller—had managed to establish a national distribution and reputation, but most brands were regional. However, as television became an increasingly powerful advertising medium, those brands that had the financial strength and the national distribution to support network television advertising gained a competitive advantage over even the strongest of the regional brands. This push for wider distribution led to a series of mergers and acquisitions, and a few failures, so that by 1960 the number of independent brewers fell to an all-time low of thirty-four. Brands such as Schlitz, Hamm's, Pabst, Falstaff, and Schaefer, all of which ranked in the top ten beers in 1957, had either disappeared completely during the 1970s or had been acquired by larger organizations.

Over the next four decades, from the early 1960s through the end of the century, two developments have changed the picture of the beer industry. First, the big brewers have steadily become much more powerful and dominant. In 1970, the top six breweries—Anheuser-Busch, Miller, Coors,

Stroh, G. Heileman, and Pabst—accounted for just over 40 percent of total industry shipments.[9] But by the year 2000, Anheuser-Busch, Miller, and Coors alone accounted for more than 80 percent of the industry's record shipments of just under two hundred million barrels.

The second development is something of a paradox. Even as the biggest brewers have continued to control an increasing share of the industry, the number of small brewers—microbreweries and brewpubs—has risen dramatically, from fewer than 100 in 1985 to more than 1,800 in 2000. From the Sunday River Brewing Company in Maine to the Ragtime Tavern and Taproom in Florida to the Hubcap Brewery and Kitchen in Colorado to the Twenty-Tank Brewery in California—these small operations have captured the fancy of beer *aficionados* across the country who search for a noncommercial brew and relish the distinction of uncovering a new, cleverly-named obscure product. While these microbreweries and brewpubs have sprung up by the score, many of them produce only enough beer to be consumed on their own premises. For all the interest they have created, altogether they account for only 2–3 percent of the beer produced in the United States.[10]

Following the end of Prohibition, overall production of beer increased steadily and rather rapidly from thirty-two million barrels in 1934 to eighty-six million barrels in 1954. For the next ten years, production grew only slowly, but then the industry entered another growth period, moving up from ninety-one million barrels in 1963 to 178 million barrels in 1983. Over the 1983–1995 period, brewing was a very mature industry, in marketing parlance, growing very little or not at all from year to year. In the past six or seven years, however, there has been a steady, if not spectacular, growth of roughly 2 percent per year. Per capita consumption figures have followed a similar pattern, increasing slightly during the periods of overall growth. Between 1983 and 1994, the figure actually declined from 23.6 to 21.5 gallons per capita. In 1994, imports of beer into the United States accounted for only .5 percent of the market.[11] By 2003, that figure had grown to more than 10 percent. Figures 3.1 and 3.2 illustrate beer industry shipments and per capita consumption figures over the last several decades.

Beer consumption patterns vary rather widely across the United States, ranging from a high per capita figure of 35.1 gallons in Nevada to a low of 12.9 in neighboring Mormon-dominated Utah. The southwestern states of Arizona, New Mexico, and Texas are all above average in beer consumption, but California, Connecticut, and New York are all below average, in part because wine consumption is higher in those states. Beer drinking in Vermont is barely above average, while neighboring New Hampshire has the second highest per capita consumption figure. Can Dartmouth students be the reason?

The dollar value of U.S. beer production in 2002 was approximately $26 billion at producers' prices. It is more difficult to compute a retail figure.

Figure 3.1
Beer Industry Shipments in Thirty-One-Gallon Barrels

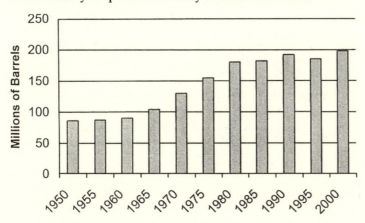

Figure 3.2
U.S. Per Capita Beer Consumption

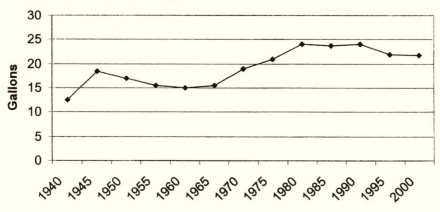

Roughly 70 percent of the beer brewed in this country is sold in cans and bottles for home consumption[12]—that is, through distributors who get perhaps a 25 percent markup and then through retailers whose markup is roughly 22 percent. The other 30 percent is sold in kegs or bottles for on-premises consumption in bars, clubs, and restaurants, a segment of the market in which the markup is very high. The best estimate of beer industry sales at retail, according to a leading analyst, is $50–55 billion.[13]

As with the other alcoholic beverages, beer industry sales have been constrained in recent years by the country's growing concern for health and fitness. Various "new age" beverages, especially flavored bottled waters and new fruit-flavored drinks, have helped to limit the growth of beer revenues. A noted beer industry analyst expects further problems for the industry: a continued decline in alcoholic beverages as a percent of discretionary expenditures. This leaves the critical question: What percent of all alcoholic beverage sales will go to the beer industry? That percent declined steadily from the end of World War II until 1972, when it turned up sharply due to the introduction of light beers and other new products, plus more convenient packaging. What this indicates is that in addition to the obvious fierce competition among the major brewers there is also the less obvious competition between beer and the other alcoholic beverages.

The Major Brewers

Anheuser-Busch is indeed "the king of beers," certainly in terms of industry leadership. The firm originated in the German immigrant settlement in St. Louis in the middle of the nineteenth century when Eberhard Anheuser acquired a local brewery and a few years later formed a partnership with his new son-in-law, Adolphus Busch. Busch family members remain major shareholders in the firm; August A. Busch III is the company's chairman and president, and August A. Busch IV is a company vice president.

Anheuser-Busch's flagship brand, Budweiser, appeared in the market in 1876, was the first beer to become a truly national brand toward the end of that century and has been the country's favorite brand ever since. The company's market share has steadily increased over the past four decades, from 8 percent in 1957 to more than 49 percent in 2002.[14] Beer and beer-related businesses (can manufacturing and malting, for example) remain the company's primary business, although there is also an entertainment division operating nine "adventure" parks around the country. Having sold off its snack food division and its ownership interest in the St. Louis Cardinals baseball team, the company has been able to concentrate almost exclusively on beer in recent years, and that focus seems to have paid real dividends. Its beer sales have increased faster than the industry-wide average; the Budweiser brand controls the regular premium beer category with a 75 percent share; Bud Light now dominates the light premium beer category with a 47.5 percent share, almost twice its nearest competitor; and the Busch and Natural Light brands hold more than 43 percent of the subpremium category.

Miller Brewing Company has an equally historic background; its roots go back to Milwaukee of the mid-nineteenth century, when Frederick Miller purchased the Plank Road Brewery. This company also remained under family leadership for more than 100 years before Philip Morris acquired it in 1969. With the marketing and financial muscle of its corporate parent, Miller increased its market share until it became the country's second largest brewer in 1976. It was Philip Morris's heavy investment in Miller's expansion that forced Anheuser-Busch and other competitors into a race for expanded capacity and accelerated the mergers and acquisitions of the 1970s. In 2000, Miller's sales of $4.3 billion and shipments of 40.6 million barrels gave it a beer industry market share of roughly 20 percent, even if its sales represented only a relatively small (5.5 percent) portion of parent company Philip Morris's overall sales.

Miller has developed a reputation of being an innovator in the industry and making new product development an important part of its marketing strategy. Its Lite beer was one of the earliest entrants in the light beer segment of the market and held the number one position among light beers until Bud Light passed it in 1994. It has also been more aggressive than its competition in introducing ice, dry, and clear beers, which are described in more detail in a later chapter.

In July 2002 Philip Morris sold its interest in Miller Brewing to British-owned SAB (South African Brewers), making the new SABMiller the second-largest brewer in the world.

Coors, like its two larger competitors, has a strong family heritage and is still owned and managed by Coors family members. Unlike Anheuser-Busch and Miller, however, until the early 1980s, Coors remained essentially a strong regional brewer with its roots in the Rocky Mountains and its strength on the West Coast, especially in the California market. Without benefit of acquisitions, Coors has been able to expand over the past twenty years into a true national competitor. From a market share in 1957 of less than 2 percent and an industry ranking of seventeenth, Coors has grown by 2002 to its number-three position and a market share of 11 percent. Beer and related operations such as can manufacturing remain the company's only business; in 2002 it did acquire the European brewer Carlsberg Brewing Company, whose brands include Carling and Grolsch. In the United States Coors's shipments held steady in 2002 at 22.7 million barrels, representing a sales volume of $2.4 billion.

Market share figures for Anheuser-Busch, Miller, and Coors are shown in figure 3.3.

DISTILLED SPIRITS

Compared to beer, the distilled spirits industry is much more difficult to define and describe. It is a confusing jumble of producers, marketers, importers, distributors, and of course retailers. Roughly two-thirds of the broad range of products is domestically produced; the balance comes from around the world. Scotch, Irish, and Canadian whiskeys are imported from their respective countries, vodka from Sweden, Finland, Russia, and other Eastern European nations, tequila from Mexico, rum from Jamaica

Figure 3.3
Major Brewers' Market Shares, 1975–2002

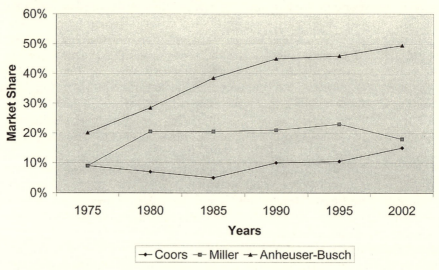

and elsewhere around the Caribbean, brandy from France and Spain, and gin from the United Kingdom.

The consumption pattern for distilled spirits in total declined steadily between 1975 and 1995. Per capita consumption for adults reached a peak in this country in 1974 at 3.14 gallons, dropped to 1.85 gallons in 1994, and has rebounded since then to approximately 2.23 gallons. Total consumption declined from just under 450 million gallons in 1981 to less than 337 million in 1994, before rebounding to roughly 390 million gallons in 2001.[15]

Among the various categories of spirits, however, the pattern has been very mixed. So-called "brown goods," whiskeys of all types, dark rum, and brandy, have shown the largest drop. In just the ten years between 1984 and 1994, the whiskey category dropped by roughly one-third. All rum, light and dark, was down 20 percent, brandy fell by 25 percent, and cordials and cocktails managed a slight gain. In the "white goods" category, gin fell by 25 percent over that same time period, even vodka showed a decline of 7 percent, and only tequila managed a significant increase of 25 percent, although it is still only a minor category compared with the other beverages.

Diageo PLC (formerly Grand Metropolitan) is the world's largest distilled spirits company with revenues in 2003 of almost $14 billion generated by the company's collection of famous brands: Guinness, Bailey's, Johnnie Walker, J&B, Jose Cuervo, Smirnoff, and Tanqueray among them.

Diageo has also teamed with Pernod Ricard SA of France to purchase the Seagram beverage brands, which had been acquired by Vivendi Universal.

Allied Domecq PLC, another British firm, is the number-two marketer of spirits in the United States, featuring Ballantine's scotch whiskey and Beefeater gin among its many brands. Brown-Forman, famous for its Jack Daniels Tennessee Sippin' whiskey, and Fortune Brands (Jim Beam bourbon, Gilbey's gin, DeKuyper cordials) are the leading U.S.-based distilled spirits producers.

At the wholesale and retail levels, the industry is no less complex. Because each state can choose to control the marketing of alcoholic beverages, the United States is split into what the industry calls license states and control states, the latter being those that control the distribution at some stage of the process. New Hampshire, Vermont, Pennsylvania, Utah, Virginia, and Washington, for example, sell distilled spirits only through state liquor stores, although in most of those states, beer and wine can be sold through private stores. In a few other states, Iowa, Michigan, and Mississippi among them, state wholesalers sell to private retailers. Montgomery County in Maryland operates its own liquor wholesalers and retailers, while throughout the rest of the state customers buy through private firms. As a result of this welter of different and changing regulations, the retail liquor business has been a difficult one for chain stores. Within some states, California for example, chains such as Liquor Barn have become well established, but throughout most of the country the sale of liquor is still the province of small, independent firms.

FRUIT OF THE VINE

The cultivation of grapes and the making of wine probably began in Mesopotamia six or seven *millennia* before Christ. Under the Greeks and later the Romans, viticulture spread first through the eastern Mediterranean regions and later to Spain, northern France, and finally Britain. By Jesus' time, wine had become an important celebratory beverage, and since then it has remained an important ritualistic element in both Jewish and Christian faiths.

During the Dark Ages, the church owned much of the grape-growing land in Europe, and individual abbeys maintained the skills of wine making (as well as beer making). Later, during the Renaissance when these lands came into the ownership of the temporal aristocracy, the great wine-growing regions of France were established—Bordeaux, Burgundy, Champagne, Medoc, and so on.

Although grapes and wine were certainly no strangers to colonial and postcolonial America, wine retained a somewhat European, and therefore elitist, image. Rum from the Caribbean and whiskey distilled from various grains, as well as home-brewed beer, became the staple alcoholic drinks of the colonies, and to this day, wine consumption in the United States has never matched the popularity that it enjoys in Europe.

Whiskeys and gin, and of course beer, remained the beverages of choice throughout the World War II years and for the next three decades. Only during the 1970s, when a sufficient number of baby boomers reached maturity and looked for a beverage that would set them apart from the cocktails and highballs of their parents, was wine "discovered." Then for the next ten years wine consumption grew dramatically, and the small, family-owned vineyards of northern California scrambled to keep up with demand.

It was not an easy task. In the years 1975–1984, production rather than marketing was the problem. Since newly planted vines require roughly five years to come into usable production, during a period of expanding demand there will necessarily be a lag before the supply can catch up. When demand did finally peak in the mid-1980s, there followed a period of overproduction, declining prices for grapes, and consolidation among the wineries.

Since the mid-1980s, overall consumption of wine in the United States fell steadily from 586 to 458 million gallons in 1994 and then rebounded to 595 million gallons in 2002. Given the gradually increasing adult population in the United States, per capita consumption fell even faster and still has not reached the peak set in 1986 at 2.4 gallons. Wine consumption has been constrained by the same forces that have affected spirits and beer: the rapid expansion of alternative beverages—such as fruit drinks, ready-to-drink teas, and bottled waters—and growing concerns over fitness and health, although the latter force would seem to have lost some of its impact since the mid-1990s.

Wine consumption varies more by state than the consumption of either spirits or beer. Annual per capita consumption in the District of Columbia at 4.8 gallons is more than two and a half times the national average and at least 30 percent more than any state. However, this high figure may be due to the unique nature of the District of Columbia: its cosmopolitan mixture of foreigners and heavy entertaining in proportion to its relatively modest population. But Nevada, New Hampshire, New Jersey, California, Massachusetts, and Connecticut are all more than 50 percent above average per capita consumption. Kentucky, South Dakota, Arkansas, Iowa, Mississippi, and Utah are all less than half the national average.[16]

Even during the Prohibition years, a number of California wineries continued to operate by producing sacramental and medicinal wines, so that when the Twenty-First Amendment was ratified, these wineries had all the necessary presses, fermenting tanks, and even inventory to begin expanding their operations. But many new start-up wineries also filed for the necessary federal permits, among them in September 1933, Ernest and Julio Gallo of Modesto. The two brothers, through clever and successful marketing strategies, came to dominate both the lower medium price levels of the industry (so-called jug wines) and also the lowest levels (Thunderbird, Night Train Express). Although Gallo has tried repeatedly to break into the upper middle price ranges with its varietal wines, this has been a tougher challenge, due in large part to consumers' difficulty in associating the name Gallo with better wines. Nevertheless, Gallo wines have managed to keep their leading market share among U.S. producers, now at roughly 32 percent, throughout the period of mergers, acquisitions, and consolidations.[17]

Second only to Gallo in wine industry market share is a name that few wine enthusiasts have ever heard of, Constellation Brands, headquartered in the Finger Lakes region of western New York. While Gallo's growth came gradually over the decades through the promotion of its own brands and the domination of the distribution network, Constellation's rise to prominence and power has come about only since 1990, the result of an aggressive acquisition strategy that brought such brands as Almaden, Inglenook, Paul Masson, Italian Swiss Colony, Taylor California Cellars, and Manischewitz into its fold. With this lineup, Constellation accounted for approximately 21 percent of the U.S. table wine business, while other divisions of the company sell sparkling wines, vodka, gin, and imported beers.

The remaining 47 percent of the domestic table wine industry is shared by a number of much smaller companies, although their brand names, among them Robert Mondavi, Sebastiani, and Beringer, may be well known to wine drinkers.

THE OPPOSITION

Opposition to alcoholic beverages lives on. Today's bias toward scientific rationalism and statistical evidence has supplanted much of the emotionalism and moral outrage that characterized the anti-alcohol movements of the late nineteenth and early twentieth centuries. Gone is the image of Carrie Nation single-handedly destroying jugs of good corn whiskey with her axe handle. Gone are the evangelical preachers and the stalwarts of the Anti-Saloon League railing against the evils of "Demon Rum." Gone are the self-righteous women of the WCTU (Women's Christian Temperance Union).

In their place are a variety of advocacy groups: organizations of young, idealistic, politically astute activists who are motivated either by the health consequences or by the social costs created by alcohol. The Center for Science in the Public Interest, for example, is especially critical of the advertising of alcoholic products and specifically of the effects of that advertising on children and teenagers. The center lobbies for more explicit warning labels on all products and in all advertising, that alcoholic beverage ads should not glamorize drinking and should not target children, that outdoor ads for alcoholic beverages should not be allowed near schools, and for an end to targeting women and minorities.

Another active and influential advocacy group is the Marin Institute for the Prevention of Alcohol and Other Drug Problems. Recent newsletters from the institute have criticized the advertising of alcoholic beverages on the Internet, the investment of state pension fund money in alcoholic beverage companies, support from the U.S. government for the export of alcoholic products, and beverage companies' trying to buy off their critics by contributing to charitable causes.

Even more focused in their approaches are Mothers Against Drunk Driving (MADD), founded in 1980, and Students Against Driving Drunk (SADD). These groups have waged an effective battle against the twin problems of drunk drivers and underage drinking for more than twenty years.

Today's anti-alcohol advocacy groups may not have the cartoon characteristics of Carrie Nation and the WCTU, but they are a force to be reckoned with for the marketers of alcoholic beverages. They maintain a constant drumbeat for higher taxes on alcohol, for restrictions on advertising, for tougher warning labels, and for stricter enforcement of existing marketing regulations. They are a constant reminder to the country as a whole, as well as to the federal and state governments, that alcoholic beverages do not enjoy the same legitimacy as most other goods and services in our economy, that to many in our society they are still socially unacceptable products.

Alcoholic beverages in the U.S. consumer economy evoke comparisons but also contrasts with their role in other cultures past and present. Without question, the same ambivalence between the good and evil of alcohol, the pleasure and the problems that troubled Noah and Falstaff permeate the consumption of beer, wine, and spirits in the United States today. But in America, alcoholic drinks have never become as natural a part of everyday consumption as they have been in Mediterranean cultures. We open a bottle of wine or beer or pour a drink of hard liquor when we are with friends, when we celebrate, when we relax after a long day, or sometimes to forget our problems and satisfy our cravings—in other words, for a special occasion or purpose. Perhaps this lack of total acceptance in the United States, or this lack of legitimacy, can be ascribed to the cyclical periods of social and religious criticism of alcohol over the last 150 years of our history, to the nineteenth-century protests of the Anti-Saloon League and the twentieth-century experiment with Prohibition.

Whatever its causes, this lack of acceptance is a constant barrier that the marketers of alcoholic beverages must try to scale. As we explore in subsequent chapters, the cloud of unacceptability that hangs over the industry imposes regulatory and social restrictions on marketing programs, closing off certain commonplace tactics that are available to marketers of mainstream products.

NOTES

1. Rev. C. H. Wright, "Biblical Encyclopedia," in *The Holy Bible* (New York: Abradale Press, 1959), 199.

2. http://www.state.me.us/sos/arc/archives/military/civilwar/dow.htm.

3. W. J. Rorabaugh, *The Alcoholic Republic: An American Tradition* (New York: Oxford University Press, 1979), notes, 256.

4. Ferdinand Cowle Iglehart, *King Alcohol Dethroned* (Westerville, OH: The American Issue Publishing Company, 1917), 362–63.

5. K. Austin Kerr, *Organized for Prohibition: A New History of the Anti-Saloon League* (New Haven, CT: Yale University Press, 1985), 185–86.

6. Iglehart, *King Alcohol Dethroned*, 291.

7. *The Gallup Poll: Public Opinion 1992*, 17–18.

8. "Retail Guide to Beer," *Beverage Dynamics*, July/August 1992, 40–42.

9. From figures compiled by R. S. Weinberg & Associates as reported in Alan Wolf, "Beer Seer," *Beverage World*, December 1991, 26.

10. Beer Institute, *Annual Report 2000–2001*, Washington, DC.

11. *Modern Brewery Age, 1994 Year in Review*.

12. By contrast, in the United Kingdom, only 23 percent of beer is consumed at home; 77 percent is consumed in taverns, pubs, and restaurants.

13. Estimated by Robert Weinberg, R. S. Weinberg & Associates, St. Louis, Missouri, in an October 6, 1995, telephone conversation with the author. Figures updated to reflect year 2002 prices.

14. Weinberg, in Wolf, "Beer Seer," 21; *Modern Brewery Age, 1994 Year in Review*, and Anheuser-Busch Companies, Inc., *Annual Report 2002*.

15. Distilled Spirits Council of the U.S. (DISCUS), *1994 Statistical Information for the U.S. Distilled Spirits Industry*, Washington, DC, 1995; from an October 13, 1995, telephone conversation between a representative of DISCUS and the author; and from the DISCUS Web site for 2001 statistics.

16. Figures from the Wine Institute as reported in Beer Institute, *Brewing Industry in the United States, Brewers Almanac 1994* (Washington, DC: Beer Institute, 1994), 44–45. Also from *Beverage World* 114, no. 1591 (May 1995): 56.

17. Daniel A. Sumner et al., *An Economic Survey of the Wine and Winegrape Industry in the United States and Canada*, University of California, Davis. Revised draft, December 2, 2001. Available at http://aic.ucdavis.edu/research/winegrape.pdf, 17.

CHAPTER 4

Handguns, Rifles, and Shotguns: The Firearms Industry

Las Vegas is the perfect site for the SHOT Show,[1] the annual extravaganza that is the principal nationwide trade show for the firearms industry. In February 2002, the huge Las Vegas Convention Center featured an estimated fourteen hundred exhibits covering nearly half a million square feet of display space and attracted a near-record crowd of 18,549 retailers and wholesalers from the industry to mingle, swap stories, and place orders with the manufacturers' reps. The western, desert scenery on the fringes of the city is a natural backdrop for all the interest in guns. The twenty-four-hours-a-day excitement and entertainment seems appropriate for this down-to-earth, fun-loving group of businesspeople, collectors, and gun enthusiasts of all kinds.

But there is something more that makes this city such an apt choice. With its emphasis on gambling, Las Vegas projects an aura of riskiness; it seems just a little bit wicked. Visitors sense they are not in the mainstream of American life, that they are somewhere out on the margin. Is the city and what it stands for really *legitimate?* What better gathering place, then, for an industry whose products and marketing practices are subject to growing social criticism, and whose own legitimacy is being called into question. For industry professionals with a chip on their collective shoulder, there could hardly be a friendlier environment.

In many ways, the SHOT Show is typical of any industry trade show. Merchandise exhibits stretch on, aisle after aisle: not just rifles, shotguns, and handguns—the standard fare of the firearms industry—but an extraordinary collection of archery products, knives of every length and description, camping equipment and accessories, and a large section devoted entirely to sporting and camping apparel, much of it in camouflage-printed fabrics.

There are the usual handouts and giveaways: bright orange tote bags, pens, notepads, lapel pins in the shape of revolvers, and "I ♥ Winchester Ammo" bumper stickers. Exhibitors vie with one another with flashing lights or videos featuring old Western movie shoot-outs or big game hunting with bow and arrow. One of the larger exhibitors recently drew a huge crowd by setting up an elaborate computer-operated rifle firing range, where two contestants could compete side by side, firing laser beams at video screens with their accuracy and scores automatically recorded on a separate monitor.

One can hardly describe the incredible diversity of products at these shows. On display are sophisticated binoculars, telescopes, and precise riflescopes, as well as decidedly unsophisticated "Huntin' Buddy" suspenders with loops to hold ammunition. There are small platforms called "tree stands," on which hunters perch high up in trees to wait for their quarry, at least nineteen different varieties of smokeless powder, even "scent traps" for attracting game: Tink's "doe-in-rut buck lure made from live white-tailed doe deer in heat" and Lee's "pure deer urine."

But most of all, there are guns: big guns like the Remington African safari model that would "bring down a rhinoceros," and tiny mini-revolvers, "unique defensive tools" much smaller than the palm of a man's hand that could be hidden in a belt or ankle holster. There are expensive guns from Perazzi: a set of four over/under shotguns with heavily etched breeches and Turkish walnut stocks to sell for $285,000; as well as inexpensive guns like the "original Russian SKS rifles in VERY GOOD condition. . . . Comes complete with bayonet, sling and oiler. . . . ONLY $99.95 each when you order three or more!"

There are guns from dozens of domestic manufacturers, as well as from Germany, Korea, the Czech Republic, England, Brazil, China, Italy, Spain, Russia, and other foreign makers. There are guns as modern as tomorrow with a Hollywood high-tech, assault-weapon look; there are muzzle loaders, reminiscent of another era; and there are the classic rifles from Winchester and Remington, and the Colt "Peacemaker"—the guns that "won the West."

There are guns from every segment of the firearms industry. For hunters, there is a wide array of rifles to bring down big game and shotguns for every imaginable hunting bird. For target shooting, depending on the level of competition, one can choose from expensive Olympic competition rifles all the way down to an inexpensive .22 or air rifle for vacant lot "plinking." There are guns for collectors: replicas of Old West favorites, and guns with fine, custom-made stocks.

And there are guns for self-defense. If hunting, target shooting, and collecting represent the upbeat side of the industry, self-defense is the darker side. At the show, manufacturers display guns for the military, for law enforcement agencies, and for civilian defensive use. Some are shot-guns—for example, the "Express" made by Remington for "home de-fense"—but most are handguns of every imaginable size and shape. Some are big and beefy, designed for "unequaled stopping power." Some are very small, designed to be easily concealed and to be used as police backup weapons. Some are designed for night use with elaborate flash-light attachments. There are personal defense pistols—PDPs—from Spring-field. But the enormous variety in product lines leaves no doubt about the size and degree of interest in the market.

In one way, however, recent SHOT Shows have been *unlike* other industry trade shows. Along with the predictable product hype, sales pitches, and promotion common to exhibitions and trade shows in every industry, these firearms shows have carried with them a strong sense that the in-dustry is under siege, that it needs to defend itself from social criticism. Just below the surface of all the usual product marketing—advertising plans, dealer displays, new product introductions, and pricing strate-gies—there is a strong political and public relations statement being tested and promoted. Exhibit after exhibit display a sign assuring visitors that the vendor is "as pro-gun as your customer." One of the best-attended seminars during a recent show featured representatives of the Bureau of Alcohol, Tobacco, and Firearms (BATF) trying to explain to a generally hostile crowd of dealers the bureau's policy of granting licenses to sell guns. And at what other trade show would there be such an interest in the intricacies of constitutional law? At the SHOT Show, interpretation of the Second Amendment is on everyone's mind, and there is little doubt how the thirty thousand dealers and exhibitors feel about "the right to bear arms."

ROMANCE AND TRAGEDY

No other product in the United States combines such romance and trag-edy[2] as does the gun. The Revolutionary-era minuteman, symbol of the country's birth, stands poised and ready, his musket at his side. Fire-arms—both the long rifle and the revolver—were synonymous with the opening and settling of the West during the nineteenth century and so share in the romantic and nostalgic images Americans have of that portion of their history. It is hard to think of such legendary characters as Daniel Boone, Sam Houston, Wyatt Earp, Annie Oakley, "Wild Bill" Hickok, Kit Carson, and "Buffalo Bill" Cody (not to mention John Wayne) without calling to mind the guns that helped to make their names famous and to give their era at least the superficial aura of romance. Riding "shot-gun" on an overland stagecoach, the shoot-out at the OK corral, the pitched gun battles between the lawmen and the masked outlaws—all

these familiar scenes lost their ugliness and painfulness in the Hollywood sanitizing process and in the reminiscences of more than 100 years
of history.

The unique history of the American West has influenced the evolution
and design of firearms. Sam Colt developed his revolver in Paterson, New
Jersey, but it was big and bulky and of little use or value in the urban
centers of the eastern United States of the 1830s, where the much smaller
derringer was preferred. However, out West where the Texas Rangers
were battling both Mexicans and Native Americans, the "six-shooter" revolvers and later the Winchester repeating rifles were the answers to the
Rangers' needs.[3]

The Tragic Dimension

The Western setting for the SHOT Show and all the normal excitement
and hoopla of a large trade exhibition are appropriate surroundings to
showcase the romantic dimension of the firearms industry. But another
group of historic figures is equally important to understanding the industry's history and especially its current circumstances. Richard Lawrence, Charles Guiteau, Leon Czolgosz, John Shrank, Giuseppe Zangara,
Lynette Fromme, Sara Jane Moore, John Hinckley, Jr., and Francisco Durand may not be household names any longer, but when John Wilkes
Booth and Lee Harvey Oswald are added to the list, the orientation becomes clear. All of the above either assassinated or shot at presidents of
the United States.

Lawrence's pistol misfired when he shot at Andrew Jackson in 1835.
Booth's pistol performed admirably and felled Abraham Lincoln at Ford's
Theater in Washington in 1865. Guiteau shot at James Garfield in 1881,
and the president later died of his wounds. Czolgosz was responsible for
the assassination of William McKinley at an exposition in Buffalo, New
York, in 1901, and only eleven years later, Schrank shot at and wounded
Theodore Roosevelt who was campaigning at the time in Milwaukee as
the Bull Moose candidate. Zangara fired at Franklin D. Roosevelt in Miami
in 1933; he missed the president, but mortally wounded Anton Cermak,
the mayor of Chicago, who was riding with Roosevelt at the time. In 1950,
two Puerto Ricans tried to assassinate Harry Truman but were shot when
they broke into Blair House, across Pennsylvania Avenue from the White
House, where the president was residing temporarily.[4]

Oswald's name and the film clips of the assassination of President Kennedy in 1963 are still etched on America's collective consciousness after
forty years. Less well remembered is that Fromme pointed a gun at Gerald
Ford in 1975, and less than a month later, Moore actually fired a shot at
the president. Even more recently in 1981, Hinckley wounded Ronald
Reagan and several others in the president's party just outside the Wash-

ington, D.C., Hilton Hotel. And as recently as 1994, Durand sprayed the White House with rounds from his rifle in broad daylight in an alleged attempt to assassinate Bill Clinton.

If we add to this list, as indeed we must, the names of Robert Kennedy, Martin Luther King, George Wallace, Malcolm X, John Lennon, and Allard Lowenstein, all of whom were either assassinated or wounded by guns in the past thirty years, we can better understand the tragic dimension of this product category we call firearms.

Romance and tragedy, schizophrenia, a love-hate relationship: At the start of a new millennium, the U.S. firearms industry is buffeted by two strong opposing crosswinds of public opinion. Caught squarely in the middle is an industry quite unlike any other.

INDUSTRY STRUCTURE

"Fragmented" is the term academicians might use to describe the firearms industry. There are no dominant competitors in the way that Philip Morris and Reynolds Tobacco dominate the cigarette industry or Anheuser-Busch and Miller dominate the beer industry. Unlike tobacco or alcoholic beverages—not to mention autos, steel, or computers—where the principal competitors can be quickly enumerated and market shares tallied, piecing together the firearms *industry* is a more difficult task. Most of the brand names from the industry's romantic past are still with us—Winchester, Colt, Remington, Browning, Smith & Wesson—but they no longer exist as independent gun manufacturers. Public policy controversy, financial woes, and severe competition both domestic and foreign, have all taken their toll. The industry now is something of a hodgepodge of small domestic firms, divisions of larger corporations or conglomerates, divisions of foreign firms, and importers of foreign-made firearms.

The famed Winchester rifles became part of Olin Corporation, predominantly a chemical firm, but they are now made under license by the U.S. Repeating Arms Co. This company, after filing for bankruptcy in 1986, became a part of GIAT, which is owned by the French government. In the late 1960s, GIAT had purchased Browning Arms, a manufacturer of high-quality shotguns, and the French firm also owns FNNH (Fabrique Nationale), a Belgian firearms manufacturer. Winchester Ammunition Co., however, remains an independent firm. Remington Arms, which claims the title "America's Oldest Gunmaker" dating back to 1816 when Eliphalet Remington fashioned a handmade rifle in his workshop, was a division of DuPont from 1980 to 1993, but then was sold to RACI Acquisitions, a New York investment firm. Smith & Wesson became a division of Lear Siegler, then of Forstmann Little, and in 1987 was acquired by Tomkins PLC of Great Britain.

Aggregate figures for the industry in units are readily available from the Bureau of Alcohol, Tobacco, and Firearms (BATF), which licenses gun manufacturers as well as dealers. As shown in table 4.1, U.S. manufacturers produced a total of 3,011,000 firearms of all types in 2001, of which 190,000 were exported and the rest were sold domestically. Handguns, that is, pistols and revolvers, made up 31 percent of the total, and rifles and shotguns combined represented 65 percent. Imports into the United States in that same year amounted to approximately 1.4 million firearms of all types; half of these were handguns, and half were long guns.[5]

Dollar figures are more difficult to compile because of the industry structure: a number of privately held firms and significant foreign ownership. Bureau of Census figures reveal that for 1999, U.S. manufacturers shipped roughly $1.3 billion worth of "small arms." Piecing this figure together with BATF statistics on unit production as well as net imports, an estimate for 1999 gun sales, both domestic and imported, would be roughly $1.7 billion at manufacturers' prices or perhaps $2.6 billion at retail.[6]

The BATF statistics shown in table 4.1 point to some interesting changes. Overall production between 1984 and 1992 changed relatively little, fluctuating between three and four million units. In 1993 and 1994, however, the figures jumped up dramatically. Production of long arms increased 28 percent between 1992 and 1994. Production of handguns jumped up 40 percent in 1993 over the previous year before settling back a bit in 1994,

Table 4.1
U.S. Firearms Production, 1980–2000

Year	Pistols	Revolvers	Rifles	Shotguns	Machine Guns
1980	760,000	1,605,000	1,936,000	1,339,000	N/A
1985	707,000	844,000	1,141,000	770,000	6,092
1990	1,376,000	462,000	1,156,000	849,000	3,809
1995	1,195,000	528,000	1,332,000	1,174,000	N/A
2000	963,000	319,000	1,583,000	898,000	47,400

Source: Department of the Treasury, Bureau of Alcohol, Tobacco, and Firearms.

still 28 percent over the 1992 level. Imports spiked even more dramatically, increasing from 721,000 units in 1991 to over three million units in 1993. These were the years preceding passage of the Brady Bill (described below), and it is clear that retailers and their gun-buying customers were increasing their purchases in advance of more restrictive gun-control regulations.

More recently, however, production in the industry has slumped. Total production in 2000 was 8 percent less than in 1995, and in 2001 production fell by 22 percent just from the previous year. The only category to show increases over the past decade has been machine guns, a frightening statistic.

Another interesting change evident in the BATF figures is in the composition of handgun production. In 1984, revolvers accounted for 58 percent of the handguns manufactured, but only 34 percent in 2001. Correspondingly, pistols jumped from 42 to 66 percent. For those concerned about crime and violence, this change is ominous and can be explained in two ways: the magazine of a pistol holds more rounds, typically eight or more, compared to only six for a revolver, giving the pistol more fire power, and the pistol is generally easier to conceal.

Dollar sales figures for individual manufacturers are difficult to find. For competitive reasons, the companies are reticent to divulge these figures, and because the businesses are for the most part divisions of larger enterprises, they are not required by the government to report them. However, the BATF does collect production figures in units from each of the domestic manufacturers and releases these a year after the aggregate numbers.

Sturm, Ruger & Co. and Remington continue to be the two largest manufacturers in the firearms industry, the former concentrating on pistols and rifles, the latter producing only long guns, both rifles and shotguns. Smith & Wesson, Beretta, Bryco, and Kel Tec manufacture only handguns, Marlin is a major competitor in the rifle classification, and O. F. Mossberg is an important manufacturer of shotguns.

Imports of firearms come from all over the world. China was the leading source through 1993, exporting some 580,000 rifles and handguns to the United States, until President Clinton banned the importation of firearms from that country. Russia, Brazil, and Austria are all important exporters of handguns and long guns to this country.

CYCLICAL PATTERNS

These figures serve to highlight the cyclical nature of the industry over past years. Guns are unusually sturdy mechanical products; they seldom wear out from use and typically last for decades. This helps to explain the steep decline in production and sales after the sudden and dramatic increase in 1993. The purchase of a firearm can rather easily be postponed, and so sales figures for the industry are sensitive to economic conditions.

The industry's swings are also strongly influenced by foreign competition. The *Wall Street Journal* of December 4, 1959,[7] reported that between 1955 and 1958, domestic firearm sales had declined by 50 percent, profits for the industry had practically vanished, and domestic employment in the industry had fallen by one-third, largely due to an increase in imports. European governments during the 1950s found themselves heavily overstocked with military hardware of all types and discovered that the U.S. market was a convenient and profitable dumping ground for their small arms. It was this particular industry downturn that prompted then senator John F. Kennedy of Massachusetts on April 28, 1958, to introduce a bill before the Senate to limit the importation of certain firearms "originally manufactured for military purposes." This was not anti-gun ideology; this was pure and simple protective legislation for the several large firearms manufacturers in the senator's home state. The tragic irony is that the proposed legislation would have barred from this country the rifle that was used to assassinate Kennedy only five years later, a 6.5 mm Mannlicher-Carcano carbine from Italy. Although the House Foreign Affairs Committee approved a companion bill by a 26–0 vote, both bills eventually died, largely due to successful lobbying by the National Rifle Association.[8]

In the mid-1980s, *Business Week* reported that the industry suffered another downswing, once again due to a combination of domestic economic problems and an upturn in imports. Especially difficult was the loss of military and law enforcement contracts for pistols to Italy's Beretta. The magazine noted three other ominous trends for the industry: the anti-gun sentiments of the younger affluent generation, discontinued sales by some of the country's largest retailers, and more costly liability insurance for manufacturers and retailers alike.[9]

As with any cyclical industry, these downturns are followed by upswings, both fueled by a combination of economic and social factors. One of those social changes is the citizenry's concern about public safety. In 1968, a national commission, chaired by Dr. Milton Eisenhower, reported that during the previous six years, sales of long guns had doubled and sales of handguns had quadrupled. The commission went on to state: "Growing interest in shooting sports may explain much of the increase in long gun sales, but it does not account for the dramatic increase in handgun sales. Fear of crime, violence, and civil disorder, and perhaps the anticipation of stricter firearms laws, appear to have stimulated sales of handguns in recent years."[10]

This explanation of the industry upturn in the 1960s was extraordinarily prophetic; precisely the same wording might well be used to describe increased industry sales in the early 1990s.

Guns are typically sold through sporting goods stores, hardware stores, general-purpose merchandisers, discounters, and specialty gun dealers. As opposition to firearms in general, and handgun sales specifically, has mounted over recent years, some of the larger retail chains, for whom guns make up only a tiny percentage of their sales and profits, have given up the category. Sears Roebuck, JCPenney, Target, Montgomery Ward, and Ames have all given up selling firearms since 1980. Kmart continues to sell long guns, but sells handguns only through its wholly owned Sports Authority division.[11] And Wal-Mart discontinued the sale of handguns in 1993. These larger retailers have been pushed to discontinue or cut back their gun sales due to increasing paperwork required by growing BATF regulations, worry that the gun seller may at some point be held liable for harm that the gun does, and a general decline in the public's sense of the *legitimacy* of the firearms trade. This has increasingly left the field to the smaller gun dealers and sporting goods stores who are served by a network of sporting goods wholesale distributors.

OPPOSITION TO GUNS

What has brought on this souring in the public's perceptions surrounding the firearms industry, this loss of legitimacy? What social forces have elevated the tragic dimension over the romance of guns? The answers can be stated simply: increased crime and violence. But the U.S. Congress historically has been slow to adopt gun-control legislation. For the first 150 years of this country's history, there were no federal restrictions at all on the sale or ownership of guns. In 1919, an excise tax was imposed on the manufacture and sale of firearms, but this was largely an effort to bolster the federal treasury after the financial strain of World War I. It was not until 1927, after sensational incidents and lurid stories of gang-war slayings, such as the St. Valentine's Day massacre in Chicago, that the U.S. Congress passed the first gun-control law. This law prohibited the shipment of concealable weapons through the mails, although gun dealers, who were required to register with the Treasury Department, were exempted.

President Franklin D. Roosevelt, when he assumed office in 1933, viewed the gangsterism of the previous decade and the resulting crime wave as a national problem requiring more stringent action at the federal level. He "proposed a series of virtually unprecedented federal anticrime bills, including a bill which would have regulated the sale and ownership of machine guns and concealable weapons." The bills remained stalled in Congress, however, until April 1934, when archcriminal John Dillinger broke out of jail and in the course of several subsequent bank robberies engaged in machine-gun battles with federal agents. "Dillinger's exploits caused a national furor, and the firearms bill and several other anticrime measures were quickly passed."[12] Through prohibitive taxes the law made it extremely difficult, although not impossible, to possess or sell machine guns, sawed-off shotguns, silencers, and a few other favorite tools of the gangsters' trade. Four years later, Roosevelt was successful in expanding the licensing requirements for gun dealers.

In the following decade, the association of guns and gangsters faded away, to be replaced by the association of guns with the duty, honor, and bravery of the armed services in World War II. The pendulum swung back to the romantic side of firearms. Legitimacy staged a recovery as every young boy had his favorite play gun—a rifle or even a machine gun modeled after the latest U.S. Army or Marine Corps issue. In the 1950s, the country seemed generally preoccupied with economic matters: good jobs, getting ahead, and acquiring material possessions that had been unavailable during the Depression and the war. Crime, while ever-present, was not a major public concern.

In the 1960s, however, the pendulum swung sharply back toward tragedy. John Kennedy's assassination in 1963 focused the country's attention on, among countless other details, the rifle that Oswald used and the ease with which he had acquired it through the mail. Lyndon Johnson, after he assumed the presidency, repeatedly urged Congress to adopt various gun-control measures, including banning the mail-order sales of firearms. But it was not until 1968, after Martin Luther King, Jr. and Senator Robert Kennedy were both gunned down, and after the rioting and burning in Los Angeles, Detroit, and Washington itself, that Congress finally passed the Gun Control Act of that year.

There were two key provisions of this law. First, it banned mail-order sales and sales to persons under the age of eighteen of rifles and shotguns. Second, it required that each licensed gun dealer record in writing the sale of every gun and include the name, age, and residence of the buyer. Gun advocates lobbied hard that the Treasury Department not maintain a permanent file of all gun owners, so it was agreed that the records of sales were to be kept by the individual dealers but were to be available for inspection by Treasury officials at any time.

It is interesting to note the care taken to avoid alienating gun owners. The law stated that its purpose was:

to provide support to . . . law enforcement officials in their fight against crime and violence, and it is not the purpose of this title to place any undue or unnecessary Federal restrictions or burdens on law-abiding citizens with respect to the acquisition, possession, or use of firearms appropriate to the purpose of hunting, trapshooting, target shooting, personal protection, or any other lawful activity, and that this title is not intended to discourage or eliminate the private ownership or use of firearms by law-abiding citizens for lawful purposes, or provide for the imposition by Federal regulations of any procedures or requirements other than those reasonably necessary to implement and effectuate the provisions of this title.[13]

Unfortunately, crime and violence have continued unabated. The National Criminal Justice Reference Service reports that homicides committed with firearms reached a total of 16,189 in 1993 compared with a figure of 10,612 in 1987, an increase of more than 52 percent in that six-year period. By 1997, the latest figures available, this total had fallen back to 13,252. Still, the United States has the unhappy distinction of leading all developed nations in per capita deaths caused by firearms. The Service noted, "Firearms homicide was the second leading cause of death for the 15- to 24-year-old group."[14]

Such statistics have stoked an acrimonious public policy debate over gun control. Advocacy groups such as Handgun Control Inc. (HCI) have lobbied for a waiting period between the time a buyer purchases a gun and the time the gun is actually delivered to the buyer. Such waiting periods are to allow time to verify that the purchaser is not a felon, mentally disabled, or otherwise disqualified for gun ownership. Other groups, such as the National Coalition to Ban Handguns have urged a total ban on the ownership of concealable weapons. While the number of formal members in these organizations is not overwhelming—HCI, the largest of the groups, reports a membership of four hundred thousand—they are bolstered by national polls which consistently show that the majority of Americans feel that some control on the sale and possession of guns, especially handguns, is necessary. The most recent assessment of public opinion reveals the following:

- a majority of the public backs all measures to regulate firearms *except* those that call for an outright ban;

- an even greater majority supports safety measures such as mandatory gun locks, safe-storage proposals, and training for all gun owners;

- a majority supports prohibiting ownership of guns by those under the age of eighteen, but does not support banning guns from households with children under that age;

- a majority backs restrictions of gun imports; and a majority opposes permissive concealed-carry laws.[15]

Anti-gun advocacy groups have faced a formidable adversary, however, in the National Rifle Association (NRA). Organized over a century ago (1871) to teach and promote long-range marksmanship to a generation that was rapidly losing the values and skills of the frontier, the NRA has evolved into an organization—and a spiritual home—for gun enthusiasts, collectors, and owners of all kinds. The NRA now claims a membership of 3.5 million and boasts an annual budget of roughly $150 million, but its influence extends far beyond these numbers. Its lobbying ability and political clout are almost legendary and reputed to be the toughest and strongest in Washington. Its very active grassroots support, its careful targeting of substantial political campaign donations, and in the end, its ability to command critical votes from so many members of the House and Senate of both political parties have earned the NRA the label "invincible" and the reputation of being the most powerful lobbying group, not only at the federal level in Washington, but also at the state and local levels.

The debate over guns, gun control, and gun registration has waxed and waned over the past two decades, spurred on or dampened by whichever party occupies the White House. Most often it is emotional rather than rational, and has pushed the ideologically opposite groups into narrow corners from which there is little room for compromise and precious little chance for mutual understanding. The policy debate splits along a number of axes. There is a split between urban and rural populations: city dwellers facing on a daily basis the violent crime in their streets support almost any measures that will reduce the number of guns in the hands of criminals, while those who live outside the cities and suburbs see such measures as a threat to their traditional use of guns for hunting and target practice. There is a regional split between the eastern United States on the one hand and western and southern areas for much the same reason.

In addition, a class or income split has developed: working class members, who are more likely to participate in hunting and outdoor sports and more likely to own a gun for self protection, set off against wealthier or more sophisticated groups for whom guns are anathema.

The public policy debate, unfortunately, has deteriorated into the two sides digging in their heels, talking past each other with no attempt to look for common ground. Gun-control advocates point to the statistics on crime in America juxtaposed against the extraordinary proliferation of guns in the country—both figures far in excess of any other industrialized country in the world—and draw the not unreasonable conclusion that fewer guns would result in fewer crimes. Gun supporters, on the other hand, argue that only 1 percent of all guns and just 2 percent of handguns are used for criminal purposes.[16] And since only a small percentage of the guns actually used to commit a crime are purchased through legitimate licensed gun dealers—they are mostly bought "on the street" or are stolen—the recommended regulations on waiting periods or other methods of control would affect criminal elements very little and only serve to inconvenience or penalize the honest.

The nature of the debate has pushed each side into extreme positions. Some gun-control advocates, as noted, want to ban all handguns and perhaps register all guns, while the gun lobby warns that *any* regulation—even on assault weapons, Saturday-night specials, or "cop-killer" bullets—is a threat to Constitutional rights and a dangerous step down the slippery slope toward universal controls. Publications of the pro-gun activists warn of "home inspections" by agents of the BATF as the next logical step if gun-control laws are not reversed.[17]

Illustrative of this deep split are the actions taken by two relatively small U.S. communities. Shortly after Reagan and a pro-gun administration took over the White House in 1981, the citizens of Morton Grove, Illinois, a small city of twenty-four thousand not far from Chicago, decided that gun control would have to be decided at the local level. When a Morton Grove resident applied for a permit to open a gun store not far from the town's junior high school, the city's trustees searched in vain for a zoning ordinance or law of any sort to block the store. "We didn't want the kids looking in the window, dreaming of guns," stated the senior trustee, Neil Cashman. And so the city passed its own law outlawing not only the sale, but also *the private possession of all handguns* in the city. Having passed what was easily the most restrictive gun-control law to be found anywhere in the country, the trustees went on to appeal to other communities across the United States to do the same. The NRA was caught by surprise, but immediately challenged the Morton Grove ordinance in the state and federal courts. To the surprise of many, the legality of the ordinance was affirmed by the circuit court of Cook County, the U.S. District Court of Northern Illinois, and twice by the U.S. Court of Appeals in Chicago.[18] And in 1983, the U.S. Supreme Court denied a request to review the Appeals Court decision. However, what Morton Grove citizens anticipated would start a groundswell of activity toward more stringent gun control proved to be a false hope. Some other communities flirted with the idea; San Francisco did in fact pass a ban on handguns, but its law was overturned by California's superior courts.[19]

Morton Grove's action stirred what might be viewed as an equal and opposite reaction at the other end of the spectrum. In 1982, Kennesaw, Georgia, population eighty-five hundred, decided to make its own statement and so passed an ordinance that read in part: "in order to provide for and protect the safety, security, and general welfare of the city and its inhabitants, every head of household residing in the city limits is required to maintain a firearm, together with ammunition therefor." The ordinance did exempt those who were mentally incompetent, paupers, or those who objected on religious grounds.[20] To increase the publicity generated by this move, Kennesaw's mayor, Darvis Purdy, wrote to Dianne Feinstein, at that time the mayor of San Francisco, and asked her to send all the weapons surrendered or confiscated in her city to Kennesaw so his town's paupers could shoulder their civic responsibility to own a gun.[21]

The Brady Bill

Jim Brady, Ronald Reagan's press secretary, was one of those wounded (Brady was permanently disabled) in the 1981 assassination attempt.

Brady's wife, Sarah, became one of the most effective spokespersons for some form of gun control, working tirelessly with Handgun Control Inc. and other gun-control groups. After eleven years of effort and countless setbacks due in large part to the political lobbying of the NRA, the Brady Bill was finally passed by a Democratic Congress in 1994 and signed into law by President Clinton. The new law outlawed assault weapons and therefore outlawed an additional thirteen specific firearms models, and also established a waiting period in the purchase of handguns for those states that did not already have such a procedure in place. The ink was hardly dry, however, before the legislation was threatened. After taking over the majority in both the House and Senate in the elections of 1994, the Republicans set as one of their early objectives the repeal or at least the wholesale change of the Brady legislation. Inevitably, the politics of gun control entered the maneuvering for the 1996 presidential nomination among the many Republican candidates. Robert Dole, then a Kansas senator whose Western constituents have little love for any form of gun control, wrote to the NRA in early 1995 that "Repealing the ill-conceived gun ban passed as part of President Clinton's crime bill last year is one of my legislative priorities."[22]

Although all components of the industry—manufacturers, dealers, distributors, the NRA—had strongly opposed the Brady legislation, the short-run effects of the debate over the bill and its eventual passage actually helped to boost industry sales. As noted above, 1994 industry sales in all categories were sharply higher as gun buyers rushed to make their purchases before the anticipated passage of the new law. This was a predictable, albeit counterproductive, feature of the legislation. Table 4.1 shows a similar situation; in 1985 the number of machine guns manufactured in the United States shot up dramatically to beat passage of the gun-control legislation of that year, which sharply restricted sales of such weapons *after* passage of the law.

In 1999, Columbine High School in Littleton, Colorado, suffered one of the most tragic gun-related events in this country's history when two students brought weapons into the school and began shooting fellow students. By the end of the affair, fifteen were dead including the two protagonists, and twenty-four were wounded. While there was a flurry of activity on the part of gun-control activists following this event to place more restrictions on the sale of guns, such efforts were short-lived and unsuccessful given Republican control of both the White House and Congress at that time.

Following the terrorist attacks of September 11, 2001, there were some efforts made by the extreme pro-gun factions to weaken the Brady Law restrictions, to allow more people to protect themselves more readily, but these efforts also had little impact.

Near the end of the 1990s, a number of major cities attempted to steal a page from the tobacco liability lawsuits. Brooklyn, Chicago, San Francisco, and at least five other cities—along with a few counties—sued the various firearms manufacturers to recover funds that those cities have had to spend because of gun-related crimes. The cities claimed that the firms had marketed their products in ways that had led to the unreasonable proliferation of guns, making it easier for criminals to acquire them. These lawsuits have had little success. A Brooklyn jury did find in favor of the city, but the decision was overturned on appeal. In 2002, however, a West Palm Beach, Florida, jury held the distributor of a handgun used in a fatal shooting responsible to the extent of 5 percent of the total award, or $1.2 million. The door seems to be at least a bit ajar, if not wide open, to pursuing this course of legal remedy.

Smith & Wesson bolted from the other firms in the industry and struck a deal with the Clinton administration under which the company would speed up gun-safety improvements in exchange for relief from the pending lawsuits. This effort hurt Smith & Wesson in the marketplace. "Led by gun-rights groups angry with the company's apparent capitulation to a government attempt at gun control, buyers stopped purchasing its products almost immediately after the March 2000 deal."[23] The gamble proved to be even more of a mistake when the Bush administration backed away from the deal.

It is perfectly clear that the number of homicides caused by firearms has been dropping since the passage of the Brady Law. Whether there is a causal relationship involved is still subject for debate. Gun-control advocates argue that there is such a relationship, and therefore, restrictions should be extended to include, for example, sales of guns at gun shows, which are not now covered by federal laws. The firearms industry, the NRA, and pro-gun advocates reject the notion that the Brady Law has led to a reduced number of homicides and oppose vehemently any further legal restrictions on the marketing and exchange of guns.

It is not surprising, then, that there was an underlying air of tension and paranoia at the SHOT Show in Las Vegas. Only those who were members of the industry, or journalists covering the show for recognized outdoor magazines, were granted passes. Other journalists, researchers, or just members of the public were not welcome. This was more than just a trade show; it was a gathering of an ideological family. It did not matter that this family included such diverse members as manufacturers of expensive over-under shotguns strictly for hunting as well as makers and importers of cheap, concealable "Saturday-night special" handguns. Nor did it matter that this family included the romantic names of our past—Winchester, Remington, Colt—as well as the unromantic "SKS" from Russia and the "CZ537" from the Czech Republic. It was us versus them, the rest of the country versus Washington bureaucrats, Constitutional freedom versus government control. This family was sticking together because all its members were being threatened, to a greater or lesser degree, by adverse public opinion. The *legitimacy* of the entire firearms industry was and is at stake, bringing about necessary changes in the marketing strategies and options available to its members.

NOTES

1. SHOT stands for Shooting, Hunting, and Outdoor Trade Show.

2. Chapter title from Jervis Anderson, *Guns in American Life* (New York: Random House, 1984).

3. Ibid., 51–54.

4. Ibid., 5–6.

5. Bureau of Alcohol, Tobacco and Firearms, Washington, DC, ATF Online (accessed October 3, 2003). Also compiled from figures from the Department of Commerce. Production figures exclude arms sold to the U.S. military, but do include sales to police and other law enforcement agencies.

6. Department of the Treasury, Bureau of Alcohol, Tobacco, and Firearms, *Commerce in Firearms in the United States*, February, 2000.

7. As reported in Carl Bakal, *The Right to Bear Arms* (New York: McGraw-Hill Book Company, 1966), 8.

8. Ibid., 7.

9. Resa W. King, "U.S. Gunmakers: The Casualties Pile Up," *Business Week,* May 19, 1986, 77–78.

10. George D. Newton, Jr. and Franklin E. Zimring, *Firearms and Violence in American Life: A Staff Report Submitted to the National Commission on the Causes & Prevention of Violence* (Washington, DC: U.S. Government Printing Office, 1968), 22.

11. Loren Berger, "Who's Minding the Gun Counter?" *Business Week,* October 25, 1993, 120–21.

12. Newton and Zimring, *Firearms and Violence,* 98.

13. Public Law 90–618, sec. 101, *U.S. Statutes at Large* 83 (1968): 1213. As quoted in *Gun Control* (Washington, DC: American Enterprise Institute for Public Policy Research, 1976).

14. See the Web site for the National Criminal Justice Reference Service, http:// www.ncjrs.org (accessed April 13, 2002).

15. Tom W. Smith, *1999 National Gun Policy Survey of the National Opinion Research Center: Research Findings* (Chicago: University of Chicago, 1999).

16. Gary Kleck, *Point Blank, Guns and Violence in America* (New York: Aldine de Gruyter, 1991), 47–48.

17. *Gun News Digest* 1, no. 1 (Spring 1995).

18. Anderson, *Guns in American Life,* 109–112.

19. Anderson, *Guns in American Life,* 114.

20. William E. Schmidt, "Georgia Town to Celebrate Mandatory Firearms," *New York Times,* April 11, 1987.

21. Anderson, *Guns in American Life,* 115.

22. *Wall Street Journal,* March 20, 1995, A4.

23. Gary Fields, "White House Retreats from Smith & Wesson Deal," *Wall Street Journal,* August 1, 2001, A4.

CHAPTER 5

Gambling in America

For an industry that still operates under a cloud of social disapproval, not to mention severe legal restrictions, gambling has experienced phenomenal growth since the 1970s. The industry has posted enviable revenue and profit figures and has muscled its way into a position of importance in the U.S. economy. In 2001, well over half a *trillion* dollars was wagered in all the various forms of legal gambling, including gross revenues[1] of $63.3 billion for the casino industry.[2] Casino revenue showed an increase of 40 percent over 1995 and a 134 percent increase over the 1991 figure, thus significantly outpacing the overall economic growth of the country. For comparison purposes, gambling revenues even in 1994 were greater than the combined spending on leisure hotels, cruise ships, spectator sports, and films at the box office.

Included in these composite gambling figures are casinos of all types (the Nevada/New Jersey variety, Indian reservations, riverboats, and deepwater cruise ships), pari-mutuel betting on horses, dogs, and jai alai games, card room and nonprofit games, legal bookmaking, and lotteries (both state-run and video lottery terminals). For our purposes, we will concentrate on casino gambling and the state lotteries, which combined account for roughly 88 percent of the entire industry.

Both of these categories have shown strong growth. In 2002, casino gambling in one form or another was available in thirty-four states,[3] and lotteries are now operated in thirty-eight states plus the District of Columbia and Puerto Rico. Pari-mutuel betting on horse and dog racing has struggled in the face of this growing competition for gamblers' dollars. Actual attendance at thoroughbred racetracks has fallen steadily for years, and until recently the sport disdained television coverage except for major events like the Kentucky Derby, the Preakness, and the Belmont Stakes. Most of the $15.1 billion wagered on horse racing, more than 86 percent, takes place in off-track betting parlors.

From relative obscurity as recently as the 1970s, gambling has mushroomed into an important economic and social factor virtually throughout the United States. Only in Hawaii, Utah, and Tennessee do adults not have access to legal gambling of some variety; in the latter state, horse racing and pari-mutuel betting have been approved, but no one has stepped forward to build a track. Table 5.1 shows the availability of different forms of gambling across the country.

There is a distinction in the long history of gambling between games of skill and games of chance. Under the Romans' Justinian Code, games of skill were tolerated, but not games of chance. The supposition is that in those days the opportunity for cheating with loaded dice, weighted coins, and marked cards was too great, and in fact such artifacts have been found. Today, however, casino games such as craps and roulette and all lotteries are based purely on chance. When blackjack players try to introduce an element of skill by counting cards and memorizing odds in an attempt to beat the house, they are not allowed to play.[4]

The factors that have either allowed, influenced, or caused the surprisingly rapid growth in gambling in the United States during just the past thirty years are many and diverse, but it is helpful to sort through the most important. The economic effects of gambling at the consumer, corporate, and government levels can hardly be overstated in this regard. For the vast majority of consumers (those who are not addicted), gambling provides a relatively inexpensive form of entertainment with the attendant supercharged thrill of potential jackpots or multimillion-dollar lottery wins. For the industry's firms, gambling provides handsome profits and returns on equity, although increased competition in recent years has led to some failures. For cash-strapped state and local governments, lotteries and casinos represent a "painless" source of tax revenue. In the almost magical world of gambling, there are enough profits and money to satisfy all three levels. A casino, or even a neighborhood bar, is happy to pay out $5,000 to buy a video lottery terminal (VLT)—a new-age slot machine on which the manufacturer makes a handsome profit—knowing that his investment will be repaid in roughly two to three weeks.[5]

Changes in the technological environment have also contributed to gambling's rapid growth. The use of computers has allowed lotteries to go online, making them much more popular and opening up the possibilities of new games such as keno. New technology has also transformed the "one-armed bandit" slot machine into a dazzling and tantalizing electronic wonder that can bring the excitement of a Las Vegas casino to a small rural tavern in South Dakota, Montana, or West Virginia. The bells,

Table 5.1
Types of Gambling by State

State	Lottery	Casinos (all types)	Racetrack, Card Rooms, etc.
Alaska			✓
Alabama			✓
Arizona	✓	✓	✓
Arkansas			✓
California	✓	✓	✓
Colorado	✓	✓	✓
Connecticut	✓	✓	✓
Delaware	✓		✓
District of Columbia	✓		✓
Florida	✓		✓
Georgia	✓		✓
Hawaii			
Idaho	✓	✓	✓
Illinois	✓	✓	✓
Indiana	✓	✓	✓
Iowa	✓	✓	✓
Kansas	✓	✓	✓
Kentucky	✓		✓
Louisiana	✓	✓	✓
Maine	✓		✓
Maryland	✓		✓
Massachusetts	✓		✓
Michigan	✓	✓	✓
Minnesota	✓	✓	✓
Mississippi		✓	✓
Missouri	✓	✓	✓
Montana	✓	✓	✓
Nebraska	✓	✓	✓
Nevada	✓	✓	✓
New Hampshire	✓		✓
New Jersey	✓	✓	✓
New Mexico	✓	✓	✓
New York	✓	✓	✓
North Carolina		✓	✓
North Dakota		✓	✓
Ohio	✓		✓
Oklahoma		✓	✓
Oregon	✓	✓	✓
Pennsylvania	✓		✓
Puerto Rico	✓	✓	✓
Rhode Island	✓	✓	✓
South Carolina			✓
South Dakota	✓	✓	✓
Tennessee			
Texas	✓		✓
Utah			
Vermont	✓		✓
Virginia	✓		✓
Washington	✓	✓	✓
West Virginia	✓	✓	✓
Wisconsin	✓	✓	✓
Wyoming			✓

whistles, and flashing colored lights grab the gambler's attention, and the wizardry of the technology keeps the patron at the machine for as long as possible. International Game Technology's (IGT) recent addition to its product line, "Winner's Choice," offers the gambler the option to play up to 100 different games. The purpose is to keep the player at the machine a little longer and spend more at each sitting. "If we don't do that, we don't sell machines," says an IGT executive.[6]

The flashy graphics and computer sounds of the VLTs have their downside, however. Just as this advanced technology turned a generation of adolescent boys into video game addicts, it is now captivating adults and exacerbating compulsive and addictive gambling that affects 1–4 percent of the population, depending on whose figures one accepts. "VLTs are the crack [cocaine] of gambling," according to the clinical director of Charter Hospital in Las Vegas. They "combine all the principles that make a game relatively addictive."[7]

Political changes have also played a role in the growth of gambling. As the federal budget came under increased pressure during the latter half of the 1980s, the states were forced to search elsewhere for money to fund their social, educational, and welfare programs. Lotteries and legalized casinos became a quick fix. And this has had something of a snowball effect. Each state that turns to gambling becomes a competitor for its neighbors, attracting discretionary spending from its neighbors' citizens as well as its own. This puts pressure on yet more states to succumb to gambling to keep that income "at home."

Changes in the U.S. social and cultural environment relative to gambling have been critical to the success of the industry. As more and more state governments give their official seal of approval to gambling by running their own lotteries and sanctioning casinos within their borders, as moral and religious objections lose some of their cutting edge, and as the tie between gambling and crime becomes more the subject of myth than of reality, gambling has become less objectionable in the eyes of Americans, and the industry has moved toward, rather than away from, legitimacy.[8] What supports and helps to propel this move is that gambling is fun, exciting, and enjoyable for large numbers of people. Strip away the objections, and gambling is bound to flourish.

Consider Chester, West Virginia. The town has a population of only 2,723, but when video slot machines were introduced in a desperate move to revive a failing racetrack, it became a "destination resort" from nearby Pennsylvania and Ohio cities. "We used to think gambling was a sin around here," says city clerk Shirley Barnhart. Now the town is more interested in the economic virtue of the slot machines combined with pari-mutuel betting.[9]

Make no mistake: the industry still has a long way to go if it is ever to be truly considered legitimate or part of the mainstream of American business. Even after the phenomenal growth of gambling enterprises since the 1970s, gambling is still an illegal activity *unless* a state government *specifically* sanctions it, and that sanction can be withdrawn. In May 2002, both South Carolina and Georgia ordered all video slot machines removed from their states. The ubiquitous office pool on football games is still illegal, as is bookmaking on all sports and unofficial numbers games. And even where legal, gambling is tightly regulated, heavily taxed, and carefully controlled by state bureaus. While our views on gambling are changing, it still belongs in this study of unacceptable products, and the marketers of casino or lottery gambling still encounter difficulties not faced by the marketers of soap, shoes, or sodas.

CASINO GAMBLING

In the 1930s, Nevada turned to legalized gambling in an attempt to generate revenue for that barren state during the Depression years. For the next forty years, all of the legal casino gambling in the United States was safely tucked away—quarantined, perhaps—in that remote state. Certainly there were plenty of country clubs around the country that would roll out slot machines whenever the law was willing to turn a blind eye, and the more adventuresome, by knowing the right people, could tap into a "permanent, floating crap game" in an abandoned warehouse or the back room of a bar. But only in Las Vegas, Reno, and a few other Nevada resort towns could true casinos be found with rows of slot machines and all the usual table games: craps, blackjack, roulette, high-stakes poker, and perhaps even baccarat.

Early on, the casinos learned that gambling plus top-name musical and comedy entertainment was a winning combination, a marketing tactic to lure players from downtown Las Vegas out to the new clubs along the "Strip": the Stardust, the Sahara, the Sands, and other grand old casino names. Thus, the glamour of Hollywood—the likes of Frank Sinatra, Liza Minelli, Dean Martin, Lena Horn, or Sammy Davis, Jr.—together with the excitement of gambling gave the major casinos a competitive advantage and established a format that has changed very little over the past decades.

In 1978, legal casino gambling broke out of the confines of Nevada. Atlantic City, New Jersey, searching for a way to turn around its economic misfortunes, authorized the operation of a number of new casinos that, everyone hoped, would tap into the heavy population centers of the East Coast. The economic effects of that decision are still being debated. Casino gambling as an industry has done well in Atlantic City, attracting what some consider excessive investments like Donald Trump's billion-dollar Taj Mahal. Atlantic City now generates gambling revenues of $4.7 billion, compared with Las Vegas's $5.4 billion, but it has not been able to rival the Nevada city for the sheer glamour and glitz of top-name entertainment and ultra high rollers. It still attracts much of its revenue from day-trippers who flood in on chartered buses from New York and Philadelphia. The economic benefits of gambling seem not to have spread much beyond the casinos. Atlantic City is still plagued with depressed, crumbling neighborhoods within a stone's throw of the palatial casinos. In Las Vegas, by contrast, there seems to be no end to the demand for new, larger, ever more palatial gambling and hotel complexes. Billion-dollar, five thousand-room mega-resorts have become almost commonplace. Even a building boom can't seem to satisfy the demand for new homes and commercial buildings, and the multiplier effect of the gambling wealth seems to have extended throughout much of the city.

Casino gambling had spread to the East Coast, but for another ten years it was confined to Nevada and Atlantic City. Then, in 1988, the town of Deadwood, South Dakota, decided that "limited stakes" blackjack and slot machines would provide the tax revenue needed to revive and restore the historic town. A few years later, Central City, Colorado, turned to casinos as the only remedy to cure its "ghost town" status. New Orleans opened a casino bigger than any in Las Vegas or Atlantic City; Chicago, Washington, D.C., Baltimore, and other cities periodically consider casinos as a source of new tax revenues.

In 1991, Iowa introduced casino gambling on Mississippi riverboats and more recently added them across the state on the Missouri River. In the ensuing years, neighboring Illinois, Missouri, Mississippi, Louisiana, Michigan, and Indiana have all launched their own riverboats, although the term "launched" may be a stretch of the imagination, as most of these casinos remain securely tied to a dock and in some cases may not even be floating.

With congressional passage of the Indian Gaming Regulatory Act of 1988 (IGRA), the door was opened to the spread of casino gambling on Indian reservations, and twenty-three states, as diverse as Arizona, Minnesota, Montana, New York, and Connecticut, have reached compacts with Native American tribes for the operation of casinos.

In 1989, *Business Week* magazine warned, "At a pace that seems almost epidemic, gambling fever is sweeping the U.S. . . . . Today gambling outlets are almost as ubiquitous and well-patronized as convenience stores. Gambling is part of the weekly, and even daily, routine of tens of millions of Americans." Quoting a gambling expert, the magazine continued, "The world seems now to be engulfed in an explosion of gambling activity," and editorialized, "Don't let the U.S. become one big casino."[10] Hyperbole? Yes, of course, but one can hardly help but be impressed with the numbers the industry is posting. With the growth in consumer spending on casino gambling averaging 12 percent from 1990 to 2000, and profit margins well above most other industries, more states and cities are sure to authorize more casinos to attract yet more customers. There will be shakeouts to be sure. Individual casinos, companies, or even cities will fail to keep pace in the increasingly competitive environment. But the early years of the twenty-first century look every bit as exciting for the casino gambling industry as were the closing years of the twentieth.

The Major Players

As casino gambling grew and matured in Nevada during the 1960s and 1970s, a symbiotic relationship developed between the gambling and entertainment businesses on the one hand and the hotels to accommodate their patrons on the other. The casino operators began getting into the hotel business to provide a captive clientele for their tables and slots, and even more rapidly the hotels began opening their own casinos to subsidize their relatively low profit operations with the high cash flows from gambling. In the latter half of the 1990s, however, there was a consolidation of the major casino operators with subsequent mergers, acquisitions, and name changes.

Park Place Entertainment, soon to be known as Caesar's Entertainment, Inc., now holds the top spot among the casino companies, with revenues in 2003 of $4.7 billion. It is an international company encompassing Caesar's Palace and Bally's Grand hotels in Las Vegas, casinos in Atlantic City and Mississippi, as well as operations in Canada, South Africa, and Uruguay. Next in line, with revenues in 2002 of just over $4 billion was MGM Mirage, a product of the merger between the MGM Grand and Mirage hotel/casinos in Las Vegas. Its other interests include the Bellagio, Treasure Island, and New York, New York casinos in Nevada, as well as gambling interests in Detroit, Mississippi, Australia, and South Africa. In third place was Harrah's, one of the original Nevada gambling trademark names, now operating twenty-six casinos in thirteen states under the Harrah's, Harvey's, Rio, and Showboat names. In addition to its own land-based casinos, Harrah's operates riverboats and manages Indian tribal casinos as well. Its 2000 revenues were just over $3.7 billion. Mandalay Resort Group is yet another major operator in Las Vegas, with the Mandalay Bay, Luxor, and Circus Circus operations generating revenues of almost $2.4 billion in 2002. Donald Trump's Trump Hotels and Casino Resorts is a major competitor in the Atlantic City market with revenues exceeding $1.2 billion.[11]

Native American Reservation Gambling

What a curious development this has been in just a short period of time: full-scale casino gambling on Native American reservations. The story has fascinating cultural, political, economic, historic, and social dimensions, but we can only skim the surface in this book.

The Seminole tribe of Florida introduced high-stakes bingo on its land in 1979, not only for its own members, but as a commercial enterprise to attract other Floridians as well. The state sued the tribe, but lost in the lower federal court. In finding for the tribe, the court established the principle that if a state criminally prohibits a form of gambling within its boundaries, then Native American tribes are also prohibited from that activity. But if a state allows some form of gambling, then the tribes also may engage in that form free of state control. Because Florida allowed various charitable groups to operate bingo games, the Seminole high-stakes bingo operation was allowed to continue.

This ruling led to an explosion of bingo operations on Native American lands during the 1980s, followed by concern on the part of various congressional committees that the situation needed some sort of control, and finally a test of the lower court ruling by the Supreme Court in 1987 in *California v. Cabazon*. The high court upheld the lower court's ruling, but also declared that Congress could limit the tribes' rights if it chose to do so.

The following year, Congress did indeed pass the Indian Gaming Regulatory Act (IGRA), which dealt with the more difficult questions over "Class III games," that is, table games, slot machines, and pari-mutuel betting, by requiring the states to negotiate compacts with tribes within their borders.[12]

Comprehensive figures on Indian gaming are difficult to find. The National Indian Gaming Association reported that as of October 2003, its members were running 321 operations in twenty-nine states. These operations generated revenues of $12.7 billion in 2001, somewhat less than 10 percent of total gambling revenues.[13]

By all counts, the most impressive of these Native American casinos is in Ledyard, Connecticut, owned by the Mashantucket Pequots. The Foxwoods Resort started in 1986 as a modest 2,100-seat bingo hall. By 2001, the operation had grown to one of the largest casinos in the world with 315,000 square feet of gambling space offering 6,700 slot machines and 300 gaming tables. More than $1.5 billion has been invested in the 1.3 million-square-foot complex, which now includes two hotels and fifteen restaurants. Foxwoods employs more than ten thousand to serve as many as sixty thousand players per day from New York, Boston, and the densely populated area within an easy drive of the casino.[14]

It did not take long for other Native Americans in Connecticut to recognize a wonderful business opportunity. In 1996, the Mohegan Tribe opened a Casino of the Earth, followed in 2001 by the Casino of the Sky. Between the two operations, the Mohegans now offer more than six thousand slot machines and 240 gaming tables.[15] In 2001 these Connecticut Indian casinos generated gambling revenue in excess of $2 billion.

THE STATE LOTTERIES

As with the various forms of casino gambling, lotteries too have a long and interesting history. They were used to help finance the Virginia Company's Jamestown settlement early in the seventeenth century[16] and continued for the next 200 years to be a popular method of raising public funds. However, the uncovering of a number of instances of gross fraud on the part of state officials and lottery middlemen led to a wave of public indignation and a decline in lottery activity after 1830.

The Civil War and the mounting need for funds during the Reconstruction period revived state lotteries. The most famous, or infamous, of this period was the Louisiana Lottery Company, chartered in 1868. Over the ensuing twenty-five years, this group flagrantly violated federal and state laws; controlled banks, newspapers, and legislatures; bribed governors and other state officials; and finally generated such a backlash of public opposition that a combination of new federal and state regulations effectively prohibited all lottery operations for the next seventy years.[17] It is interesting to note for the purposes of this book that opponents of the Louisiana Lottery criticized not only its corruption, but also its aggressive promotion of 20¢ tickets among the poor.

State lotteries were reintroduced in 1963 when New Hampshire, which was constitutionally prohibited from levying a state income tax or a state sales tax, authorized a state-operated sweepstakes "based on the outcome of horse races for the benefit of public education."[18] New York quickly followed in 1966, but neither of these early experiments lived up to expectations. New Hampshire raised only $5.7 million from the sale of its $3 tickets in its first annual sweepstakes, far short of the anticipated $10 million. Marketing mistakes were blamed: some felt the $3 ticket price was too high, and others cited the lack of promotion and excitement during the long periods between the annual (later semiannual) sweepstakes drawings. New York generated a disappointing $70 million from tickets priced at $1 and $2 in its monthly drawings in 1971. Annual per capita sales were almost identical for both states in 1970, $2.67 for New Hampshire and $2.60 for New York, and both states experienced declining sales after some initial enthusiasm.

This might have meant an early demise for state lotteries save for two factors: the continuing strong economic stimulus to search for new sources of public funds, and the introduction of a marketing approach to make the games more attractive to the players. Late in 1970, the recently formed New Jersey state lottery system placed on sale 50¢ lottery tickets for its weekly drawings, in one stroke making the tickets more affordable and enhancing the excitement of the product by increasing the frequency of play. The changes produced startling results: New Jersey's twelve-month sales totaled $124 million with per capita sales of $17. New York quickly reduced the price of its tickets to 50¢, and weekly drawings became a standard feature.

Other states could hardly ignore this new source of revenue, and in 2003, thirty-eight states plus the District of Columbia and Puerto Rico have lotteries, encompassing more than 80 percent of the country's population. The Bible Belt Southern states have been the most reluctant to succumb to the lure; Louisiana, Texas, and Georgia all began their operations in the early 1990s, and South Carolina not until 2001, but Arkansas, Alabama, Mississippi, Tennessee, Oklahoma, and North Carolina are among the twelve states that still do not have lottery operations.

In total, lottery ticket sales amounted to more than $42.4 billion in 2002; the states' take from that figure was more than $20 billion, representing 4 percent of their total revenue. New York has the biggest lottery operation, selling almost $4.8 billion of tickets in 2002; Massachusetts is only slightly behind with sales of $4.2 billion. On a per capita basis, Rhode Island heads the list; each of that state's citizens spent $1,115 on lottery tickets. Delaware, South Dakota, and Massachusetts followed, while in Nebraska and Montana, lottery ticket sales amounted to only $43 and $37 per capita, respectively (see table 5.2). All of the state lotteries in the United States have two important features in common. First, as their name indicates, they are run by the states themselves. The significance here is that it puts

Table 5.2
Per Capita Lottery Ticket Sales ($) for Selected States in 1990 and 2002

State	1990	2002	State	1990	2002
Arizona	37	54	Missouri	32	104
California	35	86	Montana	21	37
Colorado	42	92	Nebraska	N/A	43
Connecticut	87	266	New Hampshire	57	169
Delaware	82	843	New Jersey	95	246
District of Columbia	169	370	New Mexico	N/A	74
Florida	84	140	New York	74	250
Georgia	89	299	Ohio	81	175
Idaho	31	72	Oregon	145	239
Illinois	67	128	Pennsylvania	66	160
Indiana	46	105	Puerto Rico	N/A	70
Iowa	32	62	Rhode Island	105	1,115
Kansas	30	73	South Carolina	N/A	80
Kentucky	66	158	South Dakota	204	829
Louisiana	41	70	Texas	73	139
Maine	59	124	Vermont	48	134
Maryland	105	247	Virginia	67	157
Massachusetts	150	663	Washington	38	73
Michigan	72	170	West Virginia	37	469
Minnesota	30	77	Wisconsin	56	80

state governments in the position of managing and marketing an enterprise that has been morally suspect throughout much of its history. While hard-core gambling opponents may deplore the states' involvement, for others it is an official stamp of approval. And not just for lotteries. The spread and legalization of lotteries under the aegis of the states has had an impact on the acceptance of casino gambling as well. If the state itself authorizes betting on a lottery, why not slot machines, blackjack, craps, roulette, and the other casino games?

The other significant factor regarding the state lotteries is that they are monopolies, and they do precisely what we fear monopolies of all kinds will do: make exorbitant profits. Compare the payout of a typical lottery, usually in the range of 45–55 percent of the amount wagered, to the payout for a casino that averages roughly 90–93 percent across the various table games and slot machines. Critics argue that if the lotteries had to face competition, they would inevitably increase their payout figures, and the public would be getting a better value product.

A confrontation between Native American and nonnative gambling interests could change this situation. The Coeur d'Alene tribe in Idaho proposed a National Indian Lottery that would sell tickets in all jurisdictions that now run lotteries. The Native American format envisions customers buying lottery tickets by calling an 800 telephone number and paying for them with a credit card. The states have good reason to be concerned. Not only would their monopolies be threatened, but they believe a National Indian Lottery could afford higher payouts, not to mention the convenience of telephone sales and credit card payment. There are a host of legal hurdles for the Coeur d'Alenes to get over before such a lottery could begin. At present, using a telephone to sell lottery tickets, or any other form of gambling, across state lines is illegal, as is the use of credit cards for the purchase of lottery tickets in most states. But the challenge has been made, the glove has been thrown down, and over the first half of the 1990s, the Native Americans have been very successful at building gambling businesses using the IGRA as an opening wedge. Given the long history in the United States of unfair treatment of Native Americans, it is politically difficult to deny them access to this lucrative market. But at the same time, the stakes are so high that the states are not going to give up their monopoly moneymaking machines without a serious legal battle.

OPPOSITION TO GAMBLING

There is very little organized opposition to gambling in the United States. Compared to the anti-smoking groups or the handgun control advocates, for example, critics of gambling tend to mobilize or organize only when a state or municipality proposes to authorize casinos or a lottery. And yet gambling lacks the legitimacy enjoyed by mainstream U.S. industries; despite its recent resurgence and extraordinary growth, our society accepts it only with considerable reluctance and with a great many regulatory strings attached.

Objections to gambling usually fall into one of five categories: it is a regressive "tax," it is morally wrong, it can cause an addiction that often leads to tragic consequences for individuals and families, it attracts criminal elements, and it fails to deliver on its economic promises.

Gambling works like a regressive tax because, it is argued, its effects fall most heavily on the poor. While surveys show that purchasers of lottery tickets cut across all income segments, the poor are hurt most because they have little or no discretionary income and must sacrifice essentials to purchase the tickets.

The moral arguments against gambling are that it breeds sloth and idleness rather than hard work, it promotes the hope of getting something for nothing, and it glamorizes material wealth. The strongest pockets of this opposition are in the fundamentalist churches, especially in the South. As noted above, the Deep South has been the slowest region to adopt state lotteries.

The churches have opposed riverboat gambling also, but without success either in Mississippi or Missouri. During the 1992 debate over riverboats operating out of Missouri cities, all of the mainstream Christian churches—Roman Catholics, Episcopalians, Lutherans, and Methodists included—united under the banner of the Missouri Christian Leadership Forum. In their press releases, however, the churches did not argue their case against gambling on moral grounds, choosing instead the economic arguments outlined below which they must have felt would have broader appeal. In 1994, the Roman Catholic bishops in Pennsylvania announced their somewhat hedged opposition to riverboat gambling operating out of the state's ports "unless they can be assured it won't damage moral values."[19]

Church and state have been the historic defenders of public morality and would be expected, therefore, to lead the opposition to all forms of gambling. But because some church denominations, notably the Roman Catholics, have a long tradition of allowing, even encouraging, charitable bingo games, and because so many state governments are now operating and promoting their own lotteries, the opposition from these two segments of our society has been severely blunted.

Gambling addiction, however, goes beyond questions of morality. Estimates as to the number of people who are actually addicted to gambling vary widely, from 1 to 4 percent of the population, including an increasing number of teenagers, depending on whether it is someone from the industry or someone from the medical community making the estimate. But on one point there is no real disagreement: as gambling has increased so rapidly over the past three decades, the problem of gambling addiction has risen at least as rapidly if not more so. Compared with the more than four hundred thousand deaths each year related to smoking or with 17,500 alcohol-related vehicle crash deaths, the individual and social costs from gambling addiction are less dramatic and less likely to get the public's or the media's attention, but they are very real nonetheless.

The anecdotes are easy to find:

Frank won $18,000 on a basketball bet in April 1985. By the end of that week, he had lost $21,000. To finance his high-rolling habit and the late-model luxury cars and up-to-the-minute clothing that went with it, he persuaded his parents to apply for a $67,000 second mortgage on their house. He said he also persuaded a friend to take out a $150,000 first mortgage on the friend's house. Frank's former wife never knew how much he wagered. Often, he said, he bet hundreds of dollars on a football game but would tell her he had wagered only $5. . . . Somehow, he never ran out of money. "I could always find someone to con, someplace to borrow," he said. He always believed the big score was coming, but it never did. The more he gambled, the more he lost.[20]

Out-of-control gambling gripped Pete Rose, the Cincinnati Reds' batting champion, and his reputation was so tarnished that he has been denied a place in baseball's Hall of Fame. William Bennett, secretary of education in the Reagan administration and author of *The Book of Virtues*, was criticized as a hypocrite when it was discovered that he has been an addicted gambler in recent years.

Gamblers Anonymous, a self-help group along the model of Alcoholics Anonymous, claims that more than half of all pathological gamblers will turn to some form of criminal activity—bad checks, phony insurance claims, embezzlement—at some point in their search for money to support their addiction. Professional psychologists report that trying to kick the habit leads to the same sort of withdrawal symptoms experienced by smokers or drug addicts: stomach distress, sleep disorders, irritability, high blood pressure, and the like.

There are social costs as well. Gamblers are less productive at work, they call in sick more frequently, and they are distracted. Although their crimes may be white collar and nonviolent, too many addicted gamblers end up in jails and prisons, using society's resources, which are badly needed for more dangerous criminals.

Links to Crime

The continuing perception that gambling breeds or attracts criminal elements should come as no surprise. Throughout much of our history gambling has been illegal, after all, and still is in many forms and in many places. Thus, by definition, during those periods of illegality whoever organized or participated in gambling was involved in a criminal activity. There is also plenty of historical evidence to support the view: the recurring lottery scandals mentioned above and the Prohibition era association between crime gangs and numbers rackets. There are periodic reports of organized crime links to various casinos in both Nevada and Atlantic City in spite of efforts and specific regulations of the state gambling commissions to keep them out. There is some intuitive logic to support the association as well: if there is a great deal of money to be made and if the business of gambling is perceived by many to be socially unacceptable, then organized crime-related groups, presumably less concerned about the social stigma, are likely to fill the vacuum.

Organized crime's involvement in gambling activities comes to the surface often enough to validate the public's perception. In early 1995, a former president of Bally Gaming International's domestic subsidiary pleaded guilty to felony charges involving the distribution of Bally video poker machines in Louisiana. A federal grand jury indictment had alleged that members of the Marcello, Gambino, and Genovese organized crime families had engaged in racketeering in connection with the video poker machine operations.[21]

At about the same time, a former national sales manager for Gtech Holdings, a maker of lottery games and systems, claimed that the company knew about payments made in an alleged payback scheme in Kentucky. The manager was under indictment for bribery, conspiracy, fraud, and money laundering in Kentucky and New Jersey.[22]

Later in 1995, the FBI opened another investigation in Louisiana, the result of wiretap transcripts of conversations in which state legislators allegedly discussed taking bribes from video poker interests in return for preventing potentially damaging legislation from reaching a vote.[23]

There is a constant concern whether betting on athletic contests, either professional or at the college level, will compromise the sport and perhaps even result in rigged games or "shaved" point spreads. As a result, athletes at both levels are forbidden to bet, not only on their own games but on other games in their sport as well, and *any* gambling by a high-profile athlete can lead to close public scrutiny. University of Maryland quarterback Scott Milanovich was suspended by the NCAA (National Collegiate Athletic Association) from the first four football games of the 1995 season for betting on college sports. Basketball superhero Michael Jordan's gambling escapades in Atlantic City and on the golf course have been highly publicized. Jordan admitted under oath losing $57,000 to a convicted drug dealer at golf, and checks totaling almost twice that amount related to his gambling debts were found in the estate of a North Carolina businessman who was shot to death.[24]

The industry labors diligently to dispel the perception that gambling attracts criminal elements. Frank Fahrenkopf, Jr., the president of the recently formed American Gaming Association, has said that one of the goals of the industry group is to get rid of old stereotypes of gangsters being involved with legitimate gambling. Responding to criticism of gambling by Senator Paul Simon of Illinois, Fahrenkopf wrote:

As for the crime statistics, there is absolutely no credible evidence that shows the introduction of legal gaming, because of the nature of the business, increases crime. The real facts are that many non-gaming tourist attractions have higher, visitor-adjusted crime rates than do gaming-entertainment destinations. For example, when adjusted for the number of visitors, Chicago in your home state and a non-gaming community, has a higher crime rate than Las Vegas. . . . rated safer [by the FBI] than Orlando, Florida, the site of Disneyworld.[25]

Fahrenkopf's organization, the American Gaming Association, calls the link between gaming and organized crime one of the "myths" surrounding the gaming industry and dismisses it by noting how tightly regulated the industry is.[26]

On the association with crime, Harrah's reports that Atlantic City "compared favorably" with other tourist destination cities, and Las Vegas had the second lowest crime rate when visitor-adjusted population figures were used.[27] This interpretation of the statistics is of little comfort to the citizens of Atlantic City, who saw the incidence of crime increase in their city, at the same time that the visitor population swelled, with the introduction of gambling.

Economic Arguments

Finally, there is criticism of gambling because, opponents say, it fails to deliver on its economic promises. This is especially ironic because the overwhelming arguments for authorizing casino gambling or a new state lottery are, inevitably, the economic benefits that gambling will bestow. Because gambling still carries the stigma of social unacceptability, no state adopts a lottery or accepts casinos simply because they are fun and people enjoy them. We carry too much Puritanism in our psyches to allow us to do that. Always, it must be done because the economic benefits will outweigh whatever social evils are attached. Gambling will create jobs, it will bring tourists who will spend their dollars in our state or our community, it will be good for business, it will stave off the competition from neighboring states, it will keep our citizens' money at home, it will create badly needed tax revenues to support our schools, our aged, and our needy.

The state of Maryland, through an independent commission, held public hearings in the fall of 1995 and studied the advantages and disadvantages of authorizing casino gambling in Baltimore City. In connection with this proposal, the Abell Foundation, a nonprofit group, issued a preliminary report outlining the various considerations. In this twenty-four-page study, the overwhelming emphasis is on economic questions:

- What will be the effect if Maryland's neighbors to the North and South adopt casinos and/or riverboat gambling?
- Many cities with which Baltimore competes for convention business have approved or are considering casinos.
- Thousands of Maryland residents leave the state to gamble in Nevada and Atlantic City. Would neighboring states' casinos increase this outflow? Would Baltimore casinos keep the money at home?
- What would be the effects on horse racing in Maryland? On the Maryland lottery? On charitable bingo and other games?
- How many people would be employed by Baltimore casinos and at what wages?
- How much tax revenue would be created and how would that be split between the city and the state?
- How much of the casino income would come from out of the state?

In the report, barely a nod is given to the "moral issue":

Notwithstanding its increasing popularity, casino gambling is still considered distasteful, if not immoral, to many. Indeed, it is a form of "entertainment" that has been illegal in most states for decades. There are groups of residents and visitors alike who find the concept of casino gambling an affront. Would they choose to move out of the city? Would they decide to stop visiting the city? How would a casino in Baltimore City impact the city's image?[28]

Even in this very brief discussion of the moral dimension of gambling, the three questions posed are really more concerned with business-related issues than with morality. Although the report and the public debate over the casino question were weighted heavily toward economics rather than ethics, the report does raise a significant question. Would there be the same sort of public scrutiny and debate if a developer were proposing a new museum, movie theater, theme park, ski slope, or golf course? The suggestion is that because of the nature of gambling, because of its social unacceptability, a casino proposal is subjected to far more stringent economic tests, perhaps because we as a society are unwilling or uncomfortable to debate the moral arguments.

Economics continued to be the central argument in the debate surrounding gambling, both in the state of Maryland and elsewhere in the country. Newly elected Maryland Governor Robert Ehrlich, a Republican, took office in 2003 vowing to solve the state's financial problems by allowing the state's horse race tracks to add slot machines. The plan went nowhere when the Democratic-controlled legislature turned down the proposal.

Half a continent away, the longtime mayor of Okoboji, Iowa, Bob Schneider, rallied the residents of his tiny town to defeat handily a plan to establish a gambling boat on lovely Lake Okoboji, a major Midwest resort area. The argument: gambling would siphon badly needed funds away from his citizens and the surrounding farm communities simply to line the pockets of the out-of-town investment group putting up the money for the boat. The investors did not give up easily, however, because the potential profits were too enticing. They began to investigate the idea of creating a manmade lake a few miles away, near a friendlier town where they could launch the boat with its casino tables and slot machines.

PROSPECTUS

The meteoric rise of gambling in the United States since 1975 should not be taken to mean that every gambling enterprise has been successful or that the future for the industry is necessarily as bright as the past has been. Even as new riverboats were being launched up river in Indiana and Iowa in the mid-1990s, the *Grand Palais* and *Delta City Queen* in New Orleans were being shut down after only two months of operations. Their gambling revenue had been far below their expectations. A similar shake-out was taking place among the boats operating at Tunica, Mississippi.

Central City, Colorado, citizens had mixed feelings about the effects of casino gambling in their small town. True enough, the casinos did well, and the city's tax revenues increased from $500,000 to $6.5 million per year. But expenses shot up also, so that Central City's debt ballooned from $500,000 in 1988 to $20 million in 1993. "I'd tell anyone who was thinking of opening their community to casino gambling to have his head examined," rued the city manager.[29]

There are plenty of Atlantic City residents who argue that the net effects of casino gambling on that city have been negative rather than positive. And in New Orleans, only months after the country's largest casino had opened its doors, critics were calling the operation a "disaster," claiming that gambling was sucking money and profits out of small businesses, and threatening to close down the video poker machines that have proliferated in bars and truck stops around the state.[30]

Gambling suffers from another problem too as it grows so rapidly. When a state first begins a lottery operation (or a new casino), the revenue typically rises quite rapidly over the first few years. After that, however, the novelty wears off, and the state is fortunate if its lottery revenues keep up with population growth. As neighboring states commence lotteries of their own, for the competitive reasons already noted, the first state's revenues may actually decline. This can be especially painful if the state's education system, for example, has come to depend on this new fountain of tax dollars. Then the state is put in the uncomfortable position of marketing its gambling more aggressively—new games, more advertising, wider distribution, and so on—or having to reallocate its shrinking revenues.

Competition can also make it difficult for a state to impose or maintain the kinds of controls once thought appropriate. When riverboat gambling was first approved in Iowa, limits were set on the size of any single bet ($5) and how much any individual gambler could lose in a day ($200): prudent safeguards for the state's middle and lower-middle income citizens. But the limits also made it difficult for the riverboat operators to make the kind of profits they had envisioned, so after only two years the *Emerald Lady* and the *Diamond Lady* sailed away from Fort Madison, Iowa, for Biloxi, Mississippi, where the state imposed no such restrictions. Economics won out over prudence, however; Iowa removed its restrictions, new boats began operations, and revenues in 1994 were up 123 percent over the previous year.

Deadwood, South Dakota, also wanted to impose restrictions on its casino operations—no more than thirty slot machines per building—so that the casinos would remain small to conform with the nature of the town. But after several years of successful operation, the city and state came under increasing pressure to raise that restriction. One source of that pressure was a $100 million Dunbar Resort, proposed in 1994 by actor Kevin Costner, which anticipated a lavish casino operation just outside the town. In 2002, the resort was still waiting for final approval and financing, the subject of considerable opposition from a coalition of anti-gambling, anti-growth, and Native American activists.

In spite of these occasional clouds, the current forecast for gambling is for continued growth, although perhaps not at the frantic pace of the last few decades. At present, the gambling industry is a marketer's dream: strong demand, still limited supply, and practically endless variations to the product. The great unanswered question is: Can the marketing of gambling be carried on within the uncertain and unwritten constraints set by our society? The availability of online gambling adds a new dimension to this complexity and uncertainty as described in a later chapter. Gambling does still require specific legal authorization. And there is still some level of social disapproval, albeit diminishing, connected with gambling. Under these circumstances marketers are asked to exercise uncharacteristic restraint to escape past cyclical patterns and avoid throwing the industry back into a pre-1960 era of almost total prohibition.

Assuming that does not happen, a blueprint for the future of the industry, for a new dimension of gambling, already exists: at-home betting. Visionaries describe a not-too-distant interactive gambling future when players will be able to bet on a casino game, a lottery, or a horse race without leaving the comfort of their homes and just by pushing a few buttons on their television sets or their computers. Seven states already allow betting on horse races by telephone from home, using a private account and PIN (personal identification number) established by the player at a nearby track. Now two firms, TVG and Magna Entertainment, are televising round-the-clock horse racing via cable television to thirteen million homes across the country. Through their affiliates, the companies also allow at-home viewers to set up betting accounts and place bets directly from their living rooms via the Internet.[31]

And that is just the beginning. There is already a casino in cyberspace called Virtual Vegas, available through the use of a computer and a CD-ROM program featuring three-dimensional imaging, voice recognition, and other aspects of virtual reality. A player can enter a casino, walk down its aisles, select from traditional and new casino games, and talk to the computer. To date, winnings and losings are still imaginary, but the master plan calls for "on-line, real-time betting for money."[32] The National Gambling Impact Study Commission reported that in 1999 there were more than 250 online casinos, 64 lotteries, 20 bingo games, and 139 sports books, all of these categories showing a dramatic increase from just the previous year.[33] There are plenty of legal, regulatory, technological, and of course moral hurdles still to overcome before this Holy Grail of gambling—round-the-clock betting at home—is realized. But given the inherent popularity of gambling, its recent growth, the slow melting of the social stigma, the available technology, and the lure of an estimated $10 billion new segment of the industry, no one is betting against at-home gambling.

NOTES

1. "Gross gambling revenue" is the term that most closely compares to a company's or an industry's sales figure. "Handle" is a gambling term meaning the amount that is actually wagered. The handle, less what is returned to players in payouts and prizes, is the gross gambling revenue figure. For example, a gambler might take $100 to a blackjack table or a slot machine, gamble for an hour, and leave with $90. The handle would be the $100; the revenue to the casino would be $10.

2. Unless otherwise noted, industry figures are taken from the Web site of the American Gaming Association, http://www.americangaming.org/casino_entertainment/aga_facts/facts.cfm/id/8 (accessed October 3, 2003).

3. Mark Heinzl, "Place Bet, Click, Watch the Ponies on TV," *Wall Street Journal*, July 24, 2003, B1.

4. Michael Olnent, "Points of Origin," *Smithsonian* 15 (October 1984), 178–81.

5. James Cook, "Legalizing the Slots," *Forbes*, March 2, 1992, 78–79.

6. Matt Connor, "Using Technology to Keep Players in Their Seats," *International Gaming & Wagering Business*, April 1, 1995, 14.

7. William M. Bulkeley, "Video Betting, Called 'Crack of Gambling,' Is Spreading," *Wall Street Journal*, July 14, 1992, B1.

8. D. Kirk Davidson, "Losing and Regaining Legitimacy: Opposite Trends in

the Tobacco and Gambling Industries," in *Proceedings of the Fourth Annual Meeting of the International Association for Business and Society,* ed. Jean Pasquero and Denis Collins, unpublished, 291–96.

9. Francis X. Clines, "Track and Casino Turn a Rust Belt Town Green," *New York Times,* March 3, 2002, 18.

10. Chris Welles, "America's Gambling Fever," *Business Week,* April 24, 1989, 112–20, 160.

11. http://www.hoovers.com/industry (accessed April 21, 2002).

12. Henry C. Cashen and John C. Dill, "The Real Truth about Indian Gaming and the States," *State Legislatures,* March 1992, 23–25.

13. National Indian Gaming Association, http://www.indiangaming.org/library/index.html#facts (accessed October 4, 2003).

14. Paul Doocey, "A Resort to Non-Gaming Amenities: Las Vegas, Native American Style," *International Gaming & Wagering Business,* July 1, 1995, 54, 56.

15. http://www.hoovers.com/industry (accessed April 21, 2002).

16. C. T. Clotfelter and P. J. Cook, *Selling Hope: State Lotteries in America* (Cambridge, MA: Harvard University Press, 1991), 34.

17. Commission on the Review of the National Policy toward Gambling, *Gambling in America* (Washington, DC: U.S. Government Printing Office, 1976), 143–46.

18. Vicki Abt, J. F. Smith, and E. M. Christiansen, *The Business of Risk: Commercial Gambling in Mainstream America* (Lawrence, KS: University Press of Kansas, 1985), 56.

19. William Machlin, "Bishops Urge Caution on Gambling," *Philadelphia Inquirer,* August 1994.

20. James Barron, "Has the Growth of Legal Gambling Made Society the Loser?" *New York Times,* May 31, 1989, A18.

21. "Former President of Bally Gaming Unit Enters Guilty Plea," *Wall Street Journal,* January 10, 1995, B10.

22. David Stipp, "Ex-GTECH Official Tells Court Firm Knew of Payments," *Wall Street Journal,* January 11, 1995, A6.

23. Rick Wartzman, "Gambling Is Proving to Be a Poor Wager for State of Louisiana," *Wall Street Journal,* September 11, 1995, A1.

24. *Newsweek,* June 14, 1993, 73.

25. Frank J. Fahrenkopf, Jr., from a letter written to the Honorable Paul Simon, dated August 3, 1995, provided by the American Gaming Association.

26. See "Myths and Facts" on the organization's Web site, http://www.americangaming.org/casino_entertainment/aga_facts/facts.cfm/id/8 (accessed April 26, 2002).

27. *Harrah's Survey of Casino Entertainment 1995.* Harrah's publishes an annual survey of casino patrons, that is available at the company's Web site, www.harrahs.com.

28. The Abell Foundation, *Casino Gambling: Should Baltimore Roll the Dice?* (Baltimore, MD: Abell Foundation, 1994).

29. Rita Koselka and Christopher Palmeri, "Snake Eyes," *Forbes,* March 1, 1993, 70.

30. Rick Wartzman, "Gambling Is Proving to Be a Poor Wager."

31. Paul Doocey, "Gaming at Home: How Close Is It?" *International Gaming &*

Wagering Business, April 1, 1995, 1. See also Mark Heinzl, "Place Bet, Click, Watch the Ponies on TV."

32. Ibid.

33. As reported by the American Gaming Association, http://www.american gaming.org (accessed April 26, 2002).

CHAPTER 6

The Business of Pornography

To write about pornography begs a definition. But any such definition is so dependent on geography, time, and culture—and is ultimately so subjective—that I will not attempt that distracting and contentious task. Perhaps pornography is one of those commodities about which we say, "I know it when I see it."

Our purposes in this book are to treat pornography as yet another socially unacceptable product and explore how its marketing raises special problems and challenges. No doubt, because of definitional difficulties, there will be examples included here that some readers will argue should not be considered pornographic. The opposite is equally likely—that examples of other types of pornography might have been included but were not.

Sometimes there is confusion between the adjectives *pornographic* and *obscene*. We will assume that the former always refers to some aspect of sexuality, while the latter is broader and can describe, in addition to sexual material, violence, or certain physiological functions of our bodies, that is, anything that produces feelings of disgust. Much of the public policy debate—for example, how to control what is shown on the Internet and what is protected by the First Amendment—involves both obscene and pornographic material. Here we will concentrate on pornography so as to sharpen the focus on marketing issues, understanding that in movies, television, and on our computers, pornography and violence are often inseparable.

Cultural and geographic differences in the perception of pornography, or in the acceptance of sexually explicit material, are important for marketers to understand. Current standards in the United States may seem rather prudish to Europeans, who are more accustomed to seeing nudism used in outdoor advertising or on television. On the other hand, our standards seem quite relaxed to the Japanese. A Procter & Gamble television commercial for soap, which involved a fully clothed man talking to his wife (out of sight) in the bathroom, a scene totally innocent for U.S. audiences, was considered unacceptable in Japan. Or consider the problems marketers of women's lingerie face in Islamic countries. A billboard in Iran could not show a woman or lingerie, nor could it even mention the unmentionable product; it could show only the green box in which the lingerie was packaged.

Societal views on what material is considered pornographic change dramatically over time as well. Victorian England seems quaint and almost unrealistically straight-laced by today's standards. Even in our own lifetime there have been dramatic changes in what visual images are acceptable in magazines and on television, and the changes have all been in the direction of increased permissiveness.

From time to time this trend toward relaxed standards and a wider spread of pornographic material catches the attention of the federal government. In 1970, Congress found the traffic in pornography to be "a matter of national concern" and established a national commission to "study . . . the causal relationship of such materials to antisocial behavior, [and] to recommend advisable, appropriate, effective, and constitutional means to deal effectively with such traffic in obscenity and pornography."[1] Oddly enough, the majority of the commission took a rather sanguine view of the situation, questioned whether the business of pornography was indeed a "national concern," and concluded that the public was really quite "permissive about permissiveness." Theater critic Clive Barnes commented, "Few congressional commissions can have sought so eagerly to saw away at the branch they were sitting on."[2] It should be added, however, that a minority of the commission members held a sharply different view.

Sixteen years later, yet another commission was formed, this time by President Reagan's attorney general, Edwin Meese. Given the philosophy and the politics of the administration in 1986, perhaps it is not surprising that this commission came to starkly different conclusions:

More than in 1957, when the law of obscenity became inextricably part of constitutional law, more than in 1970, when the President's Commission . . . issued its report, . . . we live in a society unquestionably pervaded by sexual explicitness. In virtually every medium, from books to magazines to newspapers to music to radio to network television to cable television, matters relating to sex are discussed, described, and depicted with a frankness and an explicitness of detail that has accelerated dramatically within a comparatively short period of time.[3]

This statement might just as well have been dated 2003. For all the current news coverage of the spread of visually explicit images, we can only conclude that the acceleration has continued or perhaps increased over the past seventeen years. The only change in recent years has been the addition of another medium for pornographic material: the Internet on our computer screens.

Inevitably, there are short-term swings in the pendulum of public opinion on the subject of pornography, depending to some extent on who is doing the analysis. In 1990, the avant-garde *Village Voice* proclaimed that "puritans are on the run" because juries had refused to strike down as obscene the photography of Robert Mapplethorpe and the music of 2 Live Crew. "The market for [sexually explicit records or videotapes] is too diverse to be permanently suppressed. There's big money in sex—and in the end, Americans usually go for the gold."[4] Yet, twelve years later, there is a growing concern among liberals that the Republican Party control of the House of Representatives and the White House and the influence, if not control, of the Republican Party by the religious Right, will mean a new wave of censorship that will affect not only artistic and entertainment products, but also the content of our advertising for all products.

Such swings in public attitudes should not surprise us, although a look at history would lead us to expect long-term rather than abrupt changes. Ancient Greece and Rome were far more accepting of the human form, with or without clothing, than later cultures, and the pornographic wall frescoes of Pompeii demonstrate an open attitude to normal sexual activity as well.

The Old Testament of the Bible has plenty of lurid passages, for example, the prophet Ezekiel's descriptions of the "whoredoms" of Aholah and Aholibah and Solomon's metaphorical lyric on the pleasures of the flesh in the Song of Solomon. But the teachings leave no doubt as to the punishment awaiting individuals or communities (Sodom and Gomorrah) that surrender to such pleasures. Early Christian teachers including Paul, planted the seeds harvested centuries later in the Puritan years, that sensual pleasures were wicked and thus should be avoided by God-fearing people.

It was the invention and rapid spread of printing that led to widespread censorship. Prior to the use of printing, there was little pornography to suppress. But as books became more common, at least among the wealthy, each society and its legal system set about defining and attempting to control what its citizens could and should be permitted to see and read. Generally speaking, the classics were presumed to be acceptable, although Boccaccio's *Decameron* was occasionally intercepted, and there have been instances where even excerpted passages from the Bible have been seized as obscene, often to the eventual embarrassment of the censors. Over the past two centuries, a series of novels have created temporary scandals. John Cleland's *Fanny Hill: The Memoirs of a Woman of Pleasure*, *Lady Chatterly's Lover* by D. H. Lawrence, and Henry Miller's *Tropic of Cancer* all were labeled pornographic by the censors of the day. In the nineteenth century, the rule was indeed strict. According to the so-called Cockburn ruling in London of 1868, "a book was liable to be condemned on account of a single passage or incident or the use of one or two obscene words." And no evidence of literary, scientific, or educational merit could even be presented to the court in defense of the work.[5] This remained the standard on both sides of the Atlantic until 1933, when Judge John Woolsey of New York delivered his historic judgment in accepting James Joyce's *Ulysses*. Here, the standard shifted to whether or not the net effect of the work was obscene or whether the dominant purpose was to excite sexual impulses or lustful thoughts.

The history of censorship is also dotted with embarrassing mistakes. In the 1950s, the British Customs censorship office proved a bit overzealous when it confiscated all copies of a work entitled *Rape Round Our Coasts*, only later to discover that the subject of the work was soil erosion.[6]

Such rules, whether of Victorian England or of the United States circa 1950, now seem rather quaint and naive compared with the near "anything goes" standard of the early-twenty-first century. Even though the standards have shifted dramatically, marketers still face the problems of presenting and selling products that are opposed by significant numbers in our society.

Unlike the other product categories we have introduced in this book, pornography can claim no industry of its own. The national commission in 1970 estimated the business of pornography to be in the range of $.5–2.5 billion. By 1986, the report issued by the attorney general described pornography as an $8–10 billion business. It is reasonable to estimate, because of rapid growth and the spread into other media, that at the beginning of this new millennium the figure would be in the $20–30 billion range, but that business is spread over a number of segments of the entertainment, publishing, and communications industries. And the definitional problems mentioned above make industry statistics very difficult to pin down.

We will look briefly at pornography as it appears in movies, television, magazines, and certain forms of popular music. Because of the current level of concern, we will also look at pornography as it is made available on our computer screens (in chapter 11). Pornography comes to us in other ways as well: through 900 numbers on our telephones, through video games, through "escort services" promoted by some of our finest hotels, and sometimes even in the media advertising of mainstream products.

Child pornography—sometimes referred to as "kiddie porn"—has drawn a great deal of attention. Even people who take a relaxed, laissez-faire attitude toward pornography in general, supposing that it is a private matter for adults, can become irate over the use of children in pornographic material and also the exposure of children to adult porn. As noted below, groups advocating the control and suppression of pornography often stress the effects it is having on children, knowing that this rallying cry will gain widespread support.

We look briefly, then, at pornography as it comes to us—that is, as it is marketed—in magazines, movies, television, and popular music videos.

MAGAZINES

First there was *Esquire*.[7] Looking back on old issues of this magazine from the 1940s, they seem by today's standards rather quaint and almost innocent, certainly dated; naughty, perhaps, but it is difficult to label them as pornography. Nevertheless, the thinly clad, always buxom Varga and Petty girls, named for their artists, were shocking for the times. And *Esquire's* monthly foldout photograph, even its little mascot figure—Esky, the dapper gentleman in tuxedo with a bushy white mustache who leered appreciatively at the gorgeous cover girls—set patterns for future magazines to follow.

Esquire chose to try to be more than just a "girlie" magazine. With an almost entirely male readership, it moved to position itself as the discriminating or intelligent man's magazine, with articles on fashion and fiction by noted "macho" authors such as Norman Mailer. The magazine's naughtiness, pornography for its time, remained as a mainstay feature but became only one of several features.

This shift in emphasis on the part of *Esquire,* and the drift of publishers to experiment with more explicit material, opened the door in the 1950s for a new, much racier competitor in the form of *Playboy.* Now the monthly shock value was ratcheted up several notches. *Playboy's* totally nude centerfold and its "Playmate-of-the-month," set a new standard for pornographic material, at least as it was available in widely distributed, "slick" magazines.

Playboy also got caught up in what might be termed "the wheel of porn." It too sought to be the arbiter of good taste for well-to-do young men and began to add articles on fashion, wining and dining, the arts, serious fiction, politics, and public affairs interviews with the likes of Ralph Nader. Inevitably, this invited competition from a flock of even more explicit porn magazines such as *Penthouse, Hustler,* and *Oui.* These magazines, widely available in newsstands although sometimes with brown paper covers hiding all but the titles, have raised the pornography bar still higher. The photos explore the female models' anatomy in much more detail, feature even more erotic poses, and also portray often outlandish sexual *activity* among couples or groups.

Penthouse, Hustler, and their peers represent the current extreme in pornographic magazines with wide distribution and professional production. An almost limitless number of cheap, low-quality porn magazines can be found in sex shops, attempting to eradicate completely whatever limits might remain on erotic poses and to stretch still further the imagination of possible sexual activity.

As magazines move down this spectrum from naughty to nasty, there is a corresponding loss of legitimacy, measured in terms of distribution and types of advertising. A mainstream fashion magazine like *Cosmopolitan*, which month after month features lots of cleavage on its cover model and highlights articles on improving one's sex life, may be too "racy" for a supermarket in the Midwest. Some convenience stores will sell *Esquire* and *Playboy* but not *Penthouse* and *Hustler*. And as noted, the most graphic of the porn magazines can be found only in adult sex shops. Advertisers also must decide where to draw the line. Procter & Gamble, as a mainstream marketer, will avoid all the adult magazines, but certainly will buy space in the fashion magazines regardless of how tantalizing their covers may be. Even without Procter & Gamble, automobile manufacturers, and the other mainstream advertisers, *Playboy* and even *Penthouse* have little trouble filling up their pages with advertising aimed specifically at men: vodka, gin, tequila, rum, whiskey, and liqueurs; the major brands of cigarettes and sometimes chewing tobacco; cameras and stereo equipment; and antiperspirants and aftershaves. The cheap, sleazy magazines in the sex shops either have no advertising at all or only ads for other forms of pornography such as sex videos or 900 call-in telephone numbers for sexually explicit conversations.

FILM

Pornography in the movies comes to us in two varieties. The more legitimate of the two is produced by the major Hollywood studios complete with star-status actors and actresses, expensive productions, heavy marketing budgets, and all the panoply of directors, script writers, set designers, wardrobe consultants, and so on that Hollywood conjures up in our minds. In this case, the studios are constrained by their self-imposed rating system: the familiar G (all ages admitted), PG (parental guidance suggested—some material may not be suitable for children), PG-13 (parents strongly cautioned—some material may be inappropriate for children under thirteen), R (restricted—under seventeen requires accompanying parent or adult guardian), and NC-17 (no one seventeen and under admitted). Most major studios, members of the Motion Picture Association of America (MPAA), will not release NC-17 or unrated films, not out of concern for moral values, but for economics. Too few theaters will show NC-17 films, and too few newspapers will advertise them. The challenge

then for the major studios—from both an artistic and a marketing perspective—is how to include as much sexual content and violence as the
author and director intend and still claim the R rating.

For the Walt Disney studio, with its squeaky clean, family-oriented image, the question of ratings and appropriate subject matter is a special
problem. In 1993, Disney acquired Miramax Films so that the company
could produce and market adult films under a different name and not
hurt the Disney image. But two years later, problems stemming from the
divergent strategies of the two studios came to a boil. Miramax had acquired the rights to two films: *Priest*, a drama about a gay clergyman, and
Kids, a shocking film whose main character, a teenage boy, habitually de-
flowers young virgin girls (graphically depicted in the film) among other
acts of violence in New York. Miramax originally planned to release the
former film on Good Friday, which certainly gives new meaning to the
phrase "adding insult to injury," but when the Catholic League threatened
to boycott all Disney films and products, Miramax rescheduled the release
and scaled back the number of theaters. *Kids* posed a different problem.
In its original form it was sure to receive an NC-17 rating, but Miramax,
as a division of Disney, could not release such a film, nor could it release
an unrated film under MPAA guidelines. Miramax's options were either
to sell the film or to revise it substantially to qualify for an R rating.[8]

Of late, marketers at many studios have found a way to have their cake
and eat it too, or in marketing terms, to target more than just one market.
With the growing importance of videos, a film now has more than just its
initial life in first-run theaters. After the film's run in the theater, it will
be rented and sold in video stores, shown on cable channels, then in hotel
room systems, in foreign markets, and perhaps in other markets as well.

To meet the different demands of these distinct markets, the studios
now produce several versions of the same film. The most sexually explicit
scenes may be cut for theater runs to get an R rating; then some or all of
the scenes will be put back in the video version. While most studios refuse
to release a film without a rating, and most theaters will not run them,
video stores hold no such scruples. In fact, video stores will buy anywhere
from three to eight or nine times as many copies of an unrated film (meaning more pornography) than the rated version.[9] Even Blockbuster, the
largest of the video rental chains, which boasts that it will not stock X or
NC-17 rated films, fudges a bit by carrying unrated films regardless of
their content. This practice of marketing two or more versions of the same
film, tailoring the sexual content to different markets, dates back at least
to 1984 and the film *Crimes of Passion* starring Kathleen Turner, but the
practice is more widespread today.[10]

Another tactic of the studios for promoting R-rated films is to produce
two different trailers, the "previews of coming attractions" shown in theaters before the featured film. A so-called red-band trailer—complete with

nudity, profanity, and extreme violence—can be shown in theaters featuring an R-rated film, on the assumption that the audience is suitably mature to view such material. The other version of the trailer is sanitized somewhat and can be shown in theaters featuring PG-rated movies.

Such distinctions are blurred when studios turn to the Internet to promote their films. Sony, under pressure from the MPAA, was forced to shut down its Web site temporarily because it was showing a red-band trailer for its *Not Another Teen Movie*, with no controls in place to screen out underage viewers.[11]

That is the Hollywood variety of film pornography. The other variety needs no ratings: it is all hard-core porn, and the harder the better. It comes to us not from Hollywood, but from the San Fernando Valley on the other side of Los Angeles. There are no glamorous studios, only dingy, one-room sets where an entire video may be shot in just one day. As many as twenty-four hundred of these porn films may be produced in any given year. The stars of these video films may not be household names, but Tiffany Million, Jeanna Fine, Teri Weigel, Nikki Tyler, and Jeff Stryker have their own fans among the hard-core cognoscenti. Sticking to good marketing theory, these producers offer a product for every segment of the market, and no subject is taboo: heterosexuality, homosexuality, bestiality, incest, sex acts performed by seniors, and the list goes on and on.

The distribution channel for such films is not unlike the channel for more mundane items, hardware, candy, or other consumer goods. Wholesalers buy the films from the producing studios and turn around and market them to the thousands of video chains and independent stores across the country.

When interviewed by telephone, the president of one of the most prominent of these wholesalers, which also produces some of its own films, described his business in the following way: "If you could see our business, it would look like any other part of corporate America. We have production and distribution functions, we have accountants and bookkeepers, we have a marketing staff, telemarketers, the whole works." When asked about the problems posed by some chains (Blockbuster, for example) adopting a policy of not carrying hard-core pornography, the president replied that this gives the distributors a sales pitch to the thousands of "mom and pop" video stores across the country. Between 26 and 30 percent of the video rental business is in this hard-core porn category, a figure confirmed by two other sources, and so this distributor's sales staff markets the product to the smaller stores as a way to cover an important niche of the market left open by Blockbuster. "It becomes a matter of economics," he told me.

As long as X-rated films could be seen only in the dingy, small theaters that are usually located in the decaying areas of our metropolitan commercial districts, there was relatively little social concern or protest. The "problem" seemed to be adequately contained when it was limited to a fringe market, a handful of "dirty old men." But now that such films are as close as the corner video store, now that they so conveniently find their way into the living rooms of homes in our best neighborhoods, now that customers of the product no longer must risk the social embarrassment of patronizing one of the sleazy theaters, there is a heightened level of concern. A change in the distribution of the product has made a world of difference; the problem is no longer contained.

TELEVISION

Just as the movie theater industry is divided into a large majority of mainstream, first-run theaters that will not show NC-17 films and a small number of marginal screens that feature hard-core pornographic movies, so too is hard-core pornography on television relegated to a handful of pay-per-view cable channels. And just as with the movie industry, if this were the extent of pornography on television, there would be little criticism.

"Encroachment" is the watchword of the day; pornography is encroaching on mainstream television along four paths. First, ever more explicit scenes are creeping into network television shows. *NYPD Blue* raised a short-lived storm of protest on its inauguration some years ago when it included brief shots of nudity and equally brief shots of couples making love. Although the program is aired at 10:00 p.m., after the traditional family hours of television watching, and each segment is preceded by a stark warning to the audience that it may contain offensive language and nudity, anti-pornography groups were outraged that such material could find its way onto network television at any hour. Initially, ABC was concerned about finding enough advertisers who would be willing to buy time during the show; many refused to be associated with the program fearing some backlash or boycott of their products. However, now that the show has achieved not only critical acclaim but also high viewer ratings, selling spots before, during, and after the show is hardly a problem. With *NYPD Blue*, commercial success won out over moral concerns.

In 2002, the situation was repeated with a police drama series offered by cable TV's FX network entitled *The Shield*, which pushed the envelope of acceptable content still further; the show is "laced with raunchy language, graphic violence, and crude sexual references. . . . Just as its older sibling the Fox Broadcast network made its name by stretching the boundaries of network television, FX seems to be defining itself by pushing a little further into the realm of raciness." Burger King, General Motors, and the Subway chain decided not to run ads on the show; ads for Palm (Pilot) that appeared were pulled. "Meanwhile, FX is counting on ads from booze, beer, movie and video games companies" to take up the slack.[12]

The second path of pornography's encroachment has been into the very heart of the family viewing hours of prime-time television on popular sitcoms such as *Friends* and *Will and Grace*. Here, the material that is offensive to various groups is not explicit scenes on camera, but rather subject matter. Topics that have been taboo on television since its inception—descriptions of sexual activity, homosexuality, masturbation—are now routinely included in these family-oriented comedies.

The third path has been into the daytime talk shows. Below is a sampling of topics and show titles from a list at least ten times this long:

- On *Sally Jessy Raphael* (Multimedia Entertainment): a guest described sleeping with more than two hundred partners; a thirteen-year-old guest described her sexual experiences, which began when she was ten; a show was entitled "Wives of Rapists."

- On *Geraldo* (Tribune Entertainment): a gold-chained pimp threatened to assault a member of the studio audience as scantily clad prostitutes sat beside him; a show was entitled "Men Who Sell Themselves to Women for a Living."

- On *Maury Povich* (Paramount): eighteen-year-old Jason stated that he was in love with Calvin. Calvin was having an affair with Jamie, Jason's twin sister. Jamie was attracted to Scott, who had sex with Calvin and Tiffanie. Tiffanie had sex with everyone except Jamie.[13]

Cable television is the fourth path, with a seemingly different standard as to what is permissible and what is not, especially on the channels such as HBO, which are not in the usual packages of premium cable service and therefore require customers to request them separately. *The Sopranos*, which is aired at 8:00 p.m. on Sundays and which is one of HBO's most highly acclaimed series, is a good example. A recent segment featured full frontal nudity and graphic depictions of oral sex to accompany its notorious quotient of physical violence. *Sex and the City*, another popular HBO series, which airs at 9:00 p.m. on Wednesdays, has made its reputation by discussing in detail, and sometimes portraying, a wide assortment of heterosexual and homosexual activities. These television shows are brought to the public not by some sleazy, off-the-beaten-track porn purveyor, but by none other than AOL Time Warner, the largest media conglomerate in the United States. The idea that such content comes from the same corporation as *Time* and *Fortune* magazines gives new meaning to the concept of a diverse product line.

In the competitive market for sexual television programming, quantity wins out over quality, hands down. There seems to be a race to the bottom (no pun intended), and whoever can provide the most explicit sex will win. Just as *Playboy* has been out-porned by other magazines showing harder-core material, the Playboy cable television channel also has been upstaged by racier on-screen programming. But now Playboy Enterprises is fighting back and is acquiring three hard-core channels: Hot Zone, Hot Network, and the even more explicit Vivid TV. The *Wall Street Journal* reports, "Rich profit margins are driving the change at Playboy: Hard-core sex programming brings TV distributors nearly double the profit of Hollywood films. And consumers who pay to watch sex on TV seem to prefer the more explicit stuff: so called buy rates for hard-core porn are more than double that of soft-core porn."[14]

The nonprofit group Parents Television Council (PTC) released a report in 1999 entitled, "The Family Hour: Worse than Ever and Headed for New Lows." According to the PTC:

At the close of the century that ushered in TV, the medium's early promise has been erased by the rapid degeneration of . . . program content. Today, even shows airing in the earliest prime time hour, are sexually explicit, vulgar, and violent. Further, all indications are that, despite the growing consensus regarding media's influence on behavior—especially among the young—this trend is not only continuing, but accelerating.[15]

The PTC went on to report that its measurements of objectionable TV content during prime time hours had increased by 75 percent in just a year and a half to a rate of nearly seven incidences per hour of programming. "Among the networks, Fox [aiming at the teen and young adult market] was the clear leader in frequency of offensive material, with an average of 11 instances per hour, while 100% of its shows during the family hour contained offensive elements. . . . while CBS (3.62 per hour) was the least offensive." Overall, more than two-thirds of television programs during the family hour contained sexual material.[16]

The popularity of such shows and such topics is beyond question. Competition among the networks and production companies has become a matter of which show can introduce the most outlandish and titillating subject matter.

POPULAR MUSIC

The most severe criticism of popular music in recent years concerns the violence of its lyrics, but since this violence is often directed at women, including degradation and rape, the violence overlaps with pornography.

I dug between the chair and pulled out the machete,
She screamed, I sliced her up until her guts were like spaghetti.
A maniac, I stabbed the girl in the tits.
And to stop her nerves from jumping, I just cut her to bits.
And I'm an assassin
                    (from "Assassins," recorded by the Geto Boys)

AOL Time Warner is also one of the leading recording producers and marketers and has been battling controversy over violent content since 1993, when its Warner Records unit released the rapper Ice-T's song "Cop Killer." Criticism of the record from family-values groups was anticipated, but Time Warner was subsequently faced with police organizations picketing its stores and products, which then led to significant shareholder complaints. At first, Time Warner executives, including then chairman Gerald Levin, staunchly defended the record on the basis of artistic expression and the free speech rights guaranteed under the First Amendment. When the protests continued and the public relations heat from placard-waving uniformed police grew too intense, however, Levin eventually agreed to establish corporate standards for handling controversial music.

In 1995, Time Warner had the dubious distinction of being singled out by Republican presidential contender Robert Dole as contributing to the deterioration of values in America. The company came under criticism for its planned release of the home video version of the violent movie *Natural Born Killers*, but it is also saddled with the sins of one its divisions, Interscope Records, much as Disney is forced to deal with the nasty problems created by Miramax.

Time Warner owns 50 percent of Interscope, which in turn owns the distribution rights for Death Row Records. Not only have Death Row's founders served time in prison for various felony charges, but its star performer, rapper Snoop Doggie Dogg, has been indicted on murder charges. These legal problems aside, critics charge that the label's releases, "Dogg Food" and "Doggystyle," are prime examples of violence and pornography, advocating oral and group sex, among other things. Can there really be a big market for this kind of music? Upon its release, "Dogg Food" immediately topped the *Billboard* charts and within weeks had sold nearly three hundred thousand copies.[17]

One can hardly discuss pornography in pop music without at least mentioning Madonna. Sometimes nicknamed "The Queen of Obscene," Madonna conducted a reasonably successful one-woman drive to remove all remaining barriers to what sexual images can be brought to the video world, for example, in her 1992 release "Erotica." The publication in that same year of Madonna's book, simply entitled *Sex*, which was a large collection of mostly nude photos of her, often in various erotic poses with other nude men and women, seemed to be an effort to turn Madonna into a multimedia pornography industry all by herself. Perhaps there is a point of satiation for our society after all; in spite of extraordinary promotional efforts and an early flurry of sales, the book died a rather quiet death.

As a senator and presidential candidate, Robert Dole may have bemoaned the relaxation of values in the country. However, in his post-Senate, post-politics career, the septuagenarian is best known for his ogling of Britney Spears, the sexy teenaged pop vocalist whose scantily clad gyrations recently have been featured in Pepsi commercials. For better or worse, this is an interesting commentary on the relaxation of standards of television content in the early twenty-first century: not only will a mainstream consumer goods product like Pepsi use Britney Spears to liven up its ads with what would have been considered sexually explicit material a short decade ago, but we can joke about it by casting a respected aging political leader in the role of wishing he were sixty years younger.

THE INTERNET

If concern about pornography began in earnest with the introduction of printing, it has received another major push with the emergence of the newest communications medium, the Internet. In its cover story on pornography, *Time* magazine noted:

the modern concept of pornography was invented in the 19th century by European gentlemen whose main concern was to keep obscene material away from women and the lower classes. Things got out of hand with the spread of literacy and education, which made pornography available to anybody who could read. Now, on the computer networks, anybody with a computer and a modem cannot only consume pornography but distribute it as well.[18]

In 1995, the U.S. Senate in a rare showing of bipartisanship passed the Communications Decency Act on an 84–16 vote. The act would establish fines and prison sentences for making available or sending obscene communications to minors across electronic networks. Several states, including Maryland and Virginia, had already adopted their own statutes. One great problem with any of these laws is that the Internet is truly a medium without boundaries or borders. Denying access to the Internet for pornography in one state, or even one country, simply encourages content providers to move to a more hospitable home base. One of the more popular Web sites in the mid-1990s was a museum in the Netherlands that put online its extensive collection of erotic art, which could be downloaded in living rooms across the world.

Museum-quality art is certainly not the major problem, however. The Senate's action gained such widespread support because of the pervasiveness of the material being distributed. In 2002, a google.com search for "hard-core pornography" yielded 255,000 sites. Heading the list was a "sponsored" link (meaning it was paid for) to "Live Hardcore Porn Shows." Totaltramps.com offered a free, three-day trial and promised "raw, nasty action like you've never seen it before."

The "teensteam" Web site shows how much of the content emphasizes teenagers: "amateur teens, Asian teens, Latina teens, Club seventeen, Teen

Kitty, First timers, Teen sex, Young girls." Figure 6.1 shows the variety of sexual material, the depth of the company's product line in marketing terminology, at another Web porn site. Several screens later, there may be a statement in small print that claims all models are over the age of eighteen, but it is clear what the emphasis of the "product" is. These sites feature absolutely graphic, hard-core pictures available to anyone who visits, long before there is any need to pay a fee or join a "club." After several of these screens, the only guard against young viewers may be something like the following, "Click here to confirm that you are eighteen or older."

Pornography on the Internet is especially worrisome for several reasons. The distribution of the material is direct into our homes. We don't have to slink into an X-rated theater; we don't even have to risk being seen buying a magazine or renting a video. It also means that children have easy access to the pornographic material. At present there seem to be no effective controls, and proposed legislation raises the familiar specter of censorship. For every complaint that material currently transmitted by computer would be banned in another medium by obscenity laws,

Figure 6.1
Pornography Site Product Line (Censored)

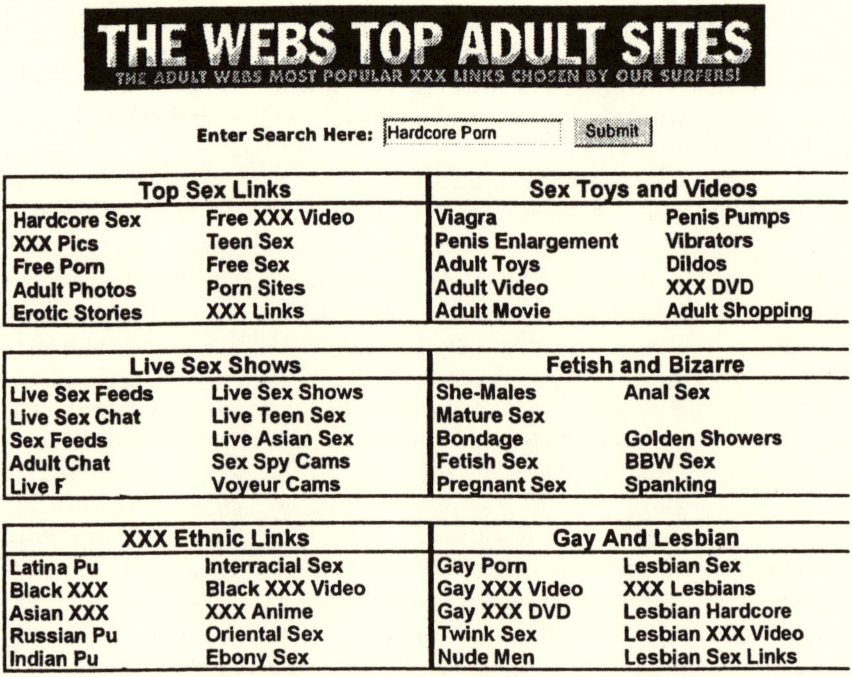

THE WEBS TOP ADULT SITES
THE ADULT WEBS MOST POPULAR XXX LINKS CHOSEN BY OUR SURFERS!

Enter Search Here: Hardcore Porn Submit

Top Sex Links		Sex Toys and Videos	
Hardcore Sex	Free XXX Video	Viagra	Penis Pumps
XXX Pics	Teen Sex	Penis Enlargement	Vibrators
Free Porn	Free Sex	Adult Toys	Dildos
Adult Photos	Porn Sites	Adult Video	XXX DVD
Erotic Stories	XXX Links	Adult Movie	Adult Shopping

Live Sex Shows		Fetish and Bizarre	
Live Sex Feeds	Live Sex Shows	She-Males	Anal Sex
Live Sex Chat	Live Teen Sex	Mature Sex	
Sex Feeds	Live Asian Sex	Bondage	Golden Showers
Adult Chat	Sex Spy Cams	Fetish Sex	BBW Sex
Live F	Voyeur Cams	Pregnant Sex	Spanking

XXX Ethnic Links		Gay And Lesbian	
Latina Pu	Interracial Sex	Gay Porn	Lesbian Sex
Black XXX	Black XXX Video	Gay XXX Video	XXX Lesbians
Asian XXX	XXX Anime	Gay XXX DVD	Lesbian Hardcore
Russian Pu	Oriental Sex	Twink Sex	Lesbian XXX Video
Indian Pu	Ebony Sex	Nude Men	Lesbian Sex Links

there are responses from civil rights groups that the Senate bill and the various state measures would ban material that has artistic or social value and that is available in print.

Much of the pornographic material now available on the Internet is free to online subscribers: bulletin board group discussions, lurid stories and pictures exchanged, and so on. However, there is also plenty of commercial activity: "kinky, nasty, bizarre, and taboo" videos for sale, as one service advertised; 900 number call-in sex lines promoted; and curiosities such as body jewelry made to hang from male and female sex organs. The extent of this activity, that is, the dollar value of merchandise bought and sold, is still relatively small. For the purposes of our inquiry, however, it is important to note that it is the lack of any constraint on those doing the marketing, either self-imposed or socially imposed, that fuels the outrage of the opposition. The Internet allows for anonymity; we do not know even who the marketers are. If there is a company name, as with the body jewelry, it is a small organization with no concern for corporate reputation. As a result, the marketing knows no bounds. Four-letter words become a part of the ad copy; graphic images of body organs and sexual activities can be used to promote the product. The absence of any need for restraint—because as consumers we do not know who is sending the message—leads to a form of competition based on shock value. Whoever sends the kinkiest, the nastiest, the most bizarre, or the most taboo message wins our attention.

THE OPPOSITION

Opponents of pornography are spread among a number of relatively small advocacy groups whose agenda is the strengthening of family values, groups most often associated in some way with political conservatives and the religious Right. A notable exception, at least in political orientation, is the Parents' Music Resource Center. One of the group's founders, Tipper Gore, wife of former vice president Al Gore, brought the prestige of her position to promote the aims of the organization, which as early as the mid-1980s successfully lobbied the music companies to put warning labels on tapes and CDs that included sexually explicit lyrics.

William Bennett, one-time secretary of education in the Reagan cabinet and editor of the best seller *The Children's Book of Virtues,* is a codirector of Empower America, that is trying to bring pressure to bear on the major television networks to clean up their talk-show smut. The National Coalition for the Protection of Children and Families has launched the "Enough Is Enough" campaign, whose goal is "to educate, motivate, and activate women to break pornography's chain of abuse." The American Family Association has published a report on the social effects of pornography and highlights some of the largest companies that profit from pornography. It singles out the leading retailers of porn magazines (Kmart, as well as convenience store groups Circle K, Dairy Mart, and National Convenience Stores, among others), leading porn advertisers (Philip Morris and RJR Nabisco for their heavy supportive advertising in *Playboy* and *Penthouse*), and the leading distributors of motel room porn movies (Holiday Inns, Hilton, ITT Sheraton, Hyatt, and Marriott). Morality in Media works "through constitutional means to curb traffic in obscenity and to uphold standards of decency in the mainstream media."[19]

There is a common theme running through the advocacy messages of all these groups. Beyond the degradation of women, as if that were not bad enough, these advocates stress the link between pornography and violent crimes such as rape, battery, maiming, pedophilia, wife abuse, murder, and drug use. For example:

Pornography appears to be the catalyst, as well as the tool that fuels this cycle of child victimization. Eighty-seven percent of molesters of female children and 77 percent of molesters of male children studied in Ontario, Canada, admitted to regular use of hard-core pornography for at least three reasons: 1) to stimulate themselves; 2) to lower the inhibitions of the child victim; and 3) as a teaching tool for the child victim to model in their real life sexual encounter with the adult.[20]

As convincing as these statistics may be, the anti-porn advocacy groups are still fighting an uphill battle. Freedom of speech under the First Amendment and the threat of censorship are tough obstacles to overcome. Beyond those hurdles, there is still the common perception that even if pornography is not exactly a victimless crime, there are more violent, serious, and pressing social ills for beleaguered law enforcement agencies to deal with first.

Furthermore, the *marketing* of pornography is becoming more professional as explicit material becomes more pervasive. In the August 1998 edition of *Adult Video News*, Mark Logan described a "Paradigm Shift: Making and Marketing Porn for the Next Millennium." He urged the industry professionals—video producers and retailers—to concentrate less on the baby boomers and focus more on the Gen-X cohort of customers, who will be the consumers of pornography for the next twenty or thirty years. New products, new stars, new forms of sex (generally kinkier and more violent is what Logan recommends), and new layouts for retail stores. For example, Logan says:

Finally, it's time to get rid of those damned video booths. . . . Gen-X kids want everything given to them to take home. . . . With the amount of streaming porn that will be available in the next year over the Internet, why on Earth would a 22-year-old guy want to come in and plunk quarters into your greasy machines when he can see the same thing at home with the click of a mouse? Not to mention those booths make your store seem seedy. There's a lot of money to be made from female customers, but you'll never get 'em in with booths on the premises.[21]

These are very familiar, perfectly rational marketing concepts applied to an industry that still has no legitimacy or social acceptability.

Whether the easy availability of pornography over the Internet serves as a shock and generates some sort of social and political backlash, or whether society's sensitivity to such material is simply dulled remains to be seen. At present, the pornography industry continues to thrive. Hard-core porn continues to creep into our lives, available more easily, in more media, more of the time. All the while, soft-core pornography becomes increasingly commonplace. Whatever line society draws in attempting to protect and promote good taste, morality, and family values has been moved radically toward the inclusive, laissez-faire end of the spectrum, if it has not been obliterated entirely.

NOTES

1. Clive Barnes, "Introduction," in *The Report of the Commission on Obscenity and Pornography* (New York: Random House, 1970).

2. Ibid.

3. *Attorney General's Commission on Pornography* (Washington, DC: Department of Justice, 1986), 277.

4. Richard Goldstein, "Doowutchyalike: In the Brave New World, Sex Sells," *Village Voice*, November 6, 1990, 49.

5. H. Montgomery Hyde, *A History of Pornography* (New York: Farrar, Straus and Giroux, 1964), 3.

6. Ibid., 9.

7. At least during the lifetime of this author, *Esquire* was the first important men's magazine with national distribution.

8. "Controversy: 'Kids' for Adults," *Newsweek*, February 20, 1995, 69. See also Thomas R. King, "Miramax Film Heightens Clash With Disney," *Wall Street Journal*, March 30, 1995, B1.

9. Lewis Beale, "Video Viewer's Choice: Rated, Unrated," *Boston Globe*, January 3, 1993, A7.

10. Ibid.

11. Bruce Orwall, "Sony Shutters Web Site Over Racy Movie Trailer," *Wall Street Journal*, August 24, 2001, B8.

12. Sally Beatty, "Advertisers Shy Away from FX's 'The Shield,'" *Wall Street Journal*, April 30, 2002, B1.

13. From material in a press release distributed by William J. Bennett and Empower America, Washington, DC, on October 26, 1995.

14. Sally Beatty, "Playboy to Acquire 3 Cable Purveyors Of Hard-Core Sex," *Wall Street Journal*, July 2, 2001, B6.

15. See the Web site for "Morality in Media," http://wwwmoralityinmedia.org/radioTvIndecency/publicInterest.htm (accessed April 28, 2002).

16. Ibid.

17. "Rapper Case Hits Glitch," *Washington Post*, November 11, 1995, C3.

18. Philip Elmer-Dewitt, "On a Screen Near You: Cyberporn," *Time*, July 3, 1995, 45.

19. Web site http://www.moralityinmedia.org (accessed April 28, 2002).

20. W. Marshall, *Report on the Use of Pornography by Sexual Offenders*, made to the Federal Department of Justice, Ottawa, Canada, 1983; included in a pamphlet from the National Coalition against Pornography, "Myths and Misconceptions about Pornography: What You Don't Know Can Hurt You," 1993.

21. Mark Logan, "Paradigm Shift: Making and Marketing Porn for the Next Millennium," *Adult Video News*, August 1998, 151–68.

CHAPTER 7

Target Marketing: Challenges and Consequences

Marketers use the term "targeting" to describe the process of focusing their efforts on the specific segments of the total market that hold the most promise and profit. The total market is enormously diverse—in terms of demographics, behavior, and geography, for example—and it is impossible to create a single marketing strategy that will be effective across this diversity. The idea is to divide up this heterogeneous mass into smaller segments, each of which has at least one element of homogeneity; marketers therefore segment the market by region, age ranges, income groupings, usage of the product, and so on. Some of the most successful marketing plans have stemmed from a creative new way to identify segments of the market.

To understand targeting, therefore, we must first understand segmenting. General Motors in the 1920s provided one of the early classic examples of segmenting. Its rival, the Ford Motor Company, manufactured and sold one basic product in one basic color (black) and through great efficiencies of mass production and cost control hoped that its low price and standardized design would appeal to a broad spectrum of the market. General Motors, by contrast, recognized the great diversity of the market and created five different motorcar divisions (Chevrolet, Pontiac, Oldsmobile, Buick, and Cadillac), each one to appeal to a different income group.

The same theory and practice hold true in the marketing of ideas. A Republican political candidate may segment the market, for example, into those who are concerned most about balancing the budget, those who give their highest priority to lower income taxes, and those who want welfare reform, and then tailor his or her campaign speech to the audience of the moment.

Targeting is the current darling of the marketing profession. There seems to be no group too narrow or obscure to escape marketers' attention if they believe there are profits to be gleaned. Various products at various times have targeted "children, women, baby boomers, yuppies, minorities, seniors, factory workers, computer owners, overweight people, dog owners, childless high-income suburban families, and practically every other demographic slice that computers can identify."[1] New technological advances—scanning equipment at checkout counters coupled with television viewing monitoring devices, for example—and compilations of "geodemographic" data that pinpoint target audiences not only by zip code but often by specific blocks in residential neighborhoods now allow marketers to identify, understand, and reach very narrow and precise segments. This then encourages marketers to design not only their products, but their promotional messages as well, with great specificity and presumably with greater efficiency.

Targeting is no less important for the industries under study here. A brewery may decide that it is fruitless and an inefficient use of its marketing resources to try to persuade non-beer-drinkers to begin drinking beer, and therefore might choose instead to target and encourage moderate beer drinkers to drink beer more often. Or the brewer may target heavy beer drinkers to persuade them to switch from a competitor's brand.

Manufacturers of rifles may want to separate the hunting and shooting competition segments of the market to design diverse products as well as promotional strategies for the two quite different groups.

Casinos will identify specific individuals as "high rollers"—the Arab sheik or the mysterious Singapore or European businessman—and offer them complimentary accommodations in a luxurious penthouse suite, limousine service, along with a round-the-clock private gambling room, if desired. Such lavish treatment is well worth the cost for such high-stakes gamblers who may wager (and lose) in the millions of dollars on a given evening. Attracting even a few members of such a clientele, while never publicized overtly, does wonders for the word-of-mouth advertising that is generated. But this is a far different "product" than that offered to the occasional, small-stakes gambler, and the promotional strategies used to attract these two disparate segments of the market are totally different as well.

There is nothing especially controversial about these examples of targeting. What does create controversy is when the markets targeted by these industries are so-called vulnerable groups. This is a phrase used to describe groups of consumers who supposedly bring to the marketplace less skill in making rational purchasing decisions, less ability to distinguish straightforward, informative advertising from puffery. Young children are probably the most often cited vulnerable group; the selling tactics of certain breakfast cereal marketers on Saturday morning television cartoon shows in promoting high-sugar, low-nutrition products have been criticized. When the children's favorite hero or heroine urges them to get Mommy to buy "Sugarblast," it is difficult for Mommy to resist.

The elderly are sometimes included as a vulnerable group, as are the disabled, racial and ethnic minorities, and even women in general.

The unifying theme here, and what leads to the term "vulnerable," is that these groups, when they enter the market as buyers, are perceived as having less chance of making informed, rational choices. In other words, they can be taken advantage of too easily. There is an imbalance in the relative power between buyer and seller, and it is the use or abuse of this power that results in unacceptable and unethical marketing behavior.

SIX EXAMPLES

Since the late 1980s, there have been a number of controversial examples of such target marketing by our industries. It is instructive to look at six of these to identify similarities and see what lessons there are to be learned by marketers.

Uptown Cigarettes

In 1989, Reynolds Tobacco launched a test market in Philadelphia for its new Uptown brand of menthol cigarettes, designed for and targeted at African American customers. The marketing plan made perfectly good sense from a straight-ahead business perspective. The rate of smoking was higher among African Americans than among whites, and fewer African Americans were giving up smoking for health reasons. Clearly, this minority group appeared to be a segment of the market worth targeting.

Research showed that black smokers had a greater preference for menthol cigarettes than did white smokers and that many blacks had a distinctive way of opening the cigarette package from the bottom. Therefore, Reynolds's product design incorporated these two features: a cigarette with heavy menthol flavor in a package designed to be opened from the bottom. The colors of the package—black and gold—and the name Uptown were selected with the African American target segment of the market in mind. Philadelphia, which had a 40 percent African American population at that time, was chosen for the test market site. Advertising for this new product was to rely mainly on magazines and outdoor billboards; the magazines selected were to be those with high African American readership such as *Jet* and *Ebony*, and the choice of billboard sites emphasized black neighborhoods. The ads themselves used African American models. Basically, this was a good, solid, well-integrated, textbook-perfect marketing plan.

Not part of the plan, however, was the firestorm of criticism that erupted. Philadelphia's African American community leaders, including pastors of a number of prominent black churches, joined with government officials—most notably, Dr. Louis Sullivan, then secretary of the U.S. Department of Health and Human Services and an African American himself—to denounce the test marketing of this new cigarette. Predictably, all of the various anti-smoking advocacy and health organizations added their weight in condemning this new product. The argument of the critics was that African Americans already suffered because they were disproportionately affected by smoking-related and other kinds of health problems. Therefore, to target them with a new cigarette product and to promote, at least implicitly, increased smoking to this particular target market was immoral and should be stopped.

Reynolds marshaled a number of logical counterarguments in response. First, the manufacturer denied that it was specifically targeting African Americans, that Uptown cigarettes were meant to be enjoyed by all smokers. This was the least credible of the company's arguments given the care and research that had gone into the design of the product. Second, Reynolds insisted that Uptown was targeted at those who were already smokers and, therefore, could not cause any increase in health problems. The company's intent was to offer a more attractive alternative than the smoker's current brand, not to encourage nonsmokers to take up the habit. Third, it would be the utmost form of patronizing to assume that African Americans could not make the same sort of adult decisions—in this case whether or not to smoke, and if so, which brand to smoke—as any other racial group in our society. To imply that African Americans needed some special form of protection was racist thinking in its worst form. Finally, Reynolds enlisted the support of other segments of the African American community, specifically those who stood to benefit from the marketing of this new product, such as African American–owned media and distribution interests.

In the end, the fire and emotion of the anti-smoking groups, the prestige of Dr. Sullivan, and perhaps most importantly, the moral weight of the Philadelphia pastors simply overwhelmed Reynolds's protestations. With a parting shot at anti-smoking "zealots" who had succeeded only in limiting the choices of African American smokers resulting in "a further erosion of the free enterprise system,"[2] Reynolds denied doing anything improper, but discontinued the test market, and eliminated Uptown from its product line.

Reynolds's unfortunate and very costly experience was not enough to dissuade a small competitor from making the same mistake several years later. In 1995, Star Tobacco Corp. agreed to withdraw its Menthol X brand of cigarettes from the market after a number of African American groups complained that the packaging targeted black smokers and exploited the name of Malcolm X. The brand was introduced shortly after the debut of the Spike Lee film about the black leader and featured a black package with a large white X. "It was just an X," said Star's president. "Call us dense if you want, but [the connection between the package and the film] didn't occur to us."[3]

Dakota Cigarettes

A second example of targeting vulnerable groups also involved Reynolds Tobacco. Statistics on smoking in the late 1980s showed that although overall smoking rates were declining in the United States, the rate among women was declining at a slower pace, and that the rate among young women may have been actually increasing. It had also been recognized that there were links between smoking rates, incomes, and levels of education. Smoking rates tended to be higher among lower income groups and among those with only a high school education compared with those who had attended or graduated from college. And Reynolds's studies showed that half of all female smokers in the eighteen to twenty-four age range smoked Marlboro cigarettes, in spite of the fact that it was difficult for some young women to identify with the Marlboro Man.

For Reynolds, this data seemed to point to an underdeveloped, potentially promising new target market. In 1990, shortly after the demise of Uptown, a story was leaked to the press that the company was planning to test a new cigarette brand, Dakota, targeted at "virile" young females with low to moderate incomes and only modest educations. The alleged customer profile of this target market went on to describe the young, virile woman as holding an entry-level job, spending her free time at tractor pulls and hot rod shows, watching television (especially *Roseanne*), going to dance clubs and bars (with a borrowed ID card if under twenty-one), cruising, or doing "whatever her boyfriend is doing." The marketing plan for Project V.F. (Virile Female) suggested promoting male strip shows and giving away premiums such as washable tattoos, "hunk-oriented" calendars, and his-and-her interlocking beer mugs. To help ensure that Dakota would steal away some of Marlboro's customers, the new brand's taste and the number of puffs per cigarette were to be identical to the industry leader.[4]

This plan too sparked immediate controversy. Once again, anti-smoking forces and health organizations, now joined by various feminist groups, denounced Dakota as a cynical attempt to exploit the vulnerability of young women with only a modest education, and to foist off on this target market a dangerous product under circumstances where the proposed customers could not make an informed choice. Anne Marie O'Keefe, a board member of Women vs. Smoking Network, commented, "What the companies have done is target the most vulnerable population. The women they describe in that document are old enough to want to assert their freedom and independence, old enough to take risks but young enough not to be able to appreciate such abstract concepts as addiction, chronic disease and mortality." Louis Sullivan was just as incensed about Dakota as he was over Uptown, "It is especially reprehensible to lure young people into smoking and potential lifelong nicotine addiction. And the risk that smoking specifically poses for women adds another tawdry dimension to any cigarette marketing effort aimed at younger women."[5]

Already bloodied by the public relations battle over Uptown, Reynolds quickly backed away from Dakota as well. The company claimed that it had never intended to market a cigarette solely to this particular target, that its plans included young men as well as young women, and that it had no knowledge of the specific documents that were leaked to the media. Reynolds initially claimed that the flap would have no effect on its plans to introduce the new product, but nothing has been heard about Dakota since 1990.

Firearms and Women

The firearms industry has also run into criticism by targeting women—not a narrow demographic segment of women this time, but females in general. Once again, the targeting decisions make perfectly good sense from a marketing textbook point of view. As might be expected, men make up the principal market for guns. The overwhelming majority of hunters are men, most of those who participate in target-shooting sports are men, and the customers for handguns, whether for legal or illegal purposes, are predominantly men. From a marketer's viewpoint, the other half of the total market, that is, women, make a very tempting target. In a mature market, which the firearms industry certainly faces, where total industry sales in most years increase only modestly, where there is stiff competition, and where any individual company's success must come at the expense of a competitor, the prospect of suddenly opening up a new, large segment is exciting.

For the marketers of rifles and shotguns, the approach taken was to promote hunting and target shooting as sports that everyone, not just men, could enjoy. And this stirred up little or no opposition.

For the marketers of handguns, however, a different approach has been taken. The promotional strategy has been to tell women that they no longer need to fear being attacked, robbed, raped, or otherwise accosted: that being armed with a handgun will "equalize" their customary weaker, more vulnerable status, and scare off any would-be attacker. A typical magazine ad will show a woman alone in a potentially hostile situation—

a deserted parking garage, for example—looking desperately over her shoulder at a menacing shadow. The copy explains that there is no longer any reason for fear, that the woman has not only the right but also the duty to protect herself by carrying a handgun for protection under such circumstances. Lorcin Company advertises a $79 handgun with a pink grip alongside two other decorative handguns with the caption: "3 Little Ladies That Get the Job Done."

This strategy of marketing handguns to women has resulted not just in targeted advertising, but in new complementary products as well. Smith & Wesson has produced an entire women's line of handguns under the name "LadySmith": pistols and revolvers with rosewood handles, smaller grips designed to fit a woman's hand, and tooled in a more feminine style. Other manufacturers now provide appropriate feminine accessories: smaller holsters made in softer fabrics, special purses (even muffs) designed with compartments for concealing a pistol, and so forth.

The opposition to this targeted marketing strategy has come from two sources. First, women's organizations have objected to preying on women's fear as a tactic for selling handguns. To the extent that women are in fact more fearful than men of being attacked, this makes them vulnerable to the marketers' persuasions and less able to make rational, informed choices as to whether or not to buy and carry a handgun. Second, anti-handgun groups have criticized the advertising campaign as promoting violence, actually endangering the woman's life rather than protecting it, and for ignoring many of the statistics associated with attacks on women. They try to remind women that most attacks come from family members and friends or acquaintances, rather than from strangers, and that the handgun the woman carries and conceals can just as often be used against her as for her own protection.

Such criticism has not caused the handgun manufacturers to back away from their strategy, or their tactics, of targeting the women's market; at best, it has convinced some mainstream women's magazines not to run the offensive ads and has discouraged the marketers from pushing their campaign any further than they have.

Malt Liquors

Yet another commonly cited and just as commonly criticized example of target marketing in our collection of industries is the brewers' choice of young African American urban males as the specific target for their malt liquors. Malt liquor differs from beer in that it has a stronger, more robust taste, and is often darker in color, but the most important distinguishing feature is that it has a 20 to 30 percent higher alcoholic content. The marketing of malt liquors takes on additional importance for the brewers because unlike the beer industry in general where sales are basically flat, these high-potency drinks have been increasing at 15 percent a year.

There is a chicken-and-egg question in this choice of target markets with this product. Have the marketers identified and nurtured a new, previously underdeveloped market segment, or are they just going where the business is, responding to what the market is already telling them? Of course the answer depends upon whom you ask.

Brewery and ad agency executives maintain that, "Targeting low-income African-Americans for malt liquor is no different from selling the Mercedes-Benz line to white, affluent suburbanites. . . . It reeks of paternalism and racism to suggest it is inappropriate. . . . Why should Colt 45 [one of the leading malt liquors and a product of Heilemann Brewing Co.] shy away from portraying its core consumers just because more than 90% of them are black?"[6] The brewers deny that they are creating a new market or that they are encouraging the targeted young men in the urban ghettos to begin drinking malt liquors; they are simply directing their marketing efforts to those who are already their prime customers.

As with the controversy over Uptown menthol cigarettes, critics of alcoholic beverage marketing have no interest in resolving the chicken-or-egg debate. What they don't like is that the breweries have targeted a specific segment of the market that "suffers disproportionately from alcohol-related disease and inadequate access to health care."[7] According to a report by the National Institute on Alcohol Abuse and Alcoholism (NIAAA) that covered ten cities in the United States, "death from cirrhosis of the liver was ten times more likely to occur among non-whites than among whites. . . . Earlier reports from the NIAAA indicate that blacks do share a disproportionate burden of other alcohol-related health problems such as alcoholism, hypertension, obstructive pulmonary disease, malnutrition and birth defects."[8] For these critics, who are joined by African American community and church leaders and by some federal health officials, notably former surgeon general Antonia Novello, targeting high-potency brews at this specific segment of the market, given this information on health problems, is morally wrong and unacceptable.

Novello rebuked all the alcoholic beverage companies—wine, beer, and liquor marketers—in "unabashedly targeting teenagers" by using "sexual imagery, cartoons, and rock and rap music" in their television and print advertising.[9]

The marketing and targeting of malt liquors has been especially controversial because of the increased potency of the product and the perceived increased vulnerability of the target. Colt 45 previously had focused on an older African American market by using prominent black actor Billy Dee Williams, beautiful women, and the tag line, "Colt 45, it works every time," to convey a message of sexual prowess associated with drinking the beverage.

But Colt 45 began to lose market share, especially to market leader Olde English 800 from Pabst, and so Heilemann switched to a younger target market and a more youthful, hip television ad campaign. Now, a young black man in shirt and tie sits on the front porch of an inner-city house, counseling an even younger black man about college while the two sip their Colt 45s: "It was a night-school thing, which is cool, because now I can do some good things. Give back what I learned. And the brothers, they see me and maybe they'll want to do something better for themselves, y' know?" Critics were incensed by the pitch to a young audience, in spite of the superficial message about going to college. Not only did the younger of the two actors look like a teenager, but the TV spot also includes a shot of a pair of sneakers hanging over a telephone line, which has special significance to young inner-city gang members.

Alcopops

"Alcopops," or "malternatives," are a more recent example of targeting problems. These are fruit-flavored, malt-based beverages, more powerful than most beers, with a 5 percent alcohol content, that critics say are aimed, at least in part, at underage drinkers. Favorite brands in this category are Mike's Hard Lemonade, Doc Otis' Hard Lemonade, and Hooper's Hooch, and they come in hip, bright, and colorful youth-oriented packaging. According to George Hacker of the Center for Science in the Public Interest (CSPI), "Booze merchants formulate the products and the design of their labeling and packaging specifically to appeal to people who don't like the taste of alcohol, which includes teenagers. 'Alcopops' are gateway drugs that ease young people into drinking."[10] A focus group of high schoolers gathered by CSPI were familiar with all the brand names and confirmed that "It's an opportunity for someone who doesn't like beer to get the same effect."[11]

In response, Jeff Becker, president of the Beer Institute, pointed out that underage drinking and drunk driving have declined, and that those problems represent a societal and family issue, "not an advertising issue."[12]

Smokeless Tobacco

The final example of target marketing that we will explore here involves smokeless tobacco: snuff, or what used to be called chewing tobacco. Smokeless tobacco still represents only a small fraction of overall tobacco industry sales, but it is the one segment of the industry that has been growing.

Whereas chewing tobacco used to be thought of as a product purchased by older men in rural areas, that perception is no longer true, and the customer profile has changed dramatically. The typical buyer and user of smokeless tobacco these days is a young man, quite likely a teenager or even younger. The reasons for this radical and rather rapid shift are not absolutely certain. One reason may be the very visible use of smokeless tobacco by baseball players on television. This free, unsolicited celebrity endorsement of the product category has certainly been a boon for the smokeless tobacco manufacturers. Another reason, perhaps following from the first, is that smokeless tobacco has taken on a certain cachet among young males. The telltale outline of the round can in the back pocket of a pair of jeans signifies that the individual is bold, a bit daring, willing to flout convention, and has crossed over some invisible barrier and is now a stage closer to manhood. Another reason for the growing popularity of smokeless tobacco among young men may be due to modifications in the product made by the manufacturers. These changes are explored in a subsequent chapter.

Whatever the cause, this dramatic shift in the customer profile opens up a wonderful opportunity for marketers, but also raises a threat. On the one hand, the market is no longer the province of tired old men; now it is alive, vibrant, young, and subject to all the excitement, imagination, and promise that youth offers to any marketer. It stirs the creative promotional juices; it calls forth all manner of marketing possibilities. On the other hand, public awareness and concern have escalated as the customer profile has changed. In the previous generation, the advertising of chewing tobacco amounted to little more than painting the brand name boldly on the sides of barns, and this generated little concern. Now, however, not only are the promotional tactics far more sophisticated, but the target is a *young* man, or as critics are likely to insist, a young boy. This raises the specter of vulnerability and changes the dynamics of the issue.

Smokeless tobacco critics had hoped that Sean Marsee's death in 1985 would frighten young snuff users and reverse the upward trend of snuff sales among teenagers. Marsee was the Oklahoma boy who began using snuff at age thirteen after receiving a free sample at a rodeo, developed mouth cancer that required the removal of a third of his tongue, and died of the disease when he was only nineteen. But his story and the warning that it represented faded rather quickly from the headlines; sales of snuff declined for only a year or two around the time of his death and then resumed their steady climb of between 3 and 4 percent a year.

This was good news for UST Inc., which controls 85 percent of the almost $2 billion smokeless tobacco market through its U.S. Smokeless Tobacco division. This company is a quiet giant, not only of the tobacco industry, but of all U.S. industries. UST boasts that it sells 1.7 million cans of its product *every day* and that each of its major brands—Copenhagen and Skoal—rings up more than $1 billion annual sales at retail. Its product may come in small cans and sell for only a couple of dollars, but it is a very profitable business. In 2000, UST's profits of $442 million on sales of

$1.548 billion represented a return on sales of 29 percent, a return on assets of 33 percent, and a remarkable return on equity of 188 percent.[13] This profit-to-sales ratio was the highest of *any* U.S. industrial company in *Business Week*'s survey of the country's top one thousand firms, almost four times the ratio for Philip Morris.[14] Since almost all of UST's sales and profits come from smokeless tobacco, the company's financial success owes much to its recent shift in target markets. With the notable exception of the Sean Marsee lawsuit following his death in the mid-1980s, which the company won, UST has avoided public scrutiny and criticism. A news article a few years ago on the company explained:

At a time when marketers of liquor and tobacco have come under increasing pressure for target marketing, UST has quietly continued the strategy. That's been possible because few of its customers are professionals, and most of its low-profile marketing efforts take place outside media centers. The company targets mostly white, blue-collar males who work in factories or on farms, or in such industries as lumber, steel, and energy.

To reach that audience, UST does little print advertising. Instead, it and other smokeless tobacco makers have learned to fish where the fishing is good. They spend millions to sponsor such events as auto racing, rodeos, monster truck shows and tractor pulls, where their blue-collar customers are likely to gather.[15]

OTHER QUESTIONABLE TARGETING PRACTICES

Certainly these are not the only examples of target marketing by our five industries, but they are the most widely publicized and arguably the most egregious. In the early 1990s, Heublein initiated a Smirnoff vodka campaign in Harlem, but was forced to end it abruptly when it came under fire from minority groups. State lottery systems have assiduously avoided targeting minority populations to escape the criticism they believe would surely be a result. And yet in states with high percentages of non-English-speaking minorities, they feel an obligation to communicate (read: promote) to these groups. In New York, the lottery system advertises in Spanish in addition to English, and in California, lottery ads are broadcast in six Asian languages as well.

Virginia Slims, one of Philip Morris's important brands, has long been criticized not only because it targets women exclusively, reminding "Baby" how far she has come, but also for its sponsorship of the Virginia Slims tennis events. Anti-smoking groups are quick to criticize any association between smoking and sports as cynical at best and unethical at worst.

Hiram Walker's Kahlua Royale sponsored *Melrose Place* parties at bars across the country, organized to attract young, female customers.

When beer makers survey their stagnant market and remind themselves that women consume only 20 percent of their product, there is the natural inclination to find products or promotion strategies to build up that underdeveloped market. But when they do, they draw a flood of criticism. Instead of using women as bikini-clad sex symbols in ads aimed at men, Michelob launched a series of television ads targeting women with vignettes such as one showing a mother with her grown daughters. Coors sponsors a professional women's baseball team appropriately called the Silver Bullets (the advertising slogan for Coors Light beer), and has experimented with various fruit-flavored brews, which it hoped would be more acceptable to women's tastes than regular beer.

These efforts met with immediate criticism, however, from health and women's organizations, which cited especially fetal alcohol syndrome, a cause of birth defects in babies born to mothers who drink. One out of every 750 babies is born with fetal alcohol syndrome, and health groups worry that the brewers' new products and marketing strategies are most likely to appeal to lower-income, poorly educated, young women who are least likely to understand the risks of drinking any alcoholic beverage while pregnant. Critics charge that too many young women believe that beer and wine are not as serious as hard liquor or are lulled into the mistake of believing that light beer or fruit-flavored beers cannot be harmful.[16]

The list could go on almost indefinitely. Reynolds came under attack when it began using billboards in Chicago's Hispanic neighborhoods to advertise its cigarettes and very quickly tore the ads down.[17] Researchers have gathered substantial evidence that tobacco companies in their efforts to attract more African American customers use billboards in black and Hispanic neighborhoods to a greater extent than in white neighborhoods. The same research shows that cigarette ads, especially for menthol cigarettes, make up a greater proportion of total advertising pages in traditional black magazines such as *Jet* and *Ebony* than in general population magazines.[18]

The Illinois lottery, in a misguided attempt to target African Americans, used billboards in black, low-income Chicago neighborhoods that read, "Go from Washington Street to Easy Street—Play the Lottery." Critics charged exploitation and the promulgation of luck over hard work, and the ad was quickly removed.

A Minnesota casino whose patrons are mostly retirees seeks to broaden its market by attracting young adults with a billboard advertising babysitting services.

TARGETING GAYS AND LESBIANS

Alcoholic beverage companies as well as the tobacco industry have long been aware that gay and lesbian communities represent especially profitable niche markets. These groups tend to be more brand loyal than the average consumer, and they are more likely to be smokers and drinkers.

Exactly how and to what extent the companies could target these markets has been an ongoing problem. Various alcoholic beverage companies have advertised in gay magazines for years, but Philip Morris was the first tobacco company to do so, when in 1992 it included *Genre*, a magazine for gay men, in the media plan for its new Benson & Hedges Special Kings. Benson & Hedges' overall market share had slipped to 3.2 percent, but it was still the second most popular brand among homosexual men, with an 11 percent share.

Marlboro, with its rugged individualist symbol, has always had a certain attraction for gay men, and it is their favorite cigarette. Philip Morris has not been reticent about capitalizing on this preference. A billboard situated between two gay bars in San Francisco's Mission District shows only a denim-clad male crotch with a carton of Marlboro cigarettes positioned at a critical, suggestive angle.

In Europe, cigarette ads targeted at gay men are less tentative. The German tobacco giant Reemstma shows its popular brand West being enjoyed at a gay marriage where the two men are embracing amidst celebrating friends.

Blatant courting of the gay community in the United States, however, evokes the same sort of criticism as the targeting of women or African Americans. Gay and lesbian health officials were quick to respond to Philip Morris's move into gay publications. "This is a community already ravaged by addiction," said Hal Offen, president of the Coalition of Lavender-Americans on Smoking and Health (CLASH), "We don't need the Marlboro Man to help pull the trigger."[19]

Philip Morris has taken a more subtle approach in trying to attract lesbian customers to Virginia Slims. A series of ads showing two women enjoying various activities and Virginia Slims together uses captions such as, "The best part of taking a break is who you take it with," "Women aren't opposed to a good line—it just all depends on what it's attached to" (showing one woman netting a fish on the other woman's line), and "If you always follow the straight and narrow, you'll never know what's around the corner" (showing one woman looking over her shoulder at another woman approaching). These ads are vague so as not to offend straight readers, but contain enough between-the-lines messages to attract lesbian readers.[20]

Hiram Walker has been much more explicit in targeting its Tuaca liqueur to lesbian women, with ads showing two women and featuring the message, "Cool girl seeks sociable silent type to share 'la dolce vita.'"

Whether creating new products for niche markets or concentrating advertising in media aimed at those specific markets, it is the *targeting* of these socially unacceptable product categories to vulnerable groups that especially incites critics. "We're opposed to any kind of targeting, whether it's to youth, women, blacks, Hispanics . . . [or] gays," said Scott Ballin of the Coalition for Smoking OR Health.[21]

Serious researchers have asked whether such targeted marketing practices, specifically relative to minorities, are the result of racism. Of course, this depends on the unresolved outcome of the chicken-and-egg debate: do specifically designed products and carefully targeted promotions create demand in the target audience or are they simply responding to pre-existing demand patterns? The answers on the racism question are twofold. There is little evidence of overt racist motivation, only the predictable drive to maximize profits. On the other hand, the results of such targeted marketing strategies may be exactly the same as if they were triggered by racism: that is, they may result in greater harm to minority groups than to others.

There are important lessons here about targeting for the marketers of socially unacceptable products. Each of the above examples has three elements: the act or process of targeting, a target market that is perceived to be vulnerable, and a product that a significant number of people believe to be potentially harmful. There is nothing *inherently* unethical or inappropriate in targeting itself; on the contrary, such pinpointed marketing in theory should provide greater value for the target customers and be more efficient for the marketers.

Nor is the problem in targeting so-called vulnerable groups. There are innumerable examples of such targeting with public service messages and even product advertising that have received quite positive reactions: for example, information on breast cancer directed at women, health effects of smoking aimed at children and teens, or hair-care products formulated especially for African Americans or Asian Americans.

But when the third element is added to the equation so that we now are looking at targeting potentially harmful products to vulnerable groups, this combination is sure to be explosive. Marketers almost certainly can expect a very powerful and emotional negative reaction from the targeted groups themselves or from their many advocates. In such a heated exchange, rational arguments based on the advertisers' rights of free speech or avoidance of paternalism and patronizing the targeted group will seldom prevail. The emotion of the advocates, and the sense that marketers are dangerously and unscrupulously influencing disadvantaged groups will win out every time.

The marketers of socially unacceptable products simply do not have the same leeway as the marketers of toothpaste or tomato soup. The former are constrained by the nature of their products. Targeting any group will be problematic; targeting any group that is perceived to be vulnerable is a surefire invitation for trouble.

NOTES

1. Michael F. Jacobson and Laurie Ann Mazur, *Marketing Madness: A Survival Guide for a Consumer Society* (Boulder, CO: Westview Press, 1995).

2. James R. Schiffman, "After Uptown, Are Some Niches Out?" *Wall Street Journal*, January 22, 1990, B1.

3. *Washington Post*, March 18, 1995, D3.

4. Alix M. Freedman and Michael J. McCarthy, "New Smoke from RJR Under Fire," *Wall Street Journal*, February 20, 1990, B1. Also, Jacobson and Mazur, *Marketing Madness*, 156.

5. Michael Specter, "Marketers Target 'Virile Female,'" *Washington Post*, February 17, 1990, A1.

6. Laura Bird, "Critics Shoot at New Colt 45 Campaign," *Wall Street Journal*, February 17, 1993, B1.

7. Ibid.

8. David J. Moore, Jerome D. Williams, and William J. Qualls, "Target Marketing of Tobacco and Alcohol Related Products to Ethnic Minority Groups in the U.S." (paper presented at the conference on Marketing and Public Policy in Atlanta, Georgia, May 1995).

9. Paul Farhi, "Novello Urges Tough Curbs on Liquor Ads," *Washington Post*, November 5, 1991, D1.

10. Center for Science in the Public Interest, "National Poll Shows 'Alcopop' Drinks Lure Teens," press release, May 9, 2001, http://www.cspinet.org/booze/alcopops_press.htm (accessed March 7, 2002).

11. Geoffrey Cowley and Anne Underwood, "Soda Pop that Packs a Punch," *Newsweek*, February 19, 2001, 45.

12. Ira Teinowitz, "Liquor Companies Accused of Targeting Children," AdAge.com, May 9, 2001, http://www.adage.com/news.cms?newsId=32347 (accessed April 5, 2002).

13. UST, Inc., *Annual Report 2000*, http://www.ussmokelesstobacco.com (accessed May 22, 2001).

14. *Business Week*, March 27, 1995, 96ff.

15. Kathleen Deveny, "With Help of Teens, Snuff Sales Rise," *Wall Street Journal*, May 3, 1990, B1.

16. Joanne Lipman, "Beer Makers Brew Controversy with Ads Targeting Women," *Wall Street Journal*, April 6, 1992, B1.

17. *Marketing News*, September 30, 1991, 15.

18. Moore, Williams, and Qualls, "Target Marketing."

19. Kevin Goebel, "Lesbians and Gays Face Tobacco Targeting," *Tobacco Control* 3 (1994): 65–67.

20. Ibid.

21. As quoted in Joanne Lipman, *Wall Street Journal*, August 13, 1992, B1.

CHAPTER 8

Product Line Management in Socially Unacceptable Industries

At the very heart of every organization—whether it is a for-profit corporation, a nonprofit agency, or a government bureau—is the product or service that it offers. The management of the organization's product line, therefore, must be the central element of its marketing strategy. This includes determining the width and depth of the product line, the importance and timing of new products, managing products in the different stages of their life cycles, positioning and repositioning products, packaging, branding, and decisions on private-label products. Other marketing activities—pricing, promoting, advertising, distributing, targeting, positioning—all evolve from and are dependant upon the product or service that the organization offers.

With socially unacceptable products, marketers constantly face the threat that their product management decisions will be challenged by some group of advocates. In other words, these decisions must pass all of the expected economic tests like return on investment, potential market share, and so forth, but they must pass social scrutiny as well.

Our five industries face all of these product strategy decisions to one degree or another. But the nature of their products—that they are harmful, dangerous, and therefore socially unacceptable for many people—influences and constrains the product decisions that their marketers make. As a result, product line changes and innovations tend to adopt the "masquerade" strategy—that is, pretend the product is something different than what it really is, or suffer serious social criticism if they offer substantive enhancements in the essential nature of the products.

In most companies, it is only natural that the products and services offered are embraced, honored, and used. Marketing people especially believe in what they are promoting and selling, but it is normal for everyone in the organization, from maintenance workers to managers, to take pride in what the firm produces. Levi Strauss employees hold in high regard the company and its denim jeans, Hershey Foods and Campbell workers are proud of their companies' chocolate or soup, New York Life Insurance agents believe in the superiority of their company's policies, and so forth.

In our five industries, however, such is not necessarily the case. The companies seem to want to distance themselves from the products they produce and market because of their controversial nature and because of society's disapproval.

Perhaps the easiest way for a company to mask its products and shield itself from censure is to change its name. In the halcyon days before the Sloan Kettering and surgeon general's reports, tobacco companies proudly identified themselves with their products. As we have seen in chapter 2, however, all the major companies have now changed their names so as to hide their association with tobacco, cigarettes, and smoking. Who would know from the names alone that B.A.T., Loew's Corporation, U.S.T. Inc., and the Brooke Group produce tobacco products? Philip Morris Companies Inc., even though it no longer markets a cigarette brand by that name in the United States, has discarded its corporate name, which originated with a nineteenth-century London tobacco shop, in favor of the inscrutable and innocuous name Altria. Conversely, how many people, how many smokers for that matter, would be able to identify the manufacturer of Marlboro cigarettes, even though it is one of the world's most recognized and popular brand names?

Philip Morris carries this strategy a step further. When it introduced a new cigarette brand called Dave's, it invented a fictitious company, Dave's Tobacco Company, to produce it. And Philip Morris asked its retailers to display the new brand anywhere but next to Marlboros. When the company's Miller Brewing Division brought Red Dog beer to market, it resurrected an unused brewery name, Plank Road, to be the nominal producer.[1] Although Philip Morris may believe that these two products need to be positioned as the folksy offerings of down-home, small town firms rather than the products of a $60 billion industrial and marketing behemoth, the result is still to distance Philip Morris Companies from the nitty-gritty of marketing cigarettes and beer and the social disapproval that goes along with it.

We noted in chapter 2 that the major tobacco companies have diversified into a number of other businesses—food, insurance, leisure-time products—and that this is also a way of disassociating themselves from producing and selling a product that carries considerable social disapproval. Another way is Reynolds's very costly and to-date unsuccessful search for a strange, elusive, new product: a cigarette that doesn't act like a cigarette—a smokeless cigarette. One of the things that nonsmokers, and even some smokers, object to most about cigarettes is the "sidestream" smoke they emit while they are being held. If this could be eliminated, there would be fewer complaints from nonsmokers and less pressure for smoking bans or restricted smoking areas.

During much of the 1980s, Reynolds experimented with a new type of cigarette under the Premier brand. It was a high-tech creation with an aluminum cylinder wrapped in tobacco that only heated the tobacco rather than burning it, thereby eliminating the smoke. Unfortunately for Reynolds, Premier had any number of disadvantages that more than offset its smokeless advantage: its carbon tip was difficult to light, requiring a special butane lighter; consumers objected to its taste and the difficulty of drawing on the cigarette; and its price was significantly higher than even the traditional premium brands. Reynolds's top management was enamored with the concept of this new idea and stuck with the research and development process far longer than most companies would have, eventually running up a bill exceeding $300 million before Premier was finally scrapped in 1989.

Even after the demise of Premier, however, the concept lives on. Five years later, Reynolds began market testing a new model of the smokeless cigarette, Eclipse, complete with new technology, but still plagued with some of the same problems that doomed Premier.[2] As if disappointing sales were not problem enough, Eclipse has been criticized as being targeted at women. Reynolds flatly denies the criticism, but ads for the low-smoke cigarette feature a woman singing the praises of a cigarette that won't stain her curtains, burn holes in her coffee table, and interfere with the perfume she has used to attract her husband.[3]

If a cigarette without smoke is still an elusive will-o'-the-wisp, what about a cigarette that doesn't smell like a cigarette? In late 1994, Reynolds introduced Salem Preferred, designed to get rid of "the lingering stale smell" in clothes, hair, furniture, and car interiors that even smokers consider offensive.[4]

This masquerade strategy is not limited to the cigarette business. The very brief and very unsuccessful "clear" beer marketing fling in 1993 was spurred, in part, by the brewers' search for a clearer, cleaner, healthier-looking product—in other words, a product that looked different from the traditional, pale-yellow, sudsy beer. The only product from that fad remaining on the shelves is Coors's Zima, but this is no longer even called a beer; it has been recast and labeled as a "unique alcohol beverage." And now the wheel has come full circle, with the introduction in 1995 of Zima Gold, a line extension that returns the amber color to this non-beer. Coors has some difficulty defining and describing what Zima is. It is easier to explain what it is not; it is not beer, it doesn't taste like beer, and it doesn't smell like beer.

Zima's quest to be different may account for its early success, but it has also led to increased criticism. Zima's smooth, soda-pop taste, lack of odor, and higher alcoholic content has made it popular with underage high schoolers, especially when a rumor was circulated that Zima could not be detected on police breath-testing equipment.[5]

One of the appeals of vodka during its surge to popularity during the 1980s was not only its lack of color, which put it in the "white goods" category as opposed to whiskeys and other spirits known as "brown goods," but also its lack of taste and smell. By ordering vodka, either on its own or in any of its almost infinite combinations, consumers make clear that what they want is the alcoholic punch, not the taste of hard liquor. The additional attribute that vodka does not leave a telltale smell on the drinker's breath has helped to make it the alcoholic beverage of choice for businesspeople at their noontime gatherings, who do not want to offend their customers or worry their bosses when they return to work.

Yet other examples of the masquerade strategy would include the subtle shift in terminology from "gambling" to "gaming." Simply by dropping two letters, the gambling industry seeks to escape the social stigma many still associate with all forms of betting. Gambling retains a dark, sinister, illicit component to its meaning, while gaming signifies lighthearted fun, excitement, even healthy competition. Prostitution has used the same name-change tactic by marketing "escort services" to hotel customers, the bulk of whom are businessmen.

The traditional gambling casinos seek to broaden their appeal by re-positioning themselves as family entertainment resorts, adding theme parks, rides, exhibits, sports events, and other attractions not normally associated with gambling. A final example of corporate hide-and-seek would be the acquisition of Miramax Films by Disney to produce and market its R-rated movies. Disney executives realized that *Beauty and the Beast, Aladdin,* and *The Lion King* by themselves, as successful as these animated children's films were, could never satisfy the studio's potential for moviemaking profits. And yet Disney dared not tarnish its name and squeaky-clean reputation. The obvious and easy solution: acquire a new studio name and identity that would sanitize Disney and yet satisfy the rest of the moviegoing public's appetite for spicier, sexier, more violent films.

PRODUCT STRATEGIES IN ALCOHOLIC BEVERAGES

The Beer Industry

Product line management in any mature business is frustrating. Growth is probably no more than population growth, which means that any gains for a particular company or brand must come at the expense of a competitor. Nowhere is this truer than in America's beer industry. The last great surge in beer industry shipments came with the introduction and growth of low-calorie light beers during the 1970s in response to Americans' growing interest in fitness and health. Since that time, light beers have continued to show strong growth. Bud Light is now the second largest selling brand of beer in the world, surpassed only by its sister brand, Budweiser. At both Miller and Coors, light beers are their top sellers.

In the 1990s, product line management for the breweries was a two-pronged effort. Most of their marketing effort and budget goes into hammering away at promoting their flagship brand names, which fall roughly into three price groups. Anheuser-Busch, for example, offers Budweiser in the premium category, Michelob as a super premium beer, and Busch at popular price points. Each of the three brands offers both regular and light varieties.

At the same time, every company in this highly competitive, mature industry is constantly on the lookout for some breakthrough idea or concept for a new product—a successor to the introduction of light beers—which ideally would stimulate an increase in sales for the entire industry and not merely steal sales from a competitor or, worse yet, cannibalize the firm's own business. This search in recent years often has meant skipping from one fad to the next, some of them lasting little more than a year. The critical marketing decisions have been when to get in and when to get out, whether to be a leader or a follower, and how much to commit to the new product type in marketing resources (ad budget, promotion expenses, etc.). Generally speaking, Miller and Coors have been the most aggressive in being the first to bring new products to market, with Anheuser-Busch holding back only long enough to learn from any mistakes the other two might make. In a classic oligopoly like the beer industry, once one competitor introduces a new product, the other major players must respond with their own versions, even if they have little faith in the idea. They cannot afford the risk of missing a new idea and being left behind. A quick look at some of the recent new types of beer is instructive.

Dry Beers

The first of these rolling fads to come (and to go) were the so-called dry beers. Ads touted these additions to each of the major brewer's lines as having a distinctive flavor with less of an aftertaste. But the concept never really took hold among beer drinkers, at its peak accounting for no more than 1 percent of shipments, and quickly leveled off at something less than that. Perhaps the biggest flaw was the inability of the industry to explain just what a *dry* beer was meant to be, and so it remained an ultimately unsuccessful oxymoron in customers' minds.

Clear Beers

This even shorter-lived curiosity was part of the clear-*everything* phenomenon that swept through U.S. marketing in 1992–94. Excited by the early success of clear fruit-flavored soft drinks, beer marketers came to believe that consumers associated lack of color with purity and therefore with health and environmental awareness. Introducing a clear product took on a "green marketing" aura, as illogical or inconsistent as that may sound, and soon consumers were bombarded with not only clear beers but clear colas, clear detergents, and clear motor oils as well.

Beer drinkers figuratively and literally didn't buy the idea, however. For them, beer just wasn't beer without its traditional and familiar pale yellow color, and clarity failed to add any appreciable value. Anheuser-Busch and Miller tested this fad under their flagship brand names, as they did with dry beers, but with little conviction and even less success. As noted above, Coors's Zima is the only clear beer product remaining on the market, although it has been cut loose from the Coors line of beers and is searching for an identity of its own.

Red Beer

If clear beer won't sell, what about red beer, or maybe amber beer? This is one of the current fads, and once again each of the major brewers has tested the idea with varying degrees of success. With red or amber beers, however, the companies often choose not to use their flagship brand names. Hoping to capitalize on the success of microbreweries, the major companies are giving red and amber beers their own catchy brand names in an attempt to convince the public that these are the products of small, distinctive breweries.

Coors has brewed and marketed Killian's Irish Red since 1981, trading on its "Irish heritage" and hoping to keep customers believing that it is really an import (which it isn't). In 1993, Killian's limited distribution shot up 58 percent, and this helped attract the attention of the rest of the industry. Within just a twelve-month period, Miller's Leinenkugel division introduced Leinenkugel Red, and Miller introduced its own Red Dog. Heileman's Henry Weinhard offered Boar's Head Red, Van Munching began distributing Tarwebok ("Red Bock" in Dutch) as a line extension of Heineken, Stroh Brewing introduced Augsburger Rot (German for "Red"), and Anheuser-Busch has really added muscle to the new concept with the roll-out of its Red Wolf brand in 1994.[6]

Non-Alcoholic Beer

Another response to the general interest in health has been the introduction and serious marketing attention given to non-alcoholic beers (technically, beer with no more than .5 percent alcohol content). Anheuser-Busch offers O'Doul's, Miller sells Sharp's, Coors's line includes Cutter, and there are a number of imported non-alcoholic beers now available in stores as well, such as Kalibur from Guinness and Buckler from Heinekin. There is some growth in this category, a higher percentage than the overall beer business, but non-alcoholic beers still represent less than 2 percent of industry shipments. In addition to covering a small niche market, however, this category offers the breweries an opportunity to score some positive public relations points. Promoting non-alcoholic beers not only sells some product, but also sends a "responsible drinking" message.

Ice Beer

On the other hand, ice beer, a moderately successful fad of 1994–95, offers customers a smooth taste and some added kick to go along with it. These beers are brewed at lower temperatures so that ice crystals form which are then filtered out, leaving a beer with an alcoholic content ranging from 4.5 to 5.6 percent, as much as 30 percent higher than regular beer. Consumers, somewhat younger but otherwise mainstream beer drinkers, probably care little about the technology involved, but they are interested in the additional kick. By the end of 1994, there were thirty-five ice beer brands on the market, most of them under the flagship brand names; by the end of the decade only one or two remained.[7]

Malt Liquor

Chapter 7 mentioned the introduction of malt liquors, with their even higher alcoholic content, some as high as 8 percent, and the controversy erupting over targeting them to African American, inner-city young men. A significant difference in the marketing of this category, in addition to the different target customer, is the branding. Whereas ice beers for the most part carry the familiar Budweiser, Lite, Molson, and Michelob labels (Icehouse brand from Miller's Plank Road Brewery is a notable exception), malt liquors are marketed under unique brand names: Olde English 800, King Cobra, Colt 45, Midnight Dragon, PowerMaster, and St. Ides. To further shield the major breweries from the controversy engendered by malt liquors, they often turn to secondary firms to do the marketing. Heilemann, for example, brews both Colt 45 and St. Ides but turns to McKenzie River Corp. to do the marketing—and take the heat. Midnight Dragon is marketed by little-known United Beers Inc. of Brooklyn.[8] These are additional examples of the masquerade strategy.

"Malternatives" or "Alcopops"

An entirely different category of malt-based beverage has become popular, and controversial, in the early years of the current decade. These are sweet, fruit-flavored drinks with catchy names such as Doc Otis' Hard Lemonade, Rick's Spiked Lemonade, Tequiza, and Hooper's Hooch. They are often marketed by the brewers in combination with distillers. Anheuser-Busch has teamed with Bacardi to market Bacardi Silver. Miller has partnered with Skyy to launch Skyy Blue, with Stolichnaya to market Stoli Citrona, with Sauza to sell a tequila drink named Sauza Diablo, and a fourth with Jack Daniels's Original Hard Cola.[9] Although the brewers that market these new beverages deny that they are aimed at teens, the ads both on the Internet and in the stores where the products are sold are invariably hip and zany, complete with fluorescent labels and psychedelic logos. "These are learner drinks," says David Jernigan of the Marin Institute for the Prevention of Alcohol and Other Drug Problems. In a poll conducted for the Center for Science in the Public Interest, 41 percent of teens age fourteen to eighteen reported trying "alcopops," twice as many fourteen- to sixteen-year-olds prefer them to beer, and 90 percent believe that companies make them taste like lemonade to lure teens into trying them.[10]

What we can conclude from this brief review of new product introductions in the beer industry is that in addition to the usual marketing concerns of break-even points, market share potential, present and future profitability, alternative uses of resources, and so on, there may be social concerns to be recognized and understood as well. Dry beers came and went without so much as a ripple of social criticism. Clear beers for the most part were dismissed as just a dumb idea, although had they been more successful and stayed around longer, the criticism that they attract underage drinkers, as has been leveled at Coors's Zima, might have been more serious.

Red beers, to the extent that they emulate the products of true microbreweries, cause little concern because the typical customer is an upscale, well-educated, reasonably affluent, twenty-five- to thirty-five-year-old male—hardly a vulnerable target market.

On the other hand, ice beers have been more problematic because their principal attribute from the consumer's standpoint, a higher alcoholic content, is the Achilles' heel of all alcoholic beverages. More alcohol equals more drunkenness, which equals more dangerous social behavior; and this quite naturally triggers a response from the health and anti-drinking advocacy groups. All the more so with malt liquors, which not only have a much higher alcoholic content, but also are promoted in forty-ounce bottles as opposed to the normal twelve-ounce size of regular beers, so that the typical unit of consumption will contain perhaps five times more alcohol, and are marketed to vulnerable target groups. And now alcopops: sweetened fruity drinks disguising the harsh taste of beer and marketed with all of the irreverence so appealing to teenagers. This is not just another typical new product; it is a surefire prescription for social criticism and advocacy group opposition regardless of the economic success the product is able to carve out in the marketplace.

Wines

For the most part, product management in the wine industry follows a traditional, uncontroversial route. In the higher price vintage wine categories, another year's harvest of grapes eventually brings to the market another year's offering of merlot or chardonnay for wine experts, real or pretending, to fuss over and declare good or not so good. Occasionally, an entrepreneurial marketer like Robert Mondavi will create a new product such as his Fumé Blanc, which is not a new product at all but merely a different name for a Sauvignon Blanc to fool the American wine-drinking public, which had shown little taste for the variety. A change of name, a new label, a little promotion, and suddenly Mondavi had a hit.

Vintners can also add to their product line by attempting to move up or down along the price scale. A smaller boutique winery can expand its sales beyond the upper price category by introducing a popular-priced line under a new label, or a big volume winery like Gallo can attempt the much more difficult job of moving into the higher price market with a new name, a spiffier label design, and a more sophisticated television campaign.

There may be an occasional change in consumers' preferences, such as the strong swing to chardonnay among white wine drinkers after the yuppies made it their wine of choice, or in the late 1990s, a swing back to red wines, which will require wineries to add new varieties to their product line if they are not already there. But in an industry where tradition is the touchstone and age is a valuable asset rather than a liability, there is comparatively little room for maneuvering in product line management.

One major exception to this was the marketing of wine coolers. In the United States, as we have noted, the market for wine is still rather small, and for Americans it is an acquired taste, which is a nice way of saying about any product that it tastes awful the first few times one tries it. The challenge then was to make wine more acceptable to the common palate, and the easiest way to do this was to mix in fruit juices and sweeteners to mask the wine taste. All wine coolers have been criticized by anti-alcohol groups, as have been the new "alcopops," because they appeal to teenagers, in large part because the wineries have *marketed* them to teens.

Fortified wines are another product entirely. Sometimes called dessert wines, these products have a high alcohol content (perhaps two or three times the alcohol of ordinary wines) and have sweet, fruity flavors to cover up the harshness. Most of this category of wine is very cheap in price and is often packaged in pocket-sized pint bottles to bring the price down to what even a homeless, skid row alcoholic can afford. For good reason, as this is the principal market for these fortified wines and another example of product line management and targeting gone awry. Anti-alcohol advocates find it shameful that wineries would actually exploit this unfortunate segment of the market with a cheap, potent product. It is quite a profitable category, however, and so the major wineries are reluctant to give them up. They do try to hide their association with these wines by using other brand names such as Thunderbird and Night Train Express (Gallo) and Wild Irish Rose and Cisco (Constellation, formerly known as Canandaigua Wine Co.).[11]

Cisco is the most widely publicized and most criticized example of the product category. Canandaigua, in addition to targeting the skid row market, has promoted Cisco as a wine cooler. It comes in a dozen flavors including strawberry, kiwi, orange, peach, black cherry, and Caribbean Sunset. With its soda-pop taste, packaged in a clear bottle, and positioned in stores alongside wine coolers, Cisco, with three times the alcohol content, was often assumed to be no stronger than the other coolers on the shelf. Or worse yet, teens recognized its potency and bought it (illegally) for the "high" and hallucination it promised. A bottle of Cisco (the smaller of the two sizes) contains the equivalent of five shots of vodka.

After a number of cases of alcohol poisoning where victims required hospital emergency room care and after numerous complaints from MADD (Mothers Against Drunk Driving), the Center for Science in the Public Interest, and the National Council on Alcohol and Drug Dependence, the Federal Trade Commission took action against Canandaigua. After some protests, the company agreed to repackage Cisco in a dark bottle so it would no longer be mistaken for a wine cooler, stop suggesting to dealers that it be marketed as a cooler, and stop promoting a bottle of Cisco as a single-serving drink.[12]

Spirits

In the late 1980s, the liquor industry jumped on the "light" product bandwagon and brought to market a number of low-alcohol cocktails. Brown-Forman offered Jack Daniels' Country Cocktails as well as Southern Comfort Cocktails, Grand Metropolitan's Heublein introduced Jose Cuervo Margaritas and Smirnoff's Quenchers, Bacardi Imports began shipping Bacardi Breezers, and American Brands' Jim Beam introduced cola laced with Jim Beam bourbon or Ronrico rum. Critics immediately charged that this would inevitably lead to more teenage drinking. According to an advisor to the federal government, "It's an easy leap from Coca-Cola to Jim Beam and cola. These are transitional products deliberately intended to blur the line between soft drinks and alcoholic drinks."[13]

In the mid-1990s, the liquor pendulum swung back to stronger drinks. Jaegermeister, an herbal-flavored German liqueur, Rumple Minze, a peppermint schnapps, Buckshot citrus liqueur, and Goldschlager schnapps (with edible flakes of gold) all have become popular with younger drinkers who favor consuming them as "shots." Bars encourage the practice by serving them in test tubes and other novel glasses. Critics cite marketing ideas such as these as luring first-time drinkers and eliminating any fear young people may have of alcohol.[14]

TOBACCO PRODUCT STRATEGIES

Once cigarettes and smoking were linked to cancer, and more recently to a steadily increasing rostrum of life-threatening medical problems, cigarette manufacturers quite naturally have been searching for product innovations that would reduce, or ideally eliminate, these health concerns. Such innovations have generally come in two areas: a reduction in the tar and nicotine content of the cigarette and improved filters that are more effective in removing the tar that is left. To introduce such improvements, however, poses a classic problem for marketers: how to praise and promote the improvement without impugning all of the existing product line. To tout a new filter or a lower tar cigarette is not simply to offer something different like a new flavor; it is saying, at least implicitly, that the new product is better and therefore that all of the other cigarettes, not only in our competitors' lines but also in our own line, are not as good. Nor do Federal Trade Commission regulations allow cigarette manufacturers to say that such innovations are safer, because there is now general agreement that no cigarette can be safe. And, of course, it would never do to promote the new product as being "less harmful" because of the implications about the firm's other cigarette products. Thus, one of the principal categories of product development for the cigarette industry—a better, safer product—is saddled with the problem of how it can be marketed.

The larger a firm's market share, the more it has to lose, and so the less likely it is to risk launching a new safer cigarette that might raise embarrassing questions about its successful existing brands. In 2000, Star Scientific, a small tobacco company, began a test market on Advance, a cigarette with sharply lower levels of cancer-causing ingredients. The following year, the smallest of the big five cigarette manufacturers, Vector, parent of Liggett Group, launched a nicotine-free cigarette under the brand name Omni.[15] From a strategy perspective, Vector had very little to lose, and Star had virtually nothing to lose, from their miniscule market shares. The upside possibilities were enormous, however, if either firm could take even a little business from Philip Morris, Reynolds, and Brown & Williamson with these new products.

New filter designs have been especially troublesome for cigarette manufacturers in that they seem to end up causing more problems than they solve. Kent's much-ballyhooed "Micronite" filter with "activated charcoal," introduced in the 1950s, was supposed to be a miracle of efficiency in removing tars from cigarette smoke. However, the substance making up the charcoal was recognized as a cancer-causing agent. In 1995, the cellulose acetate material used in most cigarette filters was blamed for depositing fragments in smokers' lungs.[16] Each of the tobacco companies faced interesting and complex marketing strategy decisions surrounding the development and introduction of filter cigarettes during the 1950s. Sadly, these decisions were based for the most part on each firm's competitive position in the industry—how much a company might gain at the expense of its competitors—not on its sense of responsibility for the health of its customers.[17]

Another important avenue for product line management and sales growth—the development of discount, generic, or private-label brands—has already been described. This avenue also poses problems for marketers. Not only is there the probability that a significant percentage of the discounted brand sales will come from the manufacturers' own brands—in other words, cannibalization—but because of the structure of pricing, costs, and discounting in the cigarette industry, the profits on the discounted brands will be but a fraction of the profits on premium brands.

Because cigarettes tend to be a commodity-type product, with little importance to the consumer to distinguish one brand from another, new product ideas tend to be merely cosmetic in nature. Cigarette manufacturers over the years have introduced longer cigarettes as product innovations. "King size" was something new and a bit strange in the 1950s; now it is the norm, and 100 mm. lengths and even 120 mm. lengths have been introduced. The longer the cigarette, the more smoking "pleasure," and the smoother the taste as well, according to some makers. Cigarettes have been made thinner (Virginia Slims, Capri) for a more delicate, feminine look, or fatter (Camel Wides) to suggest a tough-guy image. The paper used can be tan-colored (More) or a floral design (Eve). In 1991, Reynolds introduced with considerable fanfare a new package wrap that was supposed to keep the taste of its cigarettes fresher.

Beyond the major category of menthol cigarettes, manufacturers have had only limited success in promoting differences in taste. "Light" cigarettes have a lower tar content and supposedly a less harsh taste, but it has been difficult, to say the very least, to reconcile the public's interest in "lighter," that is, healthier, products to the tobacco industry. All the more so because what serious smokers really want from their cigarettes is the "punch" from the nicotine, and this in large measure is a function of the tar content. Manufacturers have tried, mostly without success, to offer lower tar without lowering the nicotine content as well. In 1992, Reynolds introduced Winston Select as a new blend of superior tobacco that would offer a smoother, milder flavor, but the tar content at 18 milligrams and 1.4 milligrams of nicotine were comparable to regular Winston cigarettes so that smokers would still get the robust taste and nicotine "hit" they were used to.[18]

Reynolds Tobacco markets five specialty flavors in its important Camel brand. Crema "delivers a hint of vanilla," Mandarin Mint adds "a touch of citrus flavor and a splash of menthol," Dark Mint "hints of chocolate," Izmir Stinger is "sweet and tart," and Twist adds "a splash of citrus flavor." Because none of these line extensions has attracted much of a following or any significant market share and many retailers do not even carry them, they have escaped the attention of the anti-tobacco critics.[19]

One of the more bizarre ideas to come from "new-age" environmental marketing is organic cigarettes. The Santa Fe Natural Tobacco Company now produces and sells American Spirit cigarettes using only organic ingredients with no chemical additives. Perhaps trying to return to the health messages of the 1940s, the company's president claims, "These are pure, unadulterated leaves, grown in the good earth, emblematic of rites as old as the Indians themselves."[20] However bizarre, this brand, which "began popping up on the shelves of organic markets and metaphysical bookstores in the late 1980s," has since become "an antiestablishment alternative to 'Big Tobacco.'" It is the only small cigarette manufacturer to market a national brand at a premium price; in fact, the brand often sells at a higher price than Marlboro and Camel. The company's sales had nearly quadrupled between 1996 and 2001, reaching roughly $100 million, when Reynolds Tobacco acquired it later that year.[21]

Fifty years ago, when the tobacco industry still enjoyed legitimacy, cigarettes were a common Christmas present. Philip Morris dared to renew the idea in November 2001, when it introduced a new brand simply called M, with the slogan "A Special Blend for a Special Season." Its counter displays featured red and green paisley backgrounds with a gift-wrapping paper look, and a company spokesperson said the purpose was to lure smokers away from rival brands during the holidays. However, the idea drew the predictable criticism from anti-tobacco advocates. Matthew Myers of the Campaign for Tobacco-Free Kids commented that, "It's selling cancer for Christmas. . . . The slogan should be, 'M is for Murder.'"[22]

Perhaps the most surprising innovations from the tobacco industry are not cigarettes at all. Given the opposition to cigarettes, the smoke they produce, and the health problems they cause, Star Scientific, one of a handful of small cigarette manufacturers, has introduced a new way for smokers to get the nicotine they crave. The company launched Ariva "cigaletts": powdered tobacco in the form of Tic Tac-sized lozenges blended with eucalyptus and mint. The introductory price in 2001 of $3 for a box of twenty lozenges was about the same as the price then for a pack of cigarettes. The potential for such a product seemed good enough that Brown & Williamson licensed the right to sell the product under its own brand name in the United States.[23]

If tobacco in the form of candy mints does not provide the same oral satisfaction as drawing on a cigarette, how about lollipops laced with nicotine? A cottage industry of independent druggists is producing lollipops in flavors such as cherry, grape, apricot, and tequila sunrise—all loaded with nicotine—and selling them under names like NicoStop, NicoPop, and Likatine to smokers who are trying to break their habit. Of course, the anti-tobacco critics complain that children may be attracted, become addicted to nicotine, and then take up smoking cigarettes, but druggists reply that the $2 or $3 price tag for these lollipops makes it highly unlikely that children would buy them. Nevertheless, Congressman Henry Waxman of California has asked the government to investigate, saying, "An addictive drug should not be masked by sweeteners and sold as a lollipop without a thorough review by FDA and strict safeguards to prevent inappropriate underage use."[24]

Product innovation in the cigarette industry, therefore, has tended to be relatively inconsequential and limited to peripheral modifications. The reason for this is the problematic nature of the product and the declining social acceptance of cigarettes.

PRODUCT MANAGEMENT IN FIREARMS

Looking through the catalog of a rifle or shotgun manufacturer, one sees model after model with slight modifications from one to another that only a gun owner and lover would appreciate. Winchester offers bolt-action or lever-action rifles, the former available with an attachment Winchester calls BOSS (for Ballistic Optimizing Shooting System). There are different calibers available in both. There are lighter weight rifles for women and younger shooters, longer or shorter barrels, stocks of choice walnut wood or synthetic Kevlar/graphite/fiberglass combinations, and plain models or more ornate rifles with extensive etching on the magazine and bolt-action sections and various "checkering" patterns on the wood stocks. There are a variety of scopes and other sighting devices for improved accuracy, smaller rifles for "plinking" or "varmint" shooting, medium size guns for deer, and bigger rifles for bear or wild boar. There are three different pump-action shotgun models designed just for wild turkey shooting, two with a camouflage design and one plain, and there are other shotgun models for upland fowl. The emphasis and tone of these rifle and shotgun catalogs is on sports: game hunting, trap, skeet, or just target shooting. Pictures or drawings of pheasants and deer stags abound; there is a healthy, wholesome, all-American, sometimes Old West tone to the catalog. And except for animal rights advocates, few people would object.

Handgun catalogs offer the same sort of diversity: a variety of sizes (.357, .41, .44, or .50 Magnum, for example), shapes (octagonal or round barrels), and finishes (perhaps eight choices ranging from gold plate to matte chrome to bright nickel to polished and blued). But the mood changes in these handgun catalogs and flyers. There may be some references to target shooting, but for the most part, these catalogs and price lists are strictly no-nonsense and utilitarian. There is a darker, more sinister feeling; for most handgun buyers, the purpose of the weapon is to defend against or to shoot *people*. Some firms promote this darker mood explicitly by incorporating drawings of shadowy, menacing intruders.

What this adds up to is that anti-gun advocates find little to complain about with cosmetic differentiation in a manufacturer's product line of long guns or even handguns for that matter. There is little or no criticism when the emphasis is on sport or invoking the memory of Buffalo Bill and Annie Oakley. But when it comes to the serious business of making handguns better and more efficient at doing what they are really created and designed to do—kill people—then the critics raise a cry of protest, and the marketers are faced with a different set of problems.

In the mid-1980s, the U.S. Department of Defense adopted the 9 mm pistol, long popular in Europe, as the standard sidearm for all the armed forces, and it then quickly became the weapon of choice for law enforcement agencies, the general public, and most criminals as well. This was good news for Italy's Beretta, which won the military contract, and bad news for Smith & Wesson, whose .38 revolver lost the business.[25] It was bad news also for anti-gun groups; all the superior product features of the 9 mm pistol that make it a deadlier, more efficient weapon—more firepower because it holds sixteen rounds instead of the revolver's six, and smaller size so that it is more easily concealable and fits more readily a woman's hand—make it all the more objectionable to gun critics.

Similarly, a firm's decision to augment its product line by making or importing the AK-47, the Tec 9, or one of the other semiautomatic weapons is not just another marketing tactic to add size, power, or efficiency to the firm's offerings. This is qualitatively different than Procter & Gamble adding a new, high-powered cleanser in a giant economy size to its line of detergents. In the firearms industry, more size, power, and efficiency add up to more death.

Certainly the same problem exists for the makers of ammunition. In the late 1980s, certain exotic versions of high-performance hollowpoint bullets came to be known as "cop-killers" and were banned by Congress even though, as the industry points out, "No police officer anywhere had ever been killed, or even shot" with such a bullet.[26] The special feature of this ammunition was that it flattened and expanded very rapidly upon impact, thus increasing the size of the wound, causing more internal damage, and providing more "stopping power."

After a particularly gruesome multiple homicide in 1993 in which Winchester Ammunition's "Black Talon" bullets were used, Senator Moynihan (D-N.Y.) condemned the bullet in a dramatic television appearance on an

NBC news program, and his proposal for a 10,000 percent tax on such "conventional" hollowpoints was seriously considered by Congress as a way to drive such products from the market. Just before Congress could act, however, Winchester voluntarily withdrew the Black Talon from the open market and restricted it for sale to police units. The company's press release read in part, "This action is being taken because the Black Talon ammunition is becoming the focal point for broader issues [prohibitive taxes and outright bans on certain ammunition] that are well beyond control of Winchester Ammunition. The controversy also threatens the good name of Winchester, which has stood for safe and responsible use of ammunition and firearms for 125 years."[27]

The company's true beliefs about the appropriateness of the product became immediately apparent, however, when it went back to the drawing board, created the Winchester Supreme SXT (for Supreme Expansion Technology) as an improved hollowpoint bullet with only slight modifications, and promoted it as "a successor to the notorious Black Talon."[28]

Regardless of the fact that such a product is still on the market, the public, or at least segments of the public, do react vociferously to such product decisions, and sometimes even to the threat or the possibility of such decisions. In December 1994, David Keen, the chief executive officer of Signature Products Corp. of Huntsville, Alabama, announced on NBC's *Today* show that his company was delaying the introduction of its "Black Rhino" bullet, ammunition that Keen claimed could not only pierce the armor worn by police officers, but also created baseball-size wounds for which there was no way to stop the bleeding. Keen said, "We're going to be a responsible manufacturer," and put the Black Rhino on hold until "we can see what the police officials really want." But he added that the public needed such new weapons because criminals now, like the police, often wear bulletproof vests. According to Keen, the Black Rhino is made of carbon-based plastics, called polymers, to escape the federal ban that prohibits such bullets made of metal.[29]

But a number of industry experts, medical specialists, and even the National Rifle Association questioned whether any bullet could create such a wound, whether the Black Rhino product even existed, or whether Keen's announcement was some bizarre publicity stunt. "This has all the trappings of a hoax," said Tanya Metaksa, chief lobbyist for the NRA.[30] Hoax or reality, the very concept was enough to arouse anti-gun activists like a swarm of angry bees.

Another curiosity, the result of social concern about firearms, is the effect that this concern has had on the *toy* gun industry. In 1988, a ten-year-old Memphis, Tennessee, boy was shot and killed by police who mistook the toy gun he was brandishing for a Colt automatic. The resulting furor resulted in a federal law mandating that toy makers decorate their toy guns with bright neon colors or some other decoration to distinguish them from real weapons.

For children, however, the fascination is in how close to reality the toy appears to be, and so for their greater enjoyment, and sometimes for their protection on the streets, they would paint out the day-glow orange with black, silver, or steely blue. In late 1994, after a Brooklyn boy was killed in much the same manner as the Memphis shooting and in response to the public outrage that ensued, Toys 'R' Us, one of the country's biggest toy retailers, announced that it would no longer sell toy guns that could be modified to look like the real thing. Sears, Target, and Kmart had already discontinued the category.[31]

GAMBLING PRODUCTS

Product line management in the gambling industry is a different sort of marketing challenge. Any form of gambling is basically a commodity product. Every roulette wheel is the same, and the odds of winning on any given number, on the black versus the red, or on numbers one through twelve are identical from one wheel to the next. The odds of rolling a seven, a "natural" four, "snake eyes," or "box cars," are exactly the same from one craps table to another. Blackjack is exactly the same game at every table, although serious gamblers might argue that one dealer, one table, or one casino was "luckier" than the next. Even lotteries, at heart, are commodities; the actual product or service—betting that a given number will be drawn randomly from a finite sample—is the same whether sponsored by the government of Spain, the state of Maryland, or the Multiple Sclerosis Foundation.

Under these circumstances—the marketing of commodity products—packaging and ancillary products or services become all-important. Competition among the Las Vegas casinos is a perfect example. Luxor's giant pyramid, MGM Grand's Hollywood surroundings, Excalibur's re-creation of King Arthur's court, Bellagio's 8.5 acre lake with dancing fountains, the fifty-story replica of the Eiffel Tower at Paris Las Vegas, Treasure Island's pirate theme—all of these are extraordinarily elaborate packages in which to house the dice tables, roulette wheels, and slot machines that are common to all of them. And if the casinos cannot really differentiate their own gambling tables from the competition, at least they can compete in offering the entertainment to go along with the gambling. Three or four times daily Treasure Island stages its Buccaneer Bay Pirate Show, a pitched battle between a pirate frigate and a British man-o'-war, complete with a live cast of a dozen or so actors, cannons booming, explosions, sails ripping, spars falling, a ship sinking into the moat surrounding the casino, sailors forced to swim for their lives—all of this live action in real-life scale taking place within 30 feet of the automobile traffic whizzing by on Las Vegas Boulevard.

If eighteenth-century sea battles are not your preference, perhaps you will be attracted to the Mirage's periodic volcano explosion and devastation, to its snow-white tiger pacing in its glass-walled cage, or to Caesar's Palace's cocktail waitresses clad in the briefest togas ever designed and serving free drinks (your choice of the most expensive liquors) to gambling patrons. There may be no way to differentiate the actual slots and the craps tables, but the diversity of the packages they come in and the services that go along with them seem endless.

The marketers of state lottery systems follow a quite different course. There may be little or no difference from one day to the next between the numbers games or from one week to the next between the lottery drawings (except when they are rolled over and the pot grows larger), but the scratch-off games are changed every four to six weeks, and a new product is rolled out to the thousands of convenience stores, bars, supermarkets, gas stations, liquor stores, and other retailers who sell lottery tickets. These scratch-off games typically incorporate some topical theme: football in the fall, baseball in the spring, Olympic competition at appropriate times, fishing in Montana, Paul Bunyan in Minnesota, and so forth.

The Maryland lottery has shown respectable increases in most years, but with the state now projecting serious budget deficits, the lottery is looking for fresh ideas to stimulate even greater participation and sales. "Officials have asked the General Assembly for permission to join with other states—or even foreign nations—to produce the mammoth jackpots that entice bored lottery players to part with their dollars."[32]

As noted in a previous chapter, the introduction of lotteries to a new state or a novel gambling delivery system such as riverboats will always stir up a greater or lesser amount of controversy. But the kind of gambling product differentiation described here has been almost totally free of criticism, even from gambling's harshest critics, for several reasons.

To date there has been no significant effort among anti-gambling groups to argue that the lavish packaging of the casinos lures non-gamblers to the gambling tables. It is accepted as a way of maintaining "brand" loyalty, of protecting market share. Nor have the different scratch-off themes been criticized as an attempt to attract new gamblers. They are quite obviously meant to stimulate gamblers' interest by continuously creating new products, thus increasing the frequency with which the gambler buys the product, but this has gone unchallenged.

The state lotteries are, of course, managed by the various states. This and the belief that profits of the lotteries are going to a good cause—to educational or welfare purposes within the state—gives the lotteries an aura of legitimacy that would not be accorded to a for-profit corporation.

Finally, and perhaps most important, casinos and especially the state lottery marketing managers have been careful, with only a few exceptions, to avoid targeting vulnerable groups. Were they even to give the impression that they were targeting women, children, or any racial or ethnic minority, this would be the trip wire that would empower the anti-gambling advocates and encourage them to seek additional governmental controls.

Even marketers of pornography find ways to enhance their product. Striptease clubs, seeking to attract higher income patrons, feature computers with stock quotes as well as car wash and shoeshine services, and now offer cranberry juice and Perrier for busy executives who must return to the office with a clear head.

SOCIAL SCREENS

This has been an informal exploration of the product strategies of our industries—glances or snapshots that can inform us as to the kinds of problems marketers in these industries face. Many of these problems involve passing the scrutiny of social critics. The social screens change from time to time, which of course makes the chance for a misstep greater, but there are some ongoing concerns—three especially—that we can identify from the material we have looked at in this chapter.

First, to repeat the lesson learned from the previous chapter, marketers must never target their products—new or old, regardless of brand name, no matter what the innovation may be—at vulnerable groups without expecting the backlash of criticism from one source or another.

Second, product management decisions in these industries must not be aimed at increasing *overall* usage of the product. This is a tough constraint to place on marketers. When PepsiCo introduces a new brand or flavor of soft drink, it hopes that it will increase to some extent total soft drink consumption, and the same hope rides along with the launch of a new motor oil or a new brand of chewing gum. But let Philip Morris introduce a new cigarette brand that might increase overall smoking, let Smith & Wesson introduce a new pistol model that might increase the prevalence of handguns, let the state of Virginia launch a new scratch-off lottery game that is perceived as attracting new gamblers or encouraging present gamblers to buy more tickets than they have in the past, and these marketers can expect an outpouring of criticism from advocacy groups.

The per capita consumption of hard liquor is down 40 percent from 1980, but the industry is hard-pressed to find a socially acceptable way to reverse that slide and increase primary demand. A proposed campaign to be run by the Distilled Spirits Council to "rebuild occasion frequency"—in the jargon of the advertising trade—elicited a predictable response. The Center for Science in the Public Interest stated that such an ad campaign would fly "in the face of a national policy to decrease alcohol consumption as part of a broad public-health initiative."[33]

The reason for this is abundantly clear. These product categories are socially unacceptable because at least certain groups believe they are harmful. To the extent that marketers develop product strategies designed to increase overall usage, greater harm is done, and the costs to society are multiplied. The only relatively safe course is to avoid any perception of increasing the market, target only those consumers who are already using the product or service, defend one's own brand, and take market share away from the competition.

Ironic though it may seem, the third and final social concern is triggered when products are designed to do the very job they are meant to do in a bigger, better, or more efficient manner. Cigarettes for the veteran smoker are a convenient delivery system for nicotine; for the beginning smoker, they are a way of gaining peer acceptance and a sense of maturity. Alcoholic beverages, at least for many imbibers, are meant to induce a mild "buzz," if not a more serious drunken condition. Gambling is meant to create excitement for the gambler. Pornography is meant to create a different sort of excitement—a titillation or arousal of sexual interest—in the reader or viewer. And most firearms, especially handguns, are meant to be defensive weapons with the distinct possibility of their threatening, wounding, or killing some other person.

When new or repositioned products come along to accomplish any of these goals in a bigger, better, or more efficient manner, there is sure to be protest. If a new cigarette were introduced that offered a bigger nicotine "hit" or if a cigarette held out the promise to young smokers of greater social acceptance, there would be strong and immediate criticism. When marketers promoted St. Ides malt liquor on the basis that a forty-ounce bottle would get its young, African American, male consumer and his girlfriend drunk faster, there arose a storm of protest. Casino operators and lottery managers dare not offer heightened gambling thrills. Gun manufacturers will invariably stir up criticism when they offer deadlier weapons. And purveyors of pornography are asking for trouble when they cross over whatever invisible line has been drawn by the local community between acceptable and unacceptable literature and graphic images.

Thus, the concept of product improvements takes on quite a different meaning with socially unacceptable products. A new toothpaste ingredient that gets teeth "even whiter" may be a fine platform for a new marketing campaign, but the makers of handguns, cigarettes, and all other products in the industries under review here must be much more circumspect. "Faster," "better," and "more efficient" in these product categories are not improvements that can be promoted. The result is that product improvements tend to be limited to cosmetic changes: a new package that will keep cigarettes fresh longer, a red or clear beer, a more elaborate casino featuring gondola rides to go along with the Venetian theme.

This is a narrow and limiting path that marketers in these industries must walk, but it comes with the territory. They simply do not have the same latitude in their product management decisions as their counterparts in mainstream consumer product categories.

NOTES

1. Suein L. Hwang, "Philip Morris Makes Dave's—But Sh! Don't Tell," *Wall Street Journal*, March 2, 1995, B1.

2. Suein L. Hwang and Alix M. Freedman, "RJR Is Testing a 'Smokeless Cigarette' after Attempt Failed Five Years Ago," *Wall Street Journal*, November 28, 1994, A5.

3. Suein L. Hwang, "Critics Say 'Smokeless' Cigarettes Are Aimed at Women," *Wall Street Journal*, May 31, 1996, B1.

4. Fara Warner, "Reynolds Launches Menthol Cigarette that Smells Better," *Wall Street Journal*, October 10, 1994, A3.

5. Jay Mathews, "Controversy Follows Coors' Zima," *Washington Post*, February 7, 1995, D1.

6. Cyndee Miller, "What's Cool and Delicious and Red All Over?" *Marketing News*, November 7, 1994, 2.

7. Skip Wollenberg, "Ice Floe in the Beer Market: Innovation of Fad?" *Marketing News*, October 10, 1994, 3.

8. Kathleen Deveny, "Malt Liquor Makers Find Lucrative Market in the Urban Young," *Wall Street Journal*, March 9, 1992, A1.

9. David Goetzl, "Hard Liquor Retreats, Malternatives Charge Forward," *AdAge.com*, March 25, 2002, QwikFIND ID: AAN31G, http://www.adage.com/news.cms?newsId = 34289 (accessed May 25, 2002). See also Hillary Chura, "Miller to Bottle Fourth Malt Beverage," *AdAge.com*, March 7, 2002, QuikFIND ID: AAN27G, http://www.adage.com/news.cms?newsId = 34187 (accessed April 5, 2002).

10. Geoffrey Cowley and Anne Underwood, "Soda Pop that Packs a Punch," *Newsweek*, February 19, 2001; and Center for Science in the Public Interest, "National Poll Shows "Alcopop" Drinks Lure Teens," press release, May 9, 2001, from the Web site http://www.cspinet.org/booze/alcopops_press.htm (accessed March 7, 2002).

11. David W. Cravens, Charles W. Lamb, Jr., and Victoria L. Crittenden, "California Valley Wine Company," in *Strategic Marketing Management Cases*, 6th ed. (Boston, MA: Irwin McGraw-Hill, 1998.)

12. Federal Trade Commission, *FTC News*, Washington, DC, March 12, 1991, 1. See also "Cisco Wine to Get New Packaging," *Washington Post*, February 9, 1991, A3; and Jim Gogek, "Racism in a Bottle: Selling Cisco to Children," *San Diego Union-Tribune*, July 26, 1993, A2.

13. Eben Shapiro, "Low Alcohol, Brightly Labeled Cocktails Stir Fears They Will Tempt Teenagers," *Wall Street Journal*, August 4, 1993, B1.

14. "'Shooters' and showy bar drinks are drawing more young imbibers," *Wall*

Street Journal, February 2, 1995, A1. See also Suein L. Hwang, "Young Drinkers Do Shots in Potent New Flavors," *Wall Street Journal,* May 13, 1994, B1.

15. Gordon Fairclough, "Smoking's Next Battleground," *Wall Street Journal,* October 2, 2000, B1. See also Gordon Fairclough, "What's Ahead for Tobacco?" *Wall Street Journal,* June 25, 2001, R15.

16. Suein L. Hwang, "Filter Bits May Lodge in Smokers' Lungs," *Wall Street Journal,* January 13, 1995, B1. See also Janice Billingsley, "Cigarette Filters May Have Added to Health Risk," *Health Scout News,* March 12, 2002, http://www.rd.yahoo.com/DailyNews/manual (accessed March 13, 2002).

17. Richard Kluger, *Ashes to Ashes: America's Hundred-Year Cigarette War, the Public Health, and the Unabashed Triumph of Philip Morris* (New York: Alfred A. Knopf, 1996). See especially chapter 6, "The Filter Tip and Other Placebos."

18. Kathleen Deveny, "RJR Tobacco Unit Plans New Version of Winston Brand," *Wall Street Journal,* March 16, 1992, B5.

19. Descriptions taken from company promotional material.

20. Kate Bohner, "Smoke and Mirrors," *Forbes,* November 8, 1993, 316.

21. http://www.biz.yahoo.com/p/r/rjr.html (accessed May 12, 2002).

22. Gordon Fairclough, "Decking the Halls with a Brand New Cigarette," *Wall Street Journal,* December 4, 2001, B1.

23. Gordon Fairclough, "Will Smokers Swallow a Different Kind of Nicotine?" *Wall Street Journal,* April 27, 2001, B1.

24. Gordon Fairclough, "Some Pharmacies Sell New Nic-Fix—Lollipops Laced with Nicotine," *Wall Street Journal,* April 3, 2002, B1.

25. Alan Farnham, "Inside the U.S. Gun Business," *Fortune,* June 3, 1991, 191.

26. Ed Sanow, *Handguns,* February 1995, 39–41, as printed in the sales literature of Winchester Ammunition.

27. Ibid.

28. Winchester Ammunition sales literature, January 1995.

29. Fox Butterfield, "Company Puts Hold on Plastic Bullet," *New York Times,* December 29, 1994, A16. See also Mike Mokrzycki, "'Black Rhino' Bullet Put on Hold," *Washington Post,* December 29, 1994, A10.

30. Ibid.

31. Stephanie Strom, "Shootings Lead Chain to Ban Toy Guns," *New York Times,* October 15, 1994, 9. See also Joseph Pereira and Barbara Carton, "Toys 'R' Us to Banish Some 'Realistic' Toy Guns," *Wall Street Journal,* October 14, 1994, B1.

32. David Nitkin, "State Lottery Hoping to Test Odds Overseas," *Baltimore Sun,* January 28, 2002, A1.

33. Vanessa O'Connell, "Distillers Weigh TV Ads Urging More Drinking," *Wall Street Journal,* February 23, 1999, B1.

CHAPTER 9

Promotion Strategies: Media and Messages

It is currently stylish to use the phrase "marketing communication" rather than the term "promotion." Perhaps the former projects a more gentile image than the latter: the sense that marketers are merely talking with their customers in some cerebral sort of way rather than getting their hands dirty in the business of actually trying to sell them some product or service. By whatever name, however, communicating or promoting remains an absolutely essential element in any marketing mix. And because they reach both customers and non-customers, promotional messages are the most pervasive and obvious points of contact between a firm or an industry and the general public.

It follows, then, that promotion activities—for most of us, that means the myriad forms of advertising that we encounter so often throughout every day—are the most likely and the quickest of all the marketing functions to trigger a response. In our five industries, in light of the critics and controversies that exist, the response to promoting these socially unacceptable products is, more often than not, strongly negative.

The harshest negative reaction from society to advertising and promotion in these industries is to prohibit or limit certain forms of it altogether, and we find this happening to some degree in four out of our five industries. Cigarette advertising was banned from radio and television in 1970 and from billboards and some other forms of outdoor advertising in 1998 in the Master Settlement Agreement (MSA). Hard liquor ads have been banned from network television under a voluntary agreement reached in 1948. Some newspapers will not accept advertising for X-rated movies, and the *Seattle Times* no longer accepts tobacco ads; some magazines refuse to print ads for firearms.

The rationale for these restrictions and prohibitions is to shield certain members of society, most often children, from whatever influence the ads would have. Since children are too young, at least in theory, to smoke or drink alcoholic beverages, the purpose is to reduce their exposure to messages that would encourage them to take up these activities. Banning or restricting ads for X-rated movies is meant to protect the newspapers' readers from material they might find offensive. The reason most often given is that, "This is a family newspaper," which can best be translated as meaning that children will be exposed to it as well as adults. The refusal to accept advertising for guns is usually based on a particular magazine's, or in some cases an influential individual's, biases against firearms.

Whatever the rationale, the effectiveness of these advertising bans is certainly open to question. Prohibiting the advertising of cigarettes on television and radio in 1970 simply meant that the manufacturers' advertising budgets were shifted to other media. It certainly did not result in any reduction in cigarette advertising. The same was true after the Master Settlement Agreement, when advertising dollars that had been allocated to billboards were simply shifted to magazines. To some extent, anything short of a total ban on advertising any given product is a bit like pushing on a balloon or a pillow: one can make a dent on one side, but it will simply expand somewhere else.

Banning cigarette and hard liquor advertising on radio and television, and continuing to allow it in newspapers and magazines, is justified by the belief that children are infrequent readers of the print media. But what about outdoor advertising, which is still available to distilled spirits? Surely, children are exposed to billboards with near the same frequency as adults. There may be some legal arguments here: that since the federal government owns or at least controls the airwaves, it is easier for Washington to impose restrictions on television and radio advertising without triggering questions about First Amendment freedom-of-speech rights. But logic is not necessarily the most important criterion when public policymakers "do something" in response to advocates' calls for action.

Discussion of the restrictions on advertising and promotions may create the impression that such advertising is relatively scarce or limited. Such is hardly the case. Cigarettes continue to be among the top two or three most heavily advertised product categories in the entire U.S. economy. Beer advertising is also huge, and as a percentage of sales, wine and spirits are heavily advertised. Firearms are not consumable convenience goods, like cigarettes and beer, and so do not lend themselves to mass media advertising, but there is no shortage of advertising of rifles, shotguns, and handguns in the media most appropriate for them—mainly men's outdoors and sports magazines. Casinos advertise heavily, but their audience is not so general, often regional, and so they do not use mass media with national coverage.

Many state lottery systems are restricted by their enabling legislation in the amount of advertising they can do. And various forms of pornography are limited in their advertising and promotion by social customs and the belief that if they were advertised more frequently and more publicly, society would react with much more stringent controls. For these two product categories, it can be argued that there are effective limitations on promotion.

In sum, the socially unacceptable products discussed in this book are advertised and promoted vigorously, in spite of certain restrictions placed on them. This chapter continues to take a closer look at the media used for this advertising, the messages that are "communicated," the symbols and graphic images that are employed, and some of the promotional tools and tactics other than mass media advertising that are used. Each of these advertising and promotion topics generates criticism and reaction from various advocacy groups. The topics, their history, and the positions of the adversaries, are important to an understanding of the challenges facing marketers in socially unacceptable industries and the restrictions under which they must work.

THE MEDIA

Choosing the proper media in which to promote a product is a critical part of any firm's marketing strategy. Every first-year marketing student learns that each area of the mass media has its own set of advantages and disadvantages. For example, network television offers a low cost per exposure although it has a very high absolute cost, and it offers very little opportunity for audience selectivity. By contrast, magazines offer terrific selectivity—that is, they can pinpoint very narrow groups such as race car enthusiasts or fashion-conscious, preteen girls—but the cost per thousand exposures for magazines may be relatively steep.

For marketers of most products, selecting an effective media mix is a relatively straightforward problem of matching these advantages and disadvantages of the various media with the nature of the product being marketed, the type of customers and their buying habits, the size and location of the markets, and so forth. In addition to these market or economic factors, however, the advertising managers in our five industries must base their decisions on the social and legal restrictions and prohibitions mentioned above.

Because cigarette advertising was banned from radio and television in 1970, for example, the tobacco industry redirected its advertising dollars to other media such as magazines and billboards, but in addition, it has been able to find more subtle ways than the traditional thirty-second spot to keep its images on the American public's television screens. These are the indirect forms of advertising. One such form is through product placement in television productions and in movies that eventually are shown on television. When the script calls for an actor to smoke or for a package of cigarettes to be visible, a cigarette manufacturer will pay the film or television producer to use its brand rather than a fictitious label. And so there it is on television, the package of Marlboro or Winston cigarettes, in spite of federal law or social sanction. There is no control over the "message" that is communicated nor any agreement as to how long the brand will be visible on the screen, but manufacturers are willing to pay hundreds of thousands of dollars to have their brands appear in movies and on television in this manner.

Brown & Williamson spent roughly a million dollars over a four-year period in the 1980s for movie (and later television) exposure. The biggest single deal was with Sylvester Stallone, who received $500,000 for product placement in five of his movies. But when a $20,000 gift resulted in only one or two seconds of exposure for Super Kool Lights in the James Bond film *Never Say Never Again,* and then the word "Kool" was illegible, the company concluded that such "advertising" expenditures were ineffective and not worth the money.[1] This helped the major tobacco manufacturers agree in 1990 to no longer place their products in movies, but critics complain nevertheless that the incidence of smoking on television and in the movies—the number of times actors are seen smoking—has been on the rise.

A much more common way for cigarette makers to subvert the law banning television advertising was to use billboards and banners at sports contests, rock concerts, and other such televised events. If the locations were carefully selected, which of course they were, such signage or the Camel or Marlboro logo on a race car could result in a surprising amount of on-air exposure. Tobacco executives professed that they had no interest in such exposure, that "The TV coverage [was] incidental."[2]

But this tobacco advertising, especially at sporting events, enraged anti-smoking advocates on two counts: first, because it was such an obvious exploitation of a loophole in the law banning TV advertising for cigarettes; and second, because of the unnatural and cynical association between smoking and sports. As a result, a combination of social and legal pressure reduced such exploitation during the 1990s. Some ballparks, bowing to public sentiment, took the initiative and no longer accepted tobacco ads on their billboards. Houston's Astrodome covered its huge centerfield Marlboro ad with black plastic for the start of the 1993 season because it had not yet lined up another advertiser to buy the space. The Seattle Kingdome dropped Marlboro from its scoreboard in 1994 and replaced it with another (more socially acceptable) advertising icon, McDonald's golden arches. Dodger Stadium in Los Angeles has not allowed tobacco advertising on its billboards since its opening in 1962, nor has it allowed cigarette advertising in the programs and on the scorecards sold at the park.[3]

Legal pressure in April 1995 brought further action. New York's Madison Square Garden entered into a consent decree, ending a lawsuit brought by the U.S. Department of Justice, to remove a large Marlboro sign from the scorers' table that was highly visible during the televised broadcasts of Knicks basketball games. The Garden also agreed not to allow cigarette ads on or adjacent to the playing area or walkways to the locker rooms. The president of the Garden claimed that the arena's decision came not because of any threat of governmental action, but because such cigarette ads were no longer consistent with the Garden's image. Marlboro once again denied that it had any interest in any resulting television exposure from such ads. According to a spokeswoman, "The one reason and only reason [the company advertises at the stadium] is to reach the very large number of adult smokers who attend games and other events at Madison Square Garden. We believe that any TV coverage of our signage is incidental and disagree with the Justice Department's opinion of this particular sign."[4]

Two months later, Philip Morris and other tobacco manufacturers also entered into a consent agreement with the government to move cigarette advertising away from the view of television cameras at more than a dozen stadiums or arenas where professional football, baseball, basketball, or hockey is played. Signs in these stadiums were not banned by the agreement, only moved from locations where it is "reasonably foreseeable" that they would appear on television broadcasts.

This type of sports advertising was a major element in the negotiations leading up to the Master Settlement Agreement. Since 1998, most outdoor advertising of cigarettes in sports arenas has been banned, although tobacco companies are still allowed a limited number of opportunities to sponsor events such as the Virginia Slims tennis tournament. But the controversy is far from over, and cigarette promotion is likely to remain on television in less obvious forms.

It has already been noted how quickly and easily the cigarette companies adapted to the ban on broadcast advertising in 1970, mainly by switching their ad budgets to print and outdoor media. Now, in the wake of the MSA, it is instructive to analyze how the companies have adapted to the new restrictions. Gone are billboard ads for cigarettes; the agreement was clear on that question. Less clear, however, was the subject of magazine advertising. A major focus of the entire agreement was to reduce the marketing of cigarettes to teens and preteens. Philip Morris, in noting its removal of billboard advertising, acknowledged that "the goal . . . is to limit the exposure of kids to tobacco advertising . . . and to help reduce the incidence of youth smoking."[5]

In the nine months immediately following the MSA, the tobacco companies actually *increased* their advertising in youth-oriented magazines by 33 percent compared with the same period in the previous year. For example, cigarette ads in *Spin* magazine (32 percent of whose readers are age twelve to seventeen) jumped more than 55 percent; in *Popular Mechanics* (18 percent of readers in the twelve to seventeen age bracket) up more than 42 percent; and in *Vibe* (42 percent of readers age twelve to seventeen) up 40 percent.[6] Overall magazine advertising by the major tobacco companies for the entire year 1999 shot up 33 percent over 1998, and almost half of this increase came in youth-oriented magazines (see table 9.1).[7]

Table 9.1
U.S. Tobacco Advertising in Millions of Dollars, 1995–2000

Company	Pre-Settlement				Post-Settlement	
	1995	1996	1997	1998	1999	2000
In 20 Youth-Oriented Magazines						
Brown & Williamson	23.8	25.8	10.7	10.7	24.7	5.9
Lorillard	5.5	5.0	4.5	6.2	5.7	6.2
Philip Morris	76.8	68.7	63.1	71.1	82.6	57.3
R. J. Reynolds	22.5	28.6	40.8	52.8	62.9	57.8
Subtotal	128.5	128.1	119.1	140.7	176.0	127.2
In 18 Adult-Oriented Magazines						
Brown & Williamson	33.1	32.0	14.1	2.0	21.6	2.7
Lorillard	1.9	1.3	1.0	3.7	3.6	4.7
Philip Morris	63.4	52.1	44.3	52.7	66.5	60.1
R. J. Reynolds	11.2	12.3	20.4	20.2	23.5	22.1
Subtotal	109.7	97.6	79.8	78.6	115.2	89.7
Total	238.2	225.7	198.9	219.3	291.2	216.9

Source: Adapted from Charles King, III, and Michael Siegel, "The Master Settlement Agreement with the Tobacco Industry and Cigarette Advertising in Magazines," *New England Journal of Medicine*, August 16, 2001.

For the year 2000, magazine advertising in total had settled back to roughly the 1998 level, and ads in youth-oriented magazines were actually about 9 percent below the pre-MSA figure (see table 9.1). But that figure is misleading. Advertising in 2000 by the three brands most popular with teens and preteens—Marlboro, Newport, and Camel—in youth-oriented magazines was at an all-time high, even *after* the Master Settlement Agreement.[8] So much for Philip Morris's commitment to the goal of reducing underage smoking.

Tobacco companies are not alone in looking for ways to circumvent restrictions on television advertising. Liquor has never been advertised on network TV, not because of statutory or regulatory restrictions, but because of a self-imposed industry code. Seagram had kept its name on the screen by advertising its mixers and coolers, and in the early 1990s, Bacardi introduced the Breezer, a rum-based cooler. This product launch included an eye-catching television ad campaign. With only about 4 percent alcoholic content, the Breezer was well within the industry's 7 percent guideline, but the ads included a controversial tagline, "Bacardi Light Rum makes the difference." Industry executives worried that this was stretching the intentions of the guidelines too far and would give alcohol critics an easy target. Sure enough, one leading anti-drinking group complained that, "These are as much rum ads as Breezer ads," and another worried that, "It's an opening wedge for distilled spirits advertising on television."[9]

The real test of this self-imposed ban on television advertising of distilled spirits came in the last few months of 2001. At that time, economists and business gurus may have been uncertain as to whether the overall economy was in a recession or not, but there was no question about the telecommunications industry and the so-called dot-com companies. These firms, if they were still alive, were struggling to reverse a pattern of sharply declining sales and mounting net losses. These were the same firms that had created a short-lived business model of spending freely on marketing and advertising—including, in some cases, Super Bowl ads by little-known companies—on the assumption that market share was all-important and profits would materialize sometime in the future. When these firms either disappeared entirely or retrenched drastically, all the media—television stations and networks, magazines, newspapers, and Internet sites—experienced a dramatic decline in advertising revenues. This led to a media scramble for new sources of ads to replace that lost revenue.

At the same time, the distilled spirits companies continued to chafe under what they perceived to be an unfair dual standard. Beer and wine products were free to advertise on television, but not distilled spirits, in spite of the fact that, as the spirits producers continued to point out to anyone who would listen, the alcoholic content of a bottle of beer or a glass of wine was the equivalent of the alcohol in a shot of rum, whiskey, or vodka.

Seagram, Bacardi, and Brown-Forman had been running commercials on local television and cable stations that would carry them, but the breakthrough came in December 2001, when NBC agreed to carry a carefully orchestrated series of commercials featuring Diageo's Smirnoff, Tanqueray, and Johnnie Walker brands. NBC's guidelines required at least four months of "social responsibility messages" before any product advertising could be run, and ads would be limited to certain time slots in an attempt to insure a mostly adult viewing audience. NBC's competitors—CBS, ABC, and Fox—all claimed they had no plans for accepting liquor ads, but indicated they would be watching the public reaction to NBC's move.[10]

Reaction indeed. Three months later, NBC was forced to reverse course. Congress threatened hearings on the issue, advocacy groups brought pressure focusing on the $1 billion of alcohol advertising already on television, a Harvard study on college binge drinking and related problems was released, and there developed some public ridicule even from NBC's own Jay Leno, who quipped that the network's initials would now stand for "Nothing But Cocktails." The network announced that, "it would not be appropriate to go forward at this time." The Distilled Spirits Council called NBC's decision a "temporary" setback and grumbled that, "a few misguided critics through their attacks on NBC have undercut this effort."[11]

If direct product advertising on network television is not yet available to the distilled spirits industry, marketers have dreamed up more creative ways to promote their brands. During the presidential campaign in late 2000, Captain Morgan (rum) got on television under the guise of a campaign ad, running for president with Playboy playmates as running mates. Cutty Sark was able to get placement of its sexy pinup ads in scenes of the Mel Gibson movie *What Women Want*. Johnnie Walker has licensed its brand name to be used on casual apparel. And Diageo has created a slick direct mail magazine, *American Mix*, to go out to its database of four hundred thousand households.[12]

Colleges and universities have grown increasingly concerned about alcohol abuse on their campuses. Dismissing complaints of censorship, the University of Notre Dame, the University of Scranton, UCLA, Washington State University, and California State University at Chico have all moved to restrict alcohol-related advertising in campus publications or have limited sponsorship of campus activities by beer companies or alcoholic beverage distributors.[13]

A pattern emerges from this collection of events: that the marketers of socially unacceptable products do not have the same open access to media advertising as do the marketers of mainstream products. Affordability, coverage, effectiveness, and other traditional economic or market criteria for choosing advertising media are not the only concerns for the firms in our five industries. Nonmarket factors—social, political, and legal forces—also affect advertising decisions and, like it or not, become a part of the firms' marketing strategies. The effects may have a major consequence (the banning of tobacco advertising from television) or only a minor consequence (no more beer ads in a campus newspaper). However, as our society grows increasingly concerned about a product category and as antagonistic advocacy groups grow in strength and numbers—in other words, as the legitimacy of that product wanes—a figurative noose is tightened, and marketers' decision making becomes more circumscribed.

As traditional media become off-limits, the search begins for new promotional outlets. Blocked from the broadcast media by law and faced with growing criticism of their print and outdoor advertising as well, the tobacco companies, especially Philip Morris and Reynolds, have developed huge data banks of information on smokers for direct-mail purposes. Each time a smoker cashes in a coupon, enters a cigarette-sponsored contest, or buys a tobacco-related cap, T-shirt, or other promotional item, that smoker's name, address, and other marketing information is recorded in the company's data bank. These millions of customer names provide Philip Morris and Reynolds with all of the usual direct-mail benefits: ease of communicating directly with customers, opportunity for informed feedback, a ready-made market for new products and line extensions, and so forth. But for the cigarette companies, the direct-mail lists now provide something more: insurance against the time when the mass media might be shut off to them by some stepped-up level of governmental, or even social, regulation.

In mid-1995, a brand new medium emerged with intriguing possibilities for all advertisers: the Internet. Of course, this new phenomenon was not originally intended for commercial purposes, but marketers were quick enough and clever enough to sniff out a potentially effective and lucrative means of communicating with customers. Even now, after eight or more years of experience, it is too early to know whether regulators, and society in general, will treat the Internet as a broadcast medium (and therefore subject to FCC regulations), as print media, or ultimately as some hybrid form of advertising with a new and different set of socially or governmentally imposed guidelines or regulations. What rules, restrictions, and provisions for customer protection should apply in cyberspace? And given the frontier, freewheeling, global nature of the Internet, how would such rules be enforced? These, and other issues relating to the Internet, are explored in chapter 11.

OTHER AVENUES

There is a strong Puritan, anti-pornography streak running through American society, and marketers of sexually explicit products and services have always had to find less noticeable, semi-obscure ways to promote or communicate with their potential customers. Some take advantage of modern technological advances. In this category, along with the advertisers on the Internet, are the dial-a-porn message sellers whose media are the 800 and 900 telephone numbers. Porn purveyors were quick to take advantage of the 900 pay-per-call system, which the telephone companies were either unable to monitor or reluctant to prohibit due to free-speech legal questions. Such adult messages accounted for more than 40 percent of the 900 services in California, generating significant revenue and profits, not only for the pornography sellers, but for Pacific Telephone as well. As soon as private citizens, as well as institutions like schools and hotels, learned that they could block access to the 900 numbers, however, the sex-sellers were just as quick to find a loophole in the law—they can enter into a "contractual agreement" with the caller—which would allow them to charge for 800-number calls. Since these calls cannot be blocked, now children at home or anyone from a business, hospital, or college can dial numbers like 1-800-HOTT-SEX or 1-800-BIG-ORGY, where the caller is urged to *enter* (orgasmic groan) his credit card number anytime. Parents have complained to the phone companies, to state regulators, and to the FCC that their children have run up bills totaling hundreds of dollars. Businesses have reported that such 800 porn calls have cost them as much as $4,000 a month.[14]

Yet another high-tech twist in the use of telephones for promoting porn messages, which makes government regulation more difficult, is giving the caller the option of dialing an international number to connect with such erotic services as the Lesbian Lust Line. The message will often originate in an obscure, off-the-beaten-track location such as the Republic of Sao Tome off the coast of Africa or Surinam in northeast South America; the resulting bill at the end of the month can cause as much excitement as the message did, ranging as high as $50 a minute.[15]

Still to come, bringing more marketing opportunities and more problems for regulators: in the age of 500-channel cable television, there will surely be room, and the customer demand, for any number of channels to be devoted to pornographic entertainment.

However, other pornography marketers use "media" that are decidedly old-fashioned. On the streets of New York, Las Vegas, and other cities with heavy tourist traffic, slightly seedy men can be seen thrusting flyers and handbills into the hands of male pedestrians. These handouts promise all sorts of sexual surprises, delights, and pleasures to be found in an out-of-the-way upstairs location, down the street, or around the corner. And, of course, these sidewalk promoters can disappear in an instant should a police officer stroll onto the scene.

Or they can be so bold as to challenge in the courts their right to hand out such material. In Las Vegas, the prime location for distributing these handbills for sexual attractions is the sidewalk in front of the Mirage and Treasure Island hotel/casinos. Those two hotels, concerned for their public image, claimed ownership of the sidewalk and sought an injunction against the Bare Elegance Entertainment Company, among others, from distributing the handbills. Bare Elegance filed a countersuit based on First Amendment rights.

No advertising medium can be more direct than simply presenting the product itself, and so prostitutes still wait on certain downtown city street corners, enticingly and sometimes minimally dressed, hoping to interest passing pedestrians or motorists, ready to duck into nearby doorways at the sight of the police. Prostitutes attracting motorists can create an entirely different set of social problems—snarled traffic—in some city areas at certain times of the day or night. In Washington, D.C., rather than arrest the women or try to chase them off the streets, police found it easier to outlaw right-hand turns for motorists in a four-block area of the city renowned as a hangout for prostitutes. This was meant to deprive "customers" the means of cruising and circling this particular area shopping for a pickup.

A somewhat more modern and discreet medium for promoting prostitution and pornography (translated as "escort services" and "adult entertainment") are the travel magazines to be found in every tourist hotel room. Here is a vehicle that goes directly to the marketers' prime target audience—traveling businessmen and conventioneers—and still it avoids attracting the attention of the general public, which might trigger some protest.

THE MESSAGES

In a previous chapter, we noted that marketers of socially unacceptable products face a particularly thorny problem: that because various groups disapprove of their product, it is dangerous to make the product bigger, better, or more efficient at what it is designed to do. Anti-alcohol critics rail when a beverage with more alcohol is introduced, handgun critics protest when a weapon is designed with more firepower, and cigarette makers would encounter a veritable buzz saw of criticism if they were to market a cigarette that delivered nicotine faster or in bigger doses.

For the same reasons, promoters of these products find it difficult to decide on what messages their advertising should communicate. Here are some of the most common messages or themes that can be found in the advertising for our five product categories:

Sex

Perhaps the most common complaint about advertising in general is the heavy-handed use of sexual images and sexual messages to sell almost anything from toothpaste to aluminum siding. Two years ago, an ad to sell diamonds pictured the nude body of a woman ensnared in a diaphanous web of the precious jewels.[16] Our five product categories are no exception. Of course sex, or the promise thereof, is a most appropriate message for the promotion of pornography, so it would be difficult if not impossible to advertise pornographic products or services without sexual messages and images. Still, it is amusing and even instructive how the advertisers of escort services (prostitution) and adult entertainment (nude dancing) clubs pull a thin veil of social propriety over their ads to avoid offending those whose standards lean more to the Puritan side.

Atlanta's Club Taj Mahal promises the "ultimate adult entertainment experience" and "continuous sensuality" in its ad in *Travel Host* magazine, which features a bosomy young woman with flowing blond hair dressed in a low-cut sequined gown. To grab the attention of the club's primary target audience, the ad also states, "Complimentary admission with hotel room key or convention badge." In the same magazine, Cabaret Platinum features the face and upper torso of a lovely, softly smiling, undressed young woman and promises "over 200 girls" and an "amateur contest Tues. night."

In Las Vegas, on the other hand, there are fewer Puritans and, therefore, fewer scruples. *Las Vegas Sundown,* which claims to be the state's "leading adult entertainment guide," displays an extraordinary number of mostly, sometimes totally, nude women's bodies in erotic poses. The center pages feature fourteen gorgeous young nude women who are "Ready and Willing to Display Their Real Great ASSets For Your Enjoyment and Pleasure. GIVE US A CALL—DON'T BE SHY—WE'RE NOT." Any one of these women can be ordered "by number" simply by calling 734-2888 (734-BUTT).

The message in some of the ads in *Las Vegas Sundown* can be coy, "You've never had room service like me," or clever, "The Only Sure Bet In Las Vegas! Call 737-1751 ask for Emma." Some hold out the promise of sexual fantasies: "Saddle Up Cowboy, I'm Ready to Ride! Roxanne 477-7731." Nearly all feature very descriptive photographs.

Nor in this age of gender equity are men left out. A page in *Las Vegas Sundown* is devoted to male strippers, "Pretty Boys, young beautiful talented clean carved muscular bodies," who, with a simple telephone call, will also visit any hotel room.

In Nevada, certain counties have legalized prostitution, and so the message of some of the promotional literature can be quite explicit. Although Las Vegas's Clark County has not made prostitution legal, it is often hard to tell, and there is plenty of advertising for the legal brothels not far across the county line. *Desert Nights,* handed out in front of the Mirage and Treasure Island hotels, promotes the brothels with considerable pride and describes some of their advantages in the following "editorial" fashion:

While gambling is being exported to all areas of the United States, the one thing that is still an exclusive in Nevada is the brothel. . . . Any one of these fine reputable establishments [the Cherry Patch Ranch, Mabel's Whorehouse, Mustang Ranch, Cherry Patch II, Cottontail Ranch, Bobbie's Buckeye Bar, etc.] have women that can make you a happy man. . . . enjoy man's last bastion of male sexuality . . . so you can brag to your friends about it later.

For tourists, where [sic] couldn't be a safer way to have sex that [sic] at one of the Amargosa Valley brothels. The girls who work at the brothels are inspected by a physician weekly for genital disease and it is virtually nonexistent.

Sex may be appropriate in advertising pornography, but it hardly seems the natural message in the ads for our other product categories. Yet it can be found in all four.

Advertising for alcoholic beverages is full of sexual messages, the most common being that drinking the product will help bring on some exciting sexual encounter. Some ads are relatively discreet and merely suggestive: a Christmas ad for Remy Martin shows a bottle of its cognac and reads: "Mistletoe gets you a kiss. Imagine what this will bring." Seagram tells us that its gin "could turn a 'maybe' into . . . 'again.'" Other ads are less discreet. A magazine ad for Canadian Mist whiskey shows a woman in a tight-fitting dress snuggling up to a tuxedo-attired man and tucking a card with her name on it into the waistband of his trousers. The copy tells us that Canadian Mist is "a great first move." More blatant still is an ad for Two Fingers Tequila aimed at college students, which shows a close-up of a dark-haired young woman standing in a provocative pose, her T-shirt pulled up high, her short shorts pulled low, saying, "Two Fingers is all it takes" and "Keep me posted."[17]

Sidney Frank Importing Co. does no media advertising for the Jaegermeister German liqueur it markets in the United States, but it has organized a squad of nearly a thousand attractive young women, the "Jaegerettes," who visit bars around the country in teams of six or eight, handing out pins, caps, megaphones, garter belts, and other trinkets to men who will down shots of the drink. Pleased with the success of this promotion, Mr. Frank went on to gather "a gaggle of Grey Goose girls" to promote his super premium vodka in similar fashion.[18] There is also a team of about 100 "Jaegerdudes," young men clad in tight biker shorts who visit predominantly gay bars.

In the Beer Institute's *Advertising & Marketing Code*, guideline Number 6 states:

Beer advertising and marketing materials should reflect generally accepted contemporary standards of good taste.

  a. Beer advertising and marketing materials should not contain any lewd or indecent language or images.

   b. Beer advertising and marketing materials should not portray sexual pas-
      sion, promiscuity or any other amorous activity as a result of consuming
      beer.

But beer marketers, catering to their mostly male consumers, are notorious for using sexual messages in their advertising. The Coors Swedish
bikini team TV ads created plenty of excitement for the brand along with
plenty of controversy from feminist groups and anti-alcohol advocates.
Spuds MacKenzie, the spokesdog for Bud Light, was constantly surrounded by a group of adoring and adorable young women. In 2003,
Miller and Coors continued to vie with each other as to which could produce the racier television commercials, the latter with its scantily clad,
blond, buxom twins, and the former with male bar patrons fantasizing
over equally sexy women engaging in a pillow fight. While these ads
captured viewers' attention, they were unsuccessful in capturing market
share for their brands.

The more powerful the brew, the more obvious the sexual message. Colt
45 malt liquor presents the product as indispensable for an evening of sex.
Handsome actor Billy Dee Williams told us in a television ad, "Part one
is the lady. Part two is the Colt. Now remember that the Colt is essential.
And part three is a little luck. Well, I've got the Colt, and I've got my lady.
So wish me luck."[19] Midnight Dragon's promotional posters showed a
scantily clad beautiful woman sipping the brew through a straw saying,
"I could suck on this all night."

Undoubtedly the most offensive example of using sexual enhancement
as a sales tool was McKenzie River's recruiting of rap singer Ice Cube to
pitch its St. Ides malt liquor to young African American men. Ice Cube's
advice in the ad: "In a black can, why don't ya grab a six-pack and get
your girl in the mood quicker, and get your jimmie thicker with St. Ides
malt liquor."[20] So much for "contemporary standards of good taste."

Cigarette advertising may be less obvious, but the sexual messages are
there to be found nonetheless. Reynolds Tobacco's Camel brand has consistently returned to the sex theme over its long history. Decades ago,
Camel's first pitch to women smokers showed a 1920s vamp leaning toward her smoking male partner inviting him to "Blow a little my way."
More recently, Camel's controversial mascot, Smokin' Joe, proves how
"cool" he is by attracting a bevy of fawning young women. And in mid-
1995, Camel's promotional theme was a return to the legendary ads of the
past as collector-item packaging. To highlight the promotion, the company
featured yet another 1920s beauty leaning provocatively toward the reader.

Gambling casinos incorporate sexual images and messages in their promoting as well. It would be hard to find a billboard or a print ad for a
casino that does not include a buxom, beautiful young woman to attract
our attention. And the casinos themselves have equally attractive women

adorning their slot and video game machines or serving drinks to those playing the machines or gambling at the tables.

And firearms? Most ads for the industry, to be sure, rely simply on pictures of the product: rifles, shotguns, handguns, and boxes of ammunition, sometimes supplemented with a flying pheasant or the head of a stag deer. However, Intratec, a Miami firearms company, distributes a promotional calendar picturing mostly nude, erotically posed female models, each brandishing one of the firm's assault pistols. Another calendar, this one from an Israeli holster manufacturer, features a woman clad only in a wet T-shirt and a holster with the caption, "The Best Home Your Weapon Could Choose."[21] In much milder fashion, a Colt full-page ad features a pretty young woman (fully clothed) on horseback, holstered revolver at her waist, with a caption promising that "Diana Baxter, Colt Catalog Cowgirl, is looking forward to signing your personal copy of the new Colt Catalog at the Colt display."[22] And an exhibitor at the industry show in Las Vegas drew attention to its service by displaying on its promotional literature a female model holding a pistol against her naked thigh and buttocks.

The use of sex in the advertising for these product categories is hardly surprising given the strong orientation toward male consumers in all five, but it is an easy target for critics. Conservative religious groups object to the display or suggestion of sex, whether obvious or veiled. The message that drinking X-brand alcoholic beverage, smoking Y-brand cigarette, or gambling at Z-brand casino will result in some erotic pleasure runs contrary even to mainstream American values. And, of course, feminist groups resent the exploitation of women in such advertising. So the potential for criticism is there, but the lure of the power and profitability of sexual messages in advertising is too often overwhelming.

Health

Society's objection to all five of our product categories is based in one way or another on potential damage the product or service can do to the user's physical or mental health. One might expect, therefore, that advertising for these products would take pains to avoid the subject of health. Handgun ads, especially those targeting women, as noted in an earlier chapter, promote the idea that owning and carrying a pistol will aid the buyer's safety (health) as well as that of her family.

Even cigarette manufacturers, who face the strongest criticism over health issues, have touched on the subject in their ads either in direct or indirect fashion. In the decades before the surgeon general's report, Camel proclaimed, "More doctors smoke Camels than any other cigarette." L & M brand went even further with its slogan, "Just what the doctor ordered." Richard Pollay, in his research on the history of advertising, estimates that fully half of all cigarette advertising between 1940 and 1960 used health as a theme.[23] Kent ran a series of ads picturing a muscular, athletic young man enjoying a cigarette in a locker room, presumably after a vigorous workout, implying a positive association between smoking and health. This is the same implication that critics find so objectionable about sponsorship of tennis tournaments by Virginia Slims and any other tobacco association with sports.

Today, Carlton stresses that it is lowest in tars, implying that it is not as bad for the smoker's health as other brands. Newport's long-running ad campaign featuring simply lovely green fields and blue skies and the slogan "Alive With Pleasure" implies health and happiness, a message that many critics find particularly cynical given cigarettes' record of causing death and disease.

The previous chapter noted the introduction of Advance and Omni, two new cigarette products based on lower levels of nitrosamines, which are known to be cancer-producing elements, and nicotine. Even if it suited the strategic objectives of these smaller tobacco companies to launch these new products, there was the problem of how to market them; the new products still contain the substances that can cause cardiovascular problems, bronchitis, and emphysema. Under these circumstances, the FTC is very reluctant to allow new products to be labeled as "safer" than others on the market. Furthermore, anti-tobacco advocates fear that such improved cigarettes will give smokers the misguided belief that there is less incentive now to give up smoking entirely. Indeed, at the end of 2001, the National Cancer Institute concluded that "low-tar" cigarettes were every bit as dangerous as regular varieties and called for an end to the use of terms such as "light" or "ultra light" in tobacco advertising. The institute study found that "smokers tend to take bigger, more frequent puffs of light cigarettes in order to inhale more nicotine."[24]

The marketers of alcoholic beverages, especially wines, are having an interesting flirtation with the health theme in their advertising. Traditionally, consumption of alcohol has been pictured as a detriment to health by anti-alcohol critics, for the damage drinking can cause to the liver and other internal organs and for behavioral problems such as drunk driving and spousal and child abuse. For this reason, federal law prohibits "any representation that the use of wine has curative or therapeutic effects." The BATF (Bureau of Alcohol, Tobacco, and Firearms) refused approval of a Geyser Peak Winery ad, which stated, "As age enhances wine, Wine enhances age," because it implied that drinking wine would prolong life. The bureau would not even allow Robert Mondavi to use a label referring to a biblical recommendation of wine drinking.[25]

The flirtation took on more serious proportions when a segment of CBS' *60 Minutes*, entitled "The French Paradox," was aired in 1961. The popular TV news program suggested that moderate wine consumption might actually be beneficial to one's health, based on the lower incidence of heart disease among the French who drink more red wine than do Americans. Wine industry marketers called the television segment "the 20 minutes that changed the industry" and looked for ways to use the information and statistics in their advertising. But the BATF would not even allow Leeward Winery, a small California vintner, to quote from the *60 Minutes* program in a newsletter sent out to the winery's customers, and the bureau forced Robert Mondavi to remove from its bottles a hang tag that quoted the program.[26]

More recently, the evidence of beneficial effects for some people of consuming one or two drinks a day has become "all but indisputable." But the government is still wary of allowing alcoholic beverage marketers to use any of these statistical data in their marketing messages because the effects, whether beneficial or detrimental, vary so widely based on the drinker's gender, family history, health conditions, and lifestyle factors such as frequency of physical exercise.[27]

Success, Prestige, Social Status, and Security

Success is such a common goal. In its many manifestations—social, economic, political, professional, intellectual, athletic—success along some dimension of our lives is something almost everyone longs and strives for regardless of age, race, culture, or gender. So it is little wonder that advertisers seize on this longing to help promote their products. In our five industries, this message takes a number of different forms, once again ranging from the subtle to the obvious.

Smokin' Joe Camel sent the message to young smokers, or would-be smokers, that smoking Camels was "cool," and therefore, the admiration of women was sure to follow. The Marlboro Man sent the message that smoking that brand would signify a "rugged" or "independent" character trait.

The very essence of gambling in all forms is to win, that is to be successful, and so the hope of winning is a major message in casino and lottery advertising. Sometimes the success promised in an ad is overstated. Lottery systems have been criticized because the large winnings that they promise are often paid out over twenty years, reducing the actual present value of the winning by one-half or more.

The slightly naughty, but definitely debonair "Osky" symbol for *Esquire* magazine of old and the *Playboy* bunny of more recent years hold the promise that by becoming readers of those magazines we too can be naughty and debonair and thereby gain some esteem from our peers. Both firearms and cigarettes hold out for women the promise of liberation and independence, which for many women are synonymous with success.

Alcoholic beverage marketers are especially notorious for sending the message that choosing a particular brand of wine, scotch whiskey, vodka, or brandy is a testament to our good taste and will magically elevate our social standing. For years, Dewar's Scotch ran its series of "profiles" of Dewar's drinkers, all high achievers who have read the hippest book, scaled Yosemite's El Capitan, or discovered a miracle-cure pharmaceutical. Television ads emphasized the admiration of friends that comes with choosing just the right Gallo wine for a special occasion. And Courvoisier Cognac billboard and poster ads invariably show its consumers dressed in tuxedos and evening gowns, surrounded by the trappings of wealth and success.

Promises of prestige and success are galling to critics of advertising in general, but when the marketers of liquor, wine, cigarettes, and the rest of our socially unacceptable products make these promises, they stimulate a double dose of social criticism and complaint.

Alcohol Content of Beer

It has been noted previously that finding an appropriate attribute of socially unacceptable products to promote is difficult because their very essence is anathema to many people. The amount of alcohol in any given beverage is a case in point. Every bottle of liquor has the "proof" on the label, a measure equal to twice the alcohol content. Every bottle of wine describes on its label the alcohol content. But until recently, such information was prohibited from the labels on beer and malt liquors by a federal law, passed shortly after the repeal of Prohibition because the government feared, justifiably, that beer would be promoted on the basis of alcoholic strength. The BATF carried this restriction to the point of ruling out the name "PowerMaster" for one of Heilemann's malt liquor brands, arguing that the name was simply another way of promoting strength.

After more than sixty years Coors challenged this law in 1987 and prevailed in the lower federal court, a decision that was affirmed by the Supreme Court in 1995. While thus opening the door to showing alcoholic content on the label, the lower court ruling upheld the ban on the use of such information in ads, and this question was not part of the Supreme Court's review.

With the introduction of its Molson Ice beer in 1991, Miller Brewing determined to test the ad ban as well. Miller not only put the beer's 5.6 percent alcoholic content on the label, but showed a close-up shot of the label in its television ads. When the BATF objected, Miller responded by covering the alcohol content with a black diamond on which was written the phrase, "If you get it, get it." This second ad, which ran in *Rolling Stone* and *Spin* magazines, seemed the perfect adversarial, tongue-in-cheek message for those magazines' readers. Neither the BATF nor the alcoholic beverage critics were amused, however, and the second ad was pulled as well.[28]

Other Controversial Messages

Critics of socially unacceptable products spend considerable time and effort analyzing the manufacturers' advertising to get behind the superficial messages and to discover what the manufacturer "really meant." What was the real intent of the ad? Intentions are hard to prove, of course, but over the years, various congressional hearings and lawsuits have surfaced internal company documents that shed some light. For example, a market research firm hired by Brown & Williamson in 1975 laid out the following strategic approach to attract "young starters" to its Viceroy cigarettes:

In the young smoker's mind a cigarette falls into the same category with wine, beer, shaving, wearing a bra (or purposely not wearing one), declaration of independence and striving for self-identity. For the young starter, a cigarette is associated with introduction to sex life, with courtship, with smoking "pot" and keeping late studying hours. Thus an attempt to reach young starters should be based, among others, on the following major parameters:

Present the cigarette as one of a few initiations into the adult world.

Present the cigarette as part of the illicit pleasure category of products and activities.

To the best of your ability (considering some legal restraints) relate the product to "pot," wine, beer, sex, etc.

Don't communicate health or health related points.[29]

Researchers have discovered through teen and preteen focus groups that one of the motivators to take up smoking is simply to drive their parents crazy.

As cynical and immoral as this report seems, such an approach may be reasonable from a strictly economic, market-driven point of view. As expected, however, Brown & Williamson denied any responsibility for the ideas and claimed that the report had no influence whatsoever on the company's advertising programs.

Finding an advertising message to carry out a company's growth and profit objectives, given the sometimes hostile social, political, and legal environments, is a bit like walking a tightrope. Marketers of cigarettes, alcoholic beverages, and gambling are continuously faced with conflicting pressures. Of course they hope to sell more of their product as a result of their ads; that is, after all, the ultimate purpose of advertising. Of course the marketers need to attract new customers; every business, especially the tobacco business where so many smokers die each year, needs a constant flow of new consumers.

In the tobacco, alcoholic beverage, and gambling industries, however, both of these goals—enlarging the overall market and attracting new consumers—are sensitive issues and are actively opposed by the industry critics. The result is that the firms in these industries justify their advertising in two ways. The first, as has been noted previously, is that their ads are only meant to protect their own brands and their own market share. In other words, the increases that they hope to get will come from their competitors. The second justification is the claim that their advertising has no effect on increasing the size of the market. Emerson Foote, a founder of Foote, Cone and Belding and one of the grand old men of the advertising world, scoffs at this idea: "The cigarette industry has been artfully maintaining that cigarette advertising has nothing to do with total sales. This is complete and utter nonsense. The industry knows it is nonsense. I am always amused by the suggestion that advertising, a function that has been shown to increase consumption of virtually every other product, somehow miraculously fails to work for tobacco products."[30]

Sometimes advertising messages are thinly veiled in the hopes of avoiding criticism and controversy. Casino and lottery operators recognize that throughout much of the United States there is still some stigma attached to gambling, and that some gamblers, therefore, would like to keep their gambling activity a secret from friends or even family. Jackpot Junction, a casino located some ninety miles from Minneapolis, sought to take advantage of gamblers' concern for privacy and turn its remote location into an asset. In 1994, it initiated a series of ads promoting itself as a "discreet" place, "Conveniently located miles from anyone you know." The thirty-second TV spots showed an elderly man's wife catching him eyeing an attractive young woman, a teacher spotting a boy throwing spitballs in class, and two young children spying on their parents embracing. Each ad included a voice-over tagline: "Ever notice life's more fun when no one's watching?" Critics lost sight of the humor, however. Mental health professionals noted that out-of-the-way places have special appeal for compulsive gamblers who often feel an acute sense of shame about their habit.[31]

Malt liquor ads, for all their bluntness, also included some hidden messages. Previously noted was the theme of alcohol potency through the surrogate use of "power": the aborted PowerMaster brand from Heilemann's, Colt 45's lightening bolt and slogan, "It's Got More," and Schlitz Red Bull's slogan, "The REAL Power!" Association with street gangs is also implied by an ad for St. Ides showing Ice Cube holding his hand with his thumb, forefinger, and little finger extended, a common gang signal. Or Olde English 800's poster showing three young, African American women clad in tight short skirts and bra tops around a pool table fondling a pool cue under the headline "8 Ball Anyone?" Mainstream Americans, if they saw the ad at all, would dismiss it as simply another all-too-obvious example of using sex to sell the brew. But in the inner city neighborhoods where the ads were posted, African Americans would pick up on the reference to drugs, "8-Ball" being slang for an eighth of an ounce of crack cocaine. The message then becomes: Olde English 800 can give you as good a "high" as crack. Not to be outdone, Ice Cube responds in another ad for St. Ides, "Forget eight ball . . . that beer makes you earl [gag] . . . I don't drink eight ball no mo' . . . eight ball aside for a stronger malt liquor."

Whether blatant or disguised, the messages in ads for all socially un-acceptable products are sure to be scrutinized and, if necessary, decoded for the public by critics and anti-product advocates. When the message is about sexual exploitation, drug use, crime gangs, or some other antisocial form of behavior, sharp criticism comes as no surprise. But even when Salem shows a smiling couple strolling hand-in-hand across a green field, when MGM Grand shows an excited crowd in its casino—when the mes-sage is as innocuous as "This product is fun"—still it will be subject to criticism. It is the very nature of these products to which critics object; therefore, even to communicate the message that gambling, inhaling nic-otine, or drinking alcohol is fun can stir up a hornet's nest of controversy.

NOTES

1. Philip J. Hilts, "$1 Million Spent to Put Cigarettes in Movies, Memos Show," *New York Times*, May 20, 1994, C18.

2. Bruce Horovitz, "Cigarette Billboards Are Striking Out at Baseball Stadi-ums," *Philadelphia Inquirer*, April 8, 1993, A1.

3. Ibid.

4. Wade Lamber, "Madison Square Garden Agrees to Keep Cigarette Ads Off the Air During Games," *Wall Street Journal*, April 5, 1995, A4.

5. As quoted in Diane Turner-Bowker and William L. Hamilton, "Cigarette Advertising Expenditures Before and After the Master Settlement Agreement: Pre-liminary Findings," May 15, 2000, http://www.state.ma.us/dph/mtcp/report/mag.htm (accessed February 27, 2002).

6. Ibid.

7. Adapted from Charles King, III, and Michael Siegel, "The Master Settlement Agreement with the Tobacco Industry and Cigarette Advertising in Magazines," *New England Journal of Medicine*, August 16, 2001. Reported by Harcourt College Publishers, http://www.hbcollege.com/business_stats/kohler/resources/stats/ch13.html (accessed March 14, 2002).

8. Ibid.

9. John B. Hinge and Kathleen Deveny, "Bacardi's TV Ads for Rum-Laced Cooler Are Under Fire," *Wall Street Journal*, July 22, 1991, B1.

10. Joe Flint, Shelly Branch, and Vanessa O'Connell, "Breaking Longtime Taboo, NBC Network Plans to Accept Liquor Ads," *Wall Street Journal*, December 14, 2001, B1.

11. Joe Flint and Shelly Branch, "In Face of Widening Backlash, NBC Gives Up Plan to Run Liquor Ads," *Wall Street Journal*, March 21, 2002, B1.

12. Theresa Howard, "Spirits Makers Mix New Ways to Market," *USA Today*, December 28, 2000, 8B.

13. Susan Dodge, "Many Colleges Move to Restrict Alcohol-Related Ads in Student Papers, Vendors' Sponsorship of Events," *Chronicle of Higher Education*, February 21, 1990, A39.

14. Cyndee Miller, "'Dial-A-Porn' Protests Spur Moves to 'Hold All Calls,'" *Marketing News*, February 1, 1988, 1. See also Jonathan Dahl, "Porn Lines Offer 800 Numbers, but These Aren't Toll-Free Kind," *Wall Street Journal*, July 13, 1994, B1; and Mary Lu Carnevale, "FCC Proposes Crackdown on '800' Lines as More Companies Charge for Calls," *Wall Street Journal*, August 3, 1994, B8.

15. Dahl, "Porn Lines Offer 800 Numbers."

16. Lynne Duke, "Advertising in a Bare Market," *Washington Post*, December 8, 2000, C1.

17. Michael F. Jacobson and Laurie Ann Mazur, *Marketing Madness* (Boulder, CO: Westview Press, Inc., 1995), 164–72.

18. Christopher Lawteon, "A Liquor Maverick Shakes Up Industry with Pricey Brands," *Wall Street Journal*, May 21, 2003, A1.

19. Ibid.

20. Kathleen Deveny, "Malt Liquor Makers Find Lucrative Market in the Urban Young," *Wall Street Journal*, March 9, 1992, A1.

21. *Female Persuasion* (Washington, DC: Violence Policy Center, 1994), 57–59.

22. *SHOT Business*, January 1995, 73.

23. Richard W. Pollay, "Themes and Tactics in Cigarette Advertising, 1938–1983: Technical Report on Methods and Measures" (working paper, History of Advertising Archives, Vancouver, British Columbia, 1987), as referenced in Jacobson and Mazur, *Marketing Madness*, 150n36.

24. Gordon Fairclough, "Risks of Light Smokes Are Highlighted," *Wall Street Journal*, November 28, 2001, B8.

25. Carrie Dolan, "Wineries and Government Clash Over Ads that Toast Health Benefits of Drinking," *Wall Street Journal*, October 19, 1992, B1.

26. Ibid.

27. Marilyn Chase, "Beneficial Drinking: After Abstinence, Before Tying One On," *Wall Street Journal*, July 3, 1995, B1.

28. Suein L. Hwang and Paul M. Barrett, "Court Allows Alcohol Levels on Beer Labels," *Wall Street Journal*, April 20, 1995, B1. See also Eben Shapiro, "Molson Ice Ads Raise Hackles of Regulators," *Wall Street Journal*, February 25, 1994, B1; and Suein L. Hwang, "Miller Brewing Gets Heat for New Ice Beer Ads," *Wall Street Journal*, October 12, 1994, B1.

29. From documents placed in the records of the hearings before the House Commerce Committee Subcommittee on Oversight and Investigations, June 25, 1981, Serial No. 97–66, as presented in Jacobson and Mazur, *Marketing Madness*, 152.

30. Jacobson and Mazur, *Marketing Madness*, 152.

31. Jim McCartney, "Casino's 'Discreet' Ad Is Latest to Inspire Critics," Saint Paul *Pioneer Press*, August 5, 1994, 1A. See also Bob Geiger, "Jackpot Junction to Make Bid for Uneasy Gamblers," Minneapolis *Star Tribune*, July 18, 1994, 2D.

CHAPTER 10

Promotion Strategies: Symbols and Other Promotional Tools

THE SYMBOLS

Every marketer's dream come true is to create some advertising element—a slogan, image, tune, or symbol—that has a life beyond the ad itself. A number of the firms in our industries have been smart enough or lucky enough to create such symbols, so recognizable that they have become a part of our everyday lives. We find them in our ordinary reading, they appear in cartoons, we refer to them in our conversations about politics, sports, business, and the weather; and all the while, without our even being conscious of it, they are doing the advertiser's job of reminding us of some product. What good fortune for the advertiser when this happens! And yet in socially unacceptable industries, there is a downside to this success: the symbol also becomes a rallying point for the product's critics. Discussed below are only a few of the most famous, or infamous, of these symbols that have generated controversy along with sales.

Smokin' Joe Camel

He was the center of attention, he was insouciant, he smirked, he attracted all the gorgeous women, he was dapper and carefree—and above all else, Joe Camel was cool.[1] Is it any wonder that Joe became such a popular figure with the young (beginning at age three) and the young at heart? After all, he was the very embodiment of so much of what adolescents and many young adults long to be.

Created by a British artist in 1974 for a Camel cigarette campaign in

France, the bulbous-nosed camel with the cigarette dangling rakishly from his mouth was brought to the United States in 1988. At that time, the venerable brand's market share had been declining for almost four decades. In 1950, Camel was this country's most popular cigarette with a 27.2 percent share of the market. By 1970, it had fallen to sixth place with a 6.3 percent market share, and by the late 1980s, Camel's share had dropped to only 2.6 percent. Joe's mission: to halt and reverse this slide and to change the brand's customer base from older, blue-collar males to young, swinging "hipsters."

Joe was successful on both fronts. The market share slide was halted, and by 1993 the brand had climbed back to around 4 percent. More importantly, Camel's market share among smokers between the ages of eighteen and twenty-four rose from 4.4 to 7.9 percent. Along with this success, however, Joe managed in his relatively brief lifetime to create more controversy, arguably, than any other advertising symbol in history.

From Joe's first cartoon-style appearance in magazine ads and on billboards, critics accused Reynolds of targeting underage smokers and of luring children to become first-time smokers. One study found that the Camel brand had increased its share of the illegal children's market from .5 to 32.8 percent. Another showed that even without the benefit of television advertising, Joe Camel was as familiar to six-year-olds as Mickey Mouse.

The controversy took on added impetus when the prestigious *Journal of the American Medical Association (JAMA)* published three surveys in late 1991. Among other things, the surveys reported that more than half of all three- to six-year-olds matched the Joe Camel logo with cigarettes, and that in spite of Reynolds's continued assertions that its advertising was targeted only at young adults, 98 percent of teenagers, when shown a picture of a Joe Camel ad, correctly identified the brand compared with only 67 percent of adults.

This was just the sort of evidence anti-smoking critics wanted to press their cause, and a storm of protest erupted. Doctors' groups and the major medical associations joined the chorus of critics, Surgeon General Antonia Novello called the use of the symbol "deplorable," the Federal Trade Commission (FTC) took the unprecedented step of calling for a ban of the image entirely, the consumer-activist group INFACT threatened a boycott on all RJR Nabisco's other popular brands—from Oreo cookies to Planters nuts—and Representative Henry Waxman (D-CA) used the opportunity in the House of Representatives to urge a total ban on all cigarette advertising.

Reynolds's response was anything but contrite. Given Joe's success, and on the theory that even the bad publicity was good for the brand, the company increased the Camel ad budget in 1963 by 63 percent over the previous year. It launched an aggressive attack on the methodology used in the *JAMA* surveys and held up a First Amendment free speech shield to ward off the FTC attack. (The FTC commissioners, after a long delay, refused to accept its staff's recommendation.) Reynolds did begin to exercise some restraint in the use of Joe Camel: it dropped plans to use the logo on bandannas to be given away at a motorcycle convention and also on in-line skates, and it vetoed a suggested image of Joe cavorting with punk camels with pink hair, all of which struck the company's legal staff as too adolescent. On the other hand, Josephine Camel and a bevy of female dromedaries were added to the ads, sparking even more criticism that now the largely male brand was going after a bigger female share.

At the peak of the controversy, James W. Johnston, chief executive officer of Reynolds Tobacco vowed, "I'll be damned if I'll pull the ads."[2] But time and the continuous need for fresh advertising approaches finally accomplished what all of tobacco's sharpest critics had failed to do. By mid-1995, Smokin' Joe was disappearing from magazine ads and billboards, and small statues of the tuxedo-clad camel were becoming collectors' items.[3]

The Marlboro Man

Less controversial, perhaps, but a longer-lasting and far more important advertising and cultural icon was Philip Morris's Marlboro Man—that rugged, handsome, independent cowboy who inhabited the mountains, prairies, and corrals of the western United States. This dashing symbol was first introduced to the American public in 1954, when he came riding across television screens throughout the United States in the most dramatic and successful product relaunch in advertising history. For thirty years, Marlboro had been a largely unsuccessful woman's cigarette. But by the mid-1950s, Philip Morris needed a new product with a filter tip to counteract the growing concerns about smoking and cancer. The company chose to keep the Marlboro name, added a filter, gave it a "rich, full" flavor, packaged it in a new, distinctive red and white flip-top box, and created the Marlboro Man as its symbol. The results were beyond the company's wildest dreams. Even though banned from television in 1970, the Marlboro Man and his horse barely stumbled; they roamed the pages of magazines and newspapers and were seen on posters and billboards on every continent. The Marlboro brand not only dominates the U.S. cigarette market, it is the best-selling cigarette brand in the world. Moreover, the Marlboro Man symbol and the red and white box are, along with Coca-Cola's distinctive script logo and red shield, the most recognizable and the most valuable advertising symbols ever created.

For better or worse, the Marlboro Man's free spirit, his independence, his rugged but seemingly happy existence in the beautiful Western locale appealed not only to adults but to young people, including underage smokers, as well. As successful as Smokin' Joe was in increasing Camel's market share, he paled in comparison with the Marlboro Man. The good news for Philip Morris was how extraordinarily popular (and profitable) the brand was (and still is). Some studies have shown that Marlboro commands as much as 75 percent of the underage and the eighteen- to twenty-four-year old markets. The bad news was that the extent of this popularity, especially among young smokers, gave critics a powerful club with which to attack the company and the industry. Philip Morris, which spends as much as $1.5 *billion* a year promoting the Marlboro brand,[4] claimed at every opportunity that its Marlboro Man was not intended to appeal to the young. But intentions aside, he did; and the critics' complaints were long and loud. As the leading brand's symbol, and with more money spent to promote him than any other cigarette brand (in recent years, more than any other consumer brand in any product category), the Marlboro Man became a lightening rod that attracted all the criticism and controversy aimed at smoking and the tobacco industry in general.

Spuds MacKenzie, Bud Man, the *Playboy* Bunny, and Others

Anheuser-Busch launched its Bud Light brand after the success of Miller Lite, confirming that the light beer category was an important one, that it was here to stay, and that the Budweiser brand needed an entry in this segment of the market. Bud Light's initial advertising campaign, that played on the double meaning of the word "light," was only modestly successful and did not have the customer appeal that could propel this latecomer to the market into a true contender with Miller Lite.

Enter Spuds MacKenzie, the adorable and cuddly, if somewhat enigmatic, little bull terrier who did little more in the Bud Light ads than surround himself with an extraordinary number of beautiful, fawning young women. The connection between a bull terrier, or any dog for that matter, and light beer was never clear. Was the message that women should flock to Bud Light as they did to Spuds because Bud Light had fewer calories? Or that hip guys should drink Bud Light and so attract as many gorgeous women as Spuds?

Here is a case where it didn't really matter what the message was; the symbol became the important element of the ads. Spuds was cute, he caught the eye and the imagination of beer drinkers, and he played a brief role in making Bud Light the best-selling light beer in the United States and second only to Budweiser in the entire beer market.

Spuds also stirred up plenty of controversy. Why else would the marketers at Budweiser use a little dog for a symbol, asked the anti-alcohol critics, if they were not trying to appeal to young drinkers or would-be young drinkers? Wasn't the attraction of women a message that would appeal to teenage boys especially? And did all those women who fawned over Spuds really look old enough to drink? In spite of the proliferation of Spuds MacKenzie stuffed animals and the look-alike contests for a real, live Spuds, Budweiser professed, of course, that its advertising and promotion were aimed only at adults, . . . well perhaps young adults, just as was its cartoon character, Bud Man, and the company dismissed out of hand any suggestions that it should discontinue using Spuds as a symbol. However, given the controversy Spuds created and Anheuser-Busch's overall attempts to position the company as a responsible and responsive beer marketer, retirement for both Spuds and the Bud Man came earlier than might otherwise have happened.

By that time, another animal symbol had already been all but retired. During the 1960s and 1970s at the height of Playboy Enterprises' expansion, its symbol or mascot, the profile of a discreet but definitely voyeuristic bunny, had become a familiar sight on and off the pages of *Playboy* magazine. As Playboy Clubs opened in major tourist cities throughout the country and also overseas, the bunny's most frequent and daring observation post was as a stick-on affixed to, and thus drawing attention to, the ample bosoms of all the Playboy Club waitresses. These shapely young women in their very low-cut, tight-fitting tank costumes were themselves made out as bunnies with rabbit ears on their heads and a round, white "cottontail" attached to the backs of their costumes that wiggled as they walked among the tables to the delight of tourists and conventioneers.

Playboy marketers were very successful in that the bunny profile came to be widely recognized and identifiable as a Playboy symbol. But just as with Joe, Spuds, and the Marlboro Man, the bunny's success was also its undoing. It quickly became a target for feminist groups as yet another example of the exploitation of women by the dominant male society.

If the use of animals and cartoon characters in the advertising of socially unacceptable products creates problems, so too does the use of real, live, honest-to-goodness celebrity endorsers. As common and effective as celebrities may be in endorsing athletic shoes, breakfast cereal, or feminine hygiene products, they can no longer be used to endorse products that are controversial. Once the link between cancer and smoking was established in the 1950s, cigarette marketers stopped using entertainment stars to endorse their brands. Although it might be effective in promoting sales, almost never does an alcoholic beverage marketer dare to use a celebrity to endorse a particular brand of beer, wine, or liquor because of the criticism it would generate. McKenzie River's use of rapper Ice Cube to promote St. Ides is a case in point. Even Miller's long-running and amusing campaign using aging, over-the-hill athletes to promote Lite beer ("Tastes great!—Less filling!") sparked criticism. And it would hardly be appropriate for a sports or entertainment hero to promote gambling or some form of pornography.

Questionable Icons

That general rule doesn't prevent entrepreneurial marketers from testing the waters in some of the less public, out-of-the-way promotional venues. At a recent Comdex show in Las Vegas (the huge exposition for stereo, video, and other electronic communication equipment), X-rated videos had their own designated area of the convention center hall. What celebrities could promote these films more effectively than the female porn stars, whose appearance at the convention center caused considerable excitement and drew nationwide media attention to an otherwise parochial marketing trade show.

Sometimes advertisers seem determined to choose symbols that are so gross or in such bad taste that they are certain to generate societal and governmental disapproval. Cabo Distributing in Southern California coined the name "Black Death" for its premium-priced vodka and chose for its symbol a grinning skull wearing a black top hat. The marketing plan also called for endorsement by Slash, at the time a prominent "heavy metal" rock guitarist, and the product was to be packaged in small wooden coffins. Surgeon General Novello "denounced the product for targeting underage drinkers with its macabre imagery and its choice of Slash as a spokesman." The BATF (Bureau of Alcohol, Tobacco, and Firearms) criticized the company because "the label mocks the real health risks which may result from the consumption of alcohol" and forced a rather modest change in the name from Black Death to Black Hat. The CEO of the company was delighted with the publicity ignited by the controversy; sales rose from five thousand to twenty thousand cases a month, and the company planned to capitalize on the momentum by introducing Black Hat tequila, replacing the top hat with a black sombrero.[5]

A month later the BATF, reacting to criticism from Native American groups and others, reversed its earlier approval and turned down an application from a small brewery to market "Crazy Horse" malt liquor. The brew's label would have featured as its symbol the profile of a Native American, the imagery of the South Dakota Black Hills, and the claim that the product "was steeped in the history of the American West," a bit of a stretch given that the brewer was located in Brooklyn. South Dakota governor George Mikkelson entered a strong protest, and the "Surgeon General called the malt 'an insensitive and malicious marketing ploy' targeted at Native Americans, who have a disproportionately high rate of alcoholism and alcohol-related illness."[6]

OTHER PROMOTIONAL TOOLS

Advertising is not the only arrow in the promotional quiver, and it is not the only source of controversy for socially unacceptable products.

Sampling, common enough in the marketing plans of salsas, sausages, sodas, or a dozen other consumables, is illegal with alcoholic beverages and restricted when it comes to cigarettes. It used to be a common element of the introduction of a new brand of cigarette to hand out free samples, usually a pack of five, on street corners or at music or sporting events. Of course, there was no effective way to prevent these free samples being given to minors. Bowing to wide-scale protest, cigarette manufacturers discontinued the practice in the United States, but still give out free samples when entering new Eastern European or Asian markets if the host countries do not specifically rule out the practice, generating renewed criticism whenever they do so.

UST, Inc. was sued by the state of Massachusetts for allegedly sending out free samples of its Skoal brand chewing tobacco to high school students, many of them minors, who sent in coupons clipped from ads for Skoal.[7]

Until the early 1990s, brewers and some spirits marketers were among the biggest sponsors of spring vacation events for college students. Hospitality tents marked by huge inflatable beer cans or tequila bottles, banners, giveaway T-shirts, other trinkets, and an occasional free sample were common promotional tactics from Fort Lauderdale, Florida, to Padre Island, Texas, to Palm Springs, California, or wherever thirsty college students gathered to party on their annual spring breaks. But a combination of anti-alcohol advocates, who were appalled at how easy it was for underage college students to participate in the promotions, and the resort communities themselves, who were tired of the vandalism caused by thousands of drunken young revelers, successfully pressured the brewers and distributors to discontinue these promotions or at the very least move them into local bars where, in theory, minors could not participate.

A "Search for Bud Man" promotion, launched nationwide by Budweiser in 1991 encouraging consumers to look for prizes among the cans of the brewer's various products, had to be scrapped in Texas because the state prohibited alcoholic beverage manufacturers from using contests or sweepstakes designed to induce consumers to buy a firm's products.

Based solely on economic considerations, there are a number of good reasons for a brewery, or even a cigarette manufacturer, to sponsor an athletic event or music concert. First, and probably most important, such events represent large gatherings of the marketers' target audiences, and exposing a brand name to these groups should be an effective manner of communication. In the case of beer, at least, there is the natural association of a cold drink after some sort of athletic workout, or the association of drinking with music and entertainment.

Such sponsorship, however—whether it is the Virginia Slims tennis tournaments, the Marlboro Indianapolis auto races, sponsorship of a women's baseball team by Coors, or Budweiser's central role in a recent concert tour of the Rolling Stones—is anathema to anti-smoking and anti-alcohol critics. Because cigarettes are, and beer can be, harmful to one's health, critics accuse the manufacturers of trying to obscure this fact by creating an association with various sports that are perceived as healthy activities. Furthermore, the critics complain that there is an implied message: If professional athletes are connected in some way to cigarettes and beer, how harmful can they be?

Sports sponsorship by alcoholic beverage makers runs into trouble not only in the United States, but across the Atlantic in Europe as well. Coors, Seagram, Bass, Carlsberg, Heineken, and Holsten-Brauerei all sponsor British soccer teams, but the notorious rowdiness of soccer fans in the United Kingdom, resulting rather frequently in riots and even some deaths, has led to serious questioning of the practice by anti-alcohol groups and even by some of the sponsors, who wonder whether associating their brand names with such violence is the sort of publicity they want. The belief that alcohol contributes to such violence is rather widely accepted. In 1991 during a European Cup match in Rotterdam, officials banned drinking at the games and closed the city's bars. Neither Denmark nor France permits alcoholic beverage sponsors for their soccer teams.[8] In the United States, professional soccer has yet to establish itself as a major league sport, compared with football, baseball, basketball, or even hockey, but there is already some controversy over the role alcohol should play. Anheuser-Busch agreed to be an important sponsor of the fledgling Major League Soccer and then was outraged when the league's organizer recommended banning beer sales in the stadiums.[9]

No less problematic is the sponsorship of rock music concerts. Anheuser-Busch boasted that it was an official sponsor of the Rolling Stones' *Voodoo Lounge* tour in late 1994 with point-of-sale promotional material, sweepstakes giving away trips and tickets to the concerts, and even selling Stones' neckties. With rock concerts, the obvious complaint of alcohol critics is that a major share of the audience is under the legal drinking age, and therefore, it is totally inappropriate and wrong for a brewery to promote itself to this group of minors.[10]

Then there are less conventional forms of promotion. Philip Morris has experimented with discount coupons on turkeys, milk, soft drinks, sunglasses, windscreen washer, cosmetics, audiotapes, books, towels, and travel offers, among other various products, to promote the sale of its Marlboro, Virginia Slims, Merit, and Benson & Hedges brands.[11] For mainstream products, such associations might seem odd but harmless. Tobacco critics, however, complain that linking cigarettes with milk or turkeys is an attempt to mask the harmfulness of one product with the wholesomeness of the other.

One final type of promotion deserves mention: the catalogs of wearing apparel and miscellaneous gift items available "free" in exchange for a designated number of cigarette package labels. This is actually a recycling of an old idea: in the 1940s and 1950s, Raleigh cigarettes offered a similar promotion. Until the Master Settlement Agreement (MSA) in 1998, Marlboro smokers could collect five "Marlboro Miles" from each package they smoked. Philip Morris distributed a twenty-five-page, full color, glossy catalog with items ranging from bandannas (only twenty-five miles) to denim shirts and jackets, gear bags, Swiss Army watches, and even a regulation size pool table (twenty-five thousand miles!). Each time a smoker cashed in some "Miles," his or her name and other information were added to Philip Morris's database for future direct mail promotional activities. Camel, not to be left behind, offered "C-notes" printed to look like a small dollar bill; on each pack was a smiling Smokin' Joe dressed in a George Washington white wig, but also with sunglasses, cool as ever. Critics were angry that such logo merchandise advertised the product without having to carry the usual warning label and was another way of deflecting the public's attention from the harmfulness of cigarettes. Most of this type of cigarette promotion has been eliminated by the MSA.

Nevada's "ranches," the euphemism for bordellos, normally keep a low profile. "As long as the brothels are low-key and out of the way (they are banned in the state's biggest cities, Las Vegas and Reno), the general wisdom [is that] everyone is happy."[12] But when the winter Olympic Games came to neighboring Utah, Bella's Hacienda Ranch couldn't resist capitalizing on the promotional possibilities. Bella's, in Wells, Nevada, launched a marketing strategy to encourage visitors at the Games to travel the 180 miles to the "ranch" by staging an Olympics/Valentine's Day promotion. Customers "were entered into a raffle to win free quality time with the sex-worker of their choice" and also "concocted Olympic-like competitions for clients and their servers—competitions best left undescribed in a family newspaper."[13]

Even major companies sometimes eschew expensive television advertising for more offbeat promotions that offer better exposure at a lower cost. Diageo, the giant distiller, created an "island nation" for its Jose Cuervo brand tequila. "It leased a tiny Caribbean island and garnered millions' worth of free TV coverage with stunts like petition drives to enter the U.N. or participate in the Olympics."[14]

It is to be expected that the marketers of socially unacceptable products, like the marketers of all products, would look to other promotional tactics and tools in addition to media advertising as effective ways to increase their business. It is all but inevitable, however, that such tactics will stir up controversy. Sampling, a tried-and-true method of pushing non-customers into the trial stage of the adoption process, is forbidden with these products, either by law or by social stigma. Society *does not want* non-buyers to become buyers, particularly of cigarettes, alcoholic beverages, and the various forms of gambling. Indeed, the whole concept of the adoption process taught in every marketing textbook, moving non-users from the awareness stage to the trial stage to the adoption (addiction?) stage, is considered out-of-bounds. For these products, once again, the promotional options available to marketers are seriously restricted.

CONTRA-ADVERTISING

One way or another, in all five of our subject industries, marketers do something quite extraordinary in the marketing profession: they expend some effort and money to urge *some* of their customers *not* to buy their product. This is the result of two conditions: that the products are potentially dangerous to their buyers and that they carry to some degree the stigma of social disapproval. Beer marketers for years have promoted "responsible" drinking and have vigorously opposed drinking and driving with ad campaigns such as "Know when to say when" and "Friends don't let friends drink and drive." The Beer Institute, a trade association for U.S. brewers, has run an ad with the headline, "Why the Brewers of America Are Spending So Much to Keep Some People from Drinking," which outlines the support given by brewers to prohibit underage drinking and to promote safe drinking among college students of legal age. More recently, the Century Council, which is supported by the alcoholic beverage industries, has begun to attack the problem of teenage drinking with ads and videos available for showing in homes, schools, and teenagers' organizations such as the Boys and Girls Clubs.[15] Federal regulations now require that all alcoholic beverages carry the following message: "GOVERNMENT WARNING: (1) According to the Surgeon General, women should not drink alcoholic beverages during pregnancy because of the risk of birth defects. (2) Consumption of alcoholic beverages impairs your ability to drive a car or operate machinery, and may cause health problems."

Casinos typically offer brochures warning of the potential problems associated with addictive gambling. Grand Casinos, which operates casinos in Minnesota and Mississippi, trains its managers and employees how to spot "problem" gamblers, bans them from further play, and offers to help them seek professional psychological guidance or marriage and work-related counseling when that is appropriate. Some state lotteries contribute to Gamblers Anonymous or similar groups.

Movies, videos, and compact disks must carry warning ratings if their scenes or lyrics are violent or sexual in nature, and children seventeen and under are banned from admission to X-rated (now NC-17 rated) movies.

It is not unusual for the more prestigious gun manufacturers to promote their products by offering free lessons in the proper and safe methods of using firearms. Recently, they have encouraged their customers to use gun locks.[16] While this is certainly not the same as encouraging customers to refrain from buying, it is an explicit recognition or warning that the product can be dangerous.

Much attention and controversy have been focused on warning labels and other forms of contra-advertising in the tobacco industry. The first serious efforts began in 1968, four years after the surgeon general's report, while cigarettes were still being advertised on television. Anti-tobacco advocates successfully petitioned under the Equal Time provisions of the Federal Communications Commission (FCC) that the government begin to run public interest television spots warning of the health risks associated with cigarettes. These spots were surprisingly effective. For the first time in forty years, per capita consumption of cigarettes actually declined, and by 1970, the tobacco companies were willing to give up television and radio advertising entirely because that would bring an end to the warning spots. It was a wise trade-off for the companies; as noted in an earlier chapter, the manufacturers simply shifted their advertising dollars into other media, and per capita consumption resumed its upward trend.

There have been other successful experiments with contra-advertising to reduce smoking. The Canadian government has been very aggressive, combining such television ads with serious increases in cigarette excise taxes, to effect a significant reduction in cigarette sales in Canada. In California, a stiff increase in the state excise tax was used to produce and air some very hard-hitting television spots, and sales to teenagers declined significantly.

The provisions of the Master Settlement Agreement dwarf all previous attempts at contra-advertising. Tobacco companies are required under the MSA to pay a minimum of $1.45 billion into a Public Education Fund for the specific purpose of reducing teen smoking and addiction to tobacco. While some states—again, California is the leading example—have had success in their efforts, a common problem has been that teens are notoriously difficult to convince of the health dangers associated with smoking, at least to the degree that will result in changed behaviors. In fact, some attempts have proved to be counterproductive; warning teens not to begin smoking has triggered their natural inclinations to resist direction from authority figures of any sort.

CONCLUSIONS

Of the "four Ps" of marketing—product, price, promotion, and place (distribution)—promotion presents the biggest challenge because it embodies the most fundamental conflict. The most important and ultimate purpose of promotion is to increase sales of a product, whereas in these five industries, various groups in our society want to *limit* sales if not eliminate them entirely. The results of this conflict are the myriad of constraints under which marketers must labor, and the constant search for new, less obvious, nontraditional promotional tactics that the companies hope will escape the advocates' attention, but which will still accomplish the basic purpose of stimulating sales.

In these chapters, we have examined two levels of constraints: those imposed informally by various social groups that can evolve into customs or codes followed by the industry, and those, usually even more restrictive, imposed by law and regulation. In promoting socially unacceptable products, marketers are certain to generate criticism if they are perceived as searching for new customers. To encourage nonsmokers to take up smoking, for example, or nondrinkers to begin drinking alcoholic beverages, to recruit new customers to casino gambling, or to encourage more people to own and carry handguns: these are tactics that will surely generate strong and immediate opposition. Nor can marketers encourage current customers to use more of their product, another standard strategy. If the message in the advertising is to smoke more, drink more alcohol, or gamble more, this too will result in some form of backlash. The least controversial message is the one that says in effect, "If you already enjoy drinking beer (or whiskey or vodka), then drink our brand." Or "If you already are a smoker, smoke our brand."

A further restriction is that marketers have difficulty promoting the essential characteristic of the product. To promote beer or liquor because it has more alcohol, or cigarettes because they have more nicotine, or guns because they are more deadly is another certain way to stir up opposition.

These are serious shackles to put on marketers, but only by living within these restraints can they continue to promote their products. In addition, marketers in these industries can defuse to a degree the social criticism by running some form of contra-advertising—by "embracing the opposition." Casinos' and state lotteries' warnings about the dangers of gambling addiction and breweries' messages about "responsible" drinking serve their nominal, superficial purposes, but for marketers, the greater value of such socially responsible advertising is to weaken the arguments of the opposition and stave off more stringent governmental controls.

This conflict at the advertising and promotion level is emblematic of the broader, more fundamental struggle waged on all the various marketing fronts between the makers of socially unacceptable products and their social critics.

NOTES

1. The statistics and some of the material in this section have been collected from the following sources: Raymond M. Jones, *Strategic Management in a Hostile Environment* (dissertation, University of Maryland, 1993); Maria Mallory, "That's One Angry Camel," *Business Week*, March 7, 1994, 94; Kevin Goldman, "A Stable of Females Has Joined Joe Camel in Controversial Cigarette Ad Campaign," *Wall*

Street Journal, February 18, 1994, B1; Eben Shapiro, "FTC Staff Recommends Ban of Joe Camel Campaign," *Wall Street Journal*, August 11, 1993, B1; Joanne Lipman, "Surgeon General Says It's High Time Joe Camel Quit," *Wall Street Journal*, March 10, 1992, B1; Kathleen Deveny, "R. J. Reynolds Battles the AMA, Defending Joe Camel Cartoon Ad," *Wall Street Journal*, February 5, 1992, B5; Kathleen Deveny, "Joe Camel Is Also Pied Piper, Research Finds," *Wall Street Journal*, December 11, 1991, B1; "Camel Cartoon Holds Allure for Children, Studies Find," Baltimore *Sun*, December 11, 1991, 1A.

2. Mallory, "That's One Angry Camel."

3. Suein Hwang, "Joe Camel Is Missing, but Who's Walking Miles to Find Him?" *Wall Street Journal*, July 14, 1995, A1.

4. Laura Zinn, "The Smoke Clears at Marlboro," *Business Week*, January 31, 1994, 76.

5. Laura Bird, "'Black Death' Becomes 'Black Hat' So that Vodka Can Stay on Shelves," *Wall Street Journal*, May 12, 1992, B6. See also Laura Bird, "U.S. Moves against Label of a New Brew," *Wall Street Journal*, April 24, 1992, B4.

6. Ibid.

7. Alix M. Freedman, "UST Faces Suit Over Free Samples Provided to Minors," *Wall Street Journal*, July 26, 1995, B7.

8. Tara Parker-Pope, "Brewers' Soccer Sponsorship Draws Fire," *Wall Street Journal*, February 27, 1995, B1.

9. John Helyar, "U.S. Pro Soccer League Falls Short of Goals," *Wall Street Journal*, November 16, 1994, B1.

10. Cyndee Miller, "Stones Strut Their Marketing Stuff," *Marketing News*, November 7, 1994, 1.

11. John Slade, "Why Unbranded Promos?" *Tobacco Control* 3 (1994): 72.

12. Evelyn Nieves, "Anxious Days in Bordello Country," *New York Times*, August 19, 2001, A16.

13. Jim Carlton, "On the Nevada Fringes, Looking for Olympic Gold," *Wall Street Journal*, February 14, 2002, B1.

14. Gerry Khermouch, "Commentary: Booze Ads: There Go the Creative Juices," *Business Week Online*, January 21, 2002, http://www.businessweek.com/magazine/content/02_03/b3766088.htm (accessed March 13, 2002).

15. Fara Warner, "Liquor Industry Tackles Teenage Drinking," *Wall Street Journal*, June 30, 1995.

16. Vanessa O'Connell, "Gun Makers to Push Use of Gun Locks," *Wall Street Journal*, May 9, 2001, B12.

CHAPTER 11

The Internet

In a relatively short period of time, the Internet has become a common and vital part of our lives. More than ninety-four million Americans had access to the Internet from home in 2000, up from fifty-seven million in 1998, and millions more used the Internet at work or in schools. As of August 2000, more than half the households in the United States had computers and the vast majority of those are now connected to the Internet (see figure 11.1).[1] Given this dramatic change in our social and economic environment, it is no wonder that marketers have rushed to use the Internet in a variety of ways with varying degrees of success. Along with airline tickets, books, and music downloads (legal or otherwise), marketers can now sell or promote cigarettes, alcoholic beverages, firearms, games of chance, or pornography.

In a previous chapter, it has been noted that buyers and sellers in our five subject industries are generally satisfied with their exchanges. It is other groups in the society—advocacy and health organizations, churches, or government agencies—that raise objections to and cast doubts on the legitimacy and social acceptance of these five product categories and the firms that produce and market them. For this reason, the Internet offers four very real advantages as a marketing tool: anonymity, direct connection to the ultimate consumer, convenience, and sophisticated database management techniques.

One example illustrates all four of these advantages. In May 2002, I received a message over the Mount Saint Mary's College e-mail service from "Wild Cats [minar@geologist.com]." The subject was simply, "Call me 06367." The message read as follows (censored slightly):

Figure 11.1
Computers and Internet Access in the Home, 1984–2000 (Civilian Noninstitutional Population)

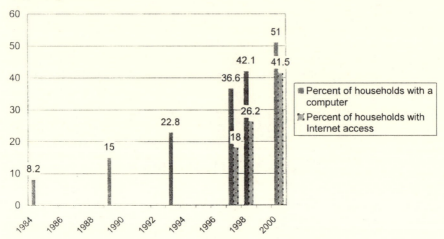

Note: Data on Internet access were not collected before 1997.
Source: U.S. Census Bureau, Current Population Survey, various years.

Hello I am your hot lil horny toy.
I am the one you dream About,
I am a very open minded person,
Love to talk about and [sic] any subject.
Fantasy is my way of life,
Ultimate in sex play.
Ummmmmmmmmmmmm
I am . . . ready for you.
It is not your looks but your imagination that matters most,
With my sexy voice I can make your dream come true . . .
Hurry Up! Call me . . .
TOLL-FREE: 1-877-451-TEEN (1-877-451-8336)
For phone billing: 1-900-993-2582.

Surprised as to how and why I should have received this message at my college and curious because of the research I was conducting at that very time on this book, I looked more closely at the address list. I discovered that the message had been sent to at least ten different "Davidsons," all associated with colleges or universities, some as remote as Denmark and New Zealand. Some database management program had allowed the sender to target a group of "academic Davidsons." As a marketer, I have questions as to how sophisticated or efficient a marketing tool this is, whether there is anything about the name "Davidson" or an affiliation with the ".edu" domain that indicates a likelihood of responding to a dial-a-porn solicitation. Nevertheless, the technology exists, much to my amazement, to pull together such a list of recipients.

To pursue the analysis, the sender of the solicitation remains totally anonymous. From a marketing perspective, I suppose that the sobriquet "Wild Cats" may have had a mildly titillating quality and thus might encourage the receiver to open the e-mail message, but the sender's address [minar@geologist.com] was a total mystery and certainly lacked any erotic quality. Finally, the Internet allowed the sender to promote this dial-a-porn service to me directly, and had I been interested in purchasing the service, I could have done so just as directly, bypassing the need to go through any intermediary. I did not need to rent a video or go to a store to buy an adult magazine; I could have experienced whatever sexual fantasies "Wild Cats" was offering conveniently from the privacy of my home.

TOBACCO

Major Companies

Tobacco's presence on the Internet is extensive and very complex. For the major cigarette manufacturers, public relations is the main function of their Web sites, and they perform this function very well. From a quick look at the Philip Morris (now Altria) home page, for example, one would never know that it is the world's largest cigarette company or that cigarettes produce the lion's share of the company's profits. There is not a sign of the Marlboro Man; no picture of the famous Marlboro package even though the brand rivals Coke as the most-recognized brand name and signature package in the entire world. The most important message from the home page is one of corporate social responsibility. Of the four "Spotlight" items, one reviews Altria's Code of Conduct, another calls attention to the company's search for "a coherent national tobacco policy," and a third tells of the company's hopes that negotiations can continue to provide for Food and Drug Administration regulation of tobacco products, something the company had fought bitterly to prevent until recently. The fourth spotlight item reviews quarterly earnings. Under "Latest Headlines" Altria tells us that its Kraft Foods division has partnered with Rainforest Alliance to work for sustainable coffee growing. And another headline reveals that the company, for all its recent shift in strategy and emphasis of responsibility, continues the "masquerade" strategy outlined in chapter 2. Altria announces that its Philip Morris division will acquire the European company Papastratos but never mentions that it is the largest manufacturer and distributor of cigarettes in Greece.[2]

The Brown & Williamson Web site emphasizes public relations also,

Figure 11.2
Brown & Williamson Home Page

Source: Courtesy of Brown & Williamson Tobacco Corporation.

although it is more creative in its design and more candid in its messages. The graphics of the site (see figure 11.2) depict a cityscape with tall buildings and roving spotlights highlighting various topics that turn out to be links to other pages—"Corporate Responsibility," "Smoking and Health," and "Youth Smoking Prevention Center" are major sections, and all include thoughtful material on those subjects. There is a section labeled "Our Brands," which brings the viewer to a page where Kool, Pall Mall, Lucky Strike, Capri, Carlton, and others are described briefly next to a picture of the package.[3]

Under "Corporate Responsibility," there is a lengthy section under the title, "Why Don't We Just Stop Making Cigarettes?" The company's answers are not surprising: cigarettes are a legal product, and consumers themselves should have the right to make the choice about smoking; prohibition doesn't work; safer cigarettes (with filter tips, for example) have been introduced, and more new improvements are on the way; and most important of all, cigarette manufacturing has an enormous positive impact on the U.S. economy. On this last point, it is important to note that the health-care costs and the costs of death and suffering are not included along with the analysis of economic benefits. While the answers may have been predictable, it is significant that the company was forthright enough to even pose the question.

In another section entitled "Business Ethics," Brown & Williamson agrees "with the judgment of public health authorities that smoking is a cause of lung cancer and other diseases," acknowledges that "many underage children and teenagers still smoke cigarettes," and admits that "as a for-profit company, any statements we make on these issues are seen as self-serving and defensive and therefore to be mistrusted." To be sure, the company goes on to give its own perspective on these areas of controversy, but its willingness to broach the subjects in a rational, candid manner is another illustration of the entire industry's new public relations approach since 1996, which is discussed in some depth in chapter 13.

Retailers

If smokers cannot actually buy cigarettes on the Internet from the major manufacturers, there are, nonetheless, plenty of opportunities to do so at other Web sites. Type in "cigarettes" or even "Marlboro," and your browser is likely to take you to a site like Nationwidesmokes.com, a five-year-old business operating out of Kilgore, Texas, which promises quick delivery to your door and discount prices because all orders are filled from a Native American reservation to avoid taxes. And if you are unwilling to pay $28.99 for a carton of Vantage cigarettes, $24.99 for Winstons, $23.99 for Camels, or $23.50 (a special) for Marlboros, you might order such unadvertised brands as Compton for $12.99, Sky Dancer for $11.99, or the new Parker brand (whose package design looks remarkably like Marlboro) for only $9.99 when ordered in quantities of five cartons.[4]

Go to http://www.discount-cigarettes.org, and you can compare prices from sixty different retailers such as Red Nation Tobacco, Indian Smokes Online, TeePee 6, CheapCigsUSA, or All of Our Butts. Both Web sites post a prominent warning about a minimum age requirement for purchasing cigarettes. Both sites also urge customers to click on a link titled "Help Us Help You, Protect Your Right to Buy Online," which connects customers to information on the legal battles the OnLine Tobacco Retailers Association is waging to ward off legislative threats to this form of marketing cigarettes.

Researchers at the University of North Carolina identified eighty-eight retailers of cigarettes on the Internet, the majority of which were housed on Native American reservations. Only 28 percent carried health warnings from the surgeon general, and almost 20 percent failed even to warn minors of minimum age requirements.[5]

In Congress, Representative Martin Meehan of Massachusetts has predicted that Internet cigarette sales will hit $10 billion by 2006, a full 20 percent of total industry sales. While most researchers feel this is an exaggerated estimate, there is concern nevertheless about the lack of regulation. Meehan has introduced a bill that would specifically bar Internet vendors from selling to minors and require health warnings, but it has made little progress.[6] New York State passed a law in 2000 actually banning sales of tobacco products by telephone, mail order, or the Internet, but the law was struck down the following year by a district court in a suit filed by Brown & Williamson claiming, among other things, that the ban would have isolated New York from the national cigarette retail market.[7]

Other Internet Exposure

Just as there is a plethora of anti-smoking information available on the Internet, so too is there plenty of pro-smoking material. Organizations such as the National Smokers Alliance (which until June 1999 was funded by Philip Morris) promote smokers' rights and oppose political candidates who want to raise taxes on cigarettes or impose other restrictions. But there are also personal Web sites where teens describe how they take up smoking to drive their parents crazy. "Allison's Teen Smoking" home page detailed a thirteen-year-old's smoking experience since she was ten, showed pictures of children and teens smoking, and generally fostered the notion that smoking is "cool." The sudden disappearance of Allison's Web site became the subject of concern in young smokers' chat groups. The speculation was that AOL "pulled the plug" on Allison under pressure from Reynolds Tobacco, incorrectly identified by the contributor as the manufacturer of Allison's favorite brand, Marlboro.[8]

ALCOHOLIC BEVERAGES

Like the tobacco manufacturers, distillers and brewers do not attempt to sell liquor and beer over the Internet. But there is plenty of promotion, and much of it is aimed at children and teens in the design and content of the online material. According to the Center for Media Education, the Jose Cuervo site features games, drawings to win T-shirts, and screen saver downloads, "all well-established techniques in marketing to teens."[9] The Budweiser site offers more screen savers, free postcards, and a contest for football tickets. Both of these sites, says the Center, "portray drinking as fun, glamorous, cool."[10] Another site, called Happy Drunks (http://www.happydrunks.com), billed itself in 1999 as the "premier site for . . . drinking and entertainment" but has now become more of a porn site featuring bare-breasted and bare-bottomed college women frolicking during spring break activities.

There are software products, such as CYBERsitter, on the market that will allow parents to filter out tobacco and alcohol Web sites, but these categories have not received much attention to date. Most of the screening efforts have been directed at pornography, as discussed below.

FIREARMS

In the public policy debate over the regulation of firearms, the Internet has become an important battleground. The Web site of Sturm, Ruger, the largest firearms manufacturer in the United States, is devoted mostly to public relations. It includes news about lawsuits against the company and industry that have been dropped, a free lock exchange program, and awards given to the company's "gold label" shotgun and 77/17 rifle. The company also includes a lengthy, thoughtful section giving its perspective on the issue of gun ownership and use in America. It begins by quoting Supreme Court Justice Louis Brandeis, who wrote, "the greatest danger to our liberty lurks when government's purposes are beneficent, [and are] promoted by men of zeal, well-meaning, but without understanding." Sturm, Ruger goes on to describe "what won't work," but also offers a ten-point "effective, measured response" including instantaneous point-of-sale background checks, prohibition of unsupervised possession of firearms by anyone under eighteen, elimination of guns in schools, "re-thinking what we accept as 'entertainment'" (showing guns on television and in movies only in connection with mayhem and gory violence), and a "reexamination of social responsibilities, values, and attitudes toward violence" (basically an exhortation to rid our streets and neighborhoods of crime).[11]

The only marketing activities on Sturm, Ruger's Web site is a section detailing the specifications and showing a picture of each of the company's products and another page offering to send the viewer a free catalog.

The National Rifle Association (NRA) Web site is all about public relations and political activity. Its "In the News" section urged members to support a Senate bill protecting the "Lawful Commerce in Arms Act." Another section, titled "Fewer Guns, More Death," told of two new reports that "prove beyond a doubt" that prohibiting citizens from carrying guns leaves them defenseless and, therefore, leads to more killings.[12]

On the other side of the issue, the Web site for the Brady Campaign to Prevent Gun Violence features sections on assault weapons, a joint effort with the Million Mom March to help the California legislature pass the strictest state gun control laws, and praise for the Ohio Supreme Court's decision upholding a ban on concealed weapons. Its "6th Annual Report Card on State Gun Laws" tells that many states are still not doing enough to prevent children's deaths from firearms even though the overall figure has declined. Many of the items on this Web site take direct aim at the actions of the NRA.[13]

GAMBLING

In 1996, a Boston Consulting Group study reported that only a year after the first online casino opened its virtual doors there were 452 gambling-related sites on the Internet operating out of such obscure havens as Turks and Caicos Islands and Belize.[14] Six years later, a Google search for "gambling on the Internet" connected me with the Internet Gaming Commission (IGC), which claimed there were then more than thirteen hundred gambling sites available. A search engine allowed me to enter my game of choice (I selected craps), the amount I wanted to bet ($10), and I was then offered a list of 301 establishments from which to choose. I selected the very first, Sands of the Caribbean, licensed in Antigua and Barbuda, and I was whisked off to a dazzling Web site with flashing lights, a red and gold background, and pictures of attractive women at the gambling tables.

One method of operation requires that the player deposit money in advance into an offshore account, bets are placed, and any winnings are deposited to the account. The IGC warns that some unlicensed operations have been negligent or downright criminal in reimbursing bettors for their winnings or making it difficult, if not impossible, to repatriate the funds from the account.

The economics of running a gambling operation on the Internet are very attractive. To build a new casino in Las Vegas to compete with Bellagio or New York, New York might cost up to $1 billion and require a thousand or more to staff and manage. When Internet Casinos, Inc. (ICI) opened its virtual doors in 1995 offering eighteen casino games and a link to the National Indian Lottery, it invested all of $1.5 million and employed seventeen people. To make the bottom line even fatter, the "house" cut for ICI was 24 percent compared to a figure of only 8 percent for a typical Nevada or Atlantic City bricks-and-mortar casino.

There are no accurate figures on the extent of casino gambling on the Internet because much of the activity is illegal. A federal law bans interstate gambling over telephone lines. Exempt from this law, however, is betting on horse racing, where figures show that online betting has grown from only $5 million in 1998 to an estimated $300 million in 2002.[15] Such rapid growth is due, no doubt, to the ease of gambling online. In fact, a letter from the chairman of the IGC promoting its services stated, "You can even enter national lotteries from around the world. More than 1300 Internet gaming establishments are operating in more than thirty countries . . . from Antigua and Australia to Trinidad and Venezuela. And, your computer can take you there. No travel arrangements, no costly accommodations."[16] A 2000 survey conducted by the American Gaming Association found that 2 percent of those who participated in some form of gambling, slightly over two million people in the United States, did so on the Internet.[17] Putting these pieces of information together—the high profits of online gambling on a minimum investment, the rapid growth of online horse race betting, the ease of access for gamblers to online betting (no need to even leave the comfort of your home), and the number of people now participating—it is reasonable to estimate that annual online casino and lottery gambling now amounts to several billion dollars and will grow very rapidly over the next few years.

PORNOGRAPHY

As noted in chapter 6, there has always been a stigma attached to the purchasing of pornographic material, whether buying an adult magazine at a newsstand, renting an XXX-rated video, buying sex paraphernalia, or purchasing the services of a companion from an escort service. Such market exchanges are usually transacted out of the limelight, away from the attention of others, except perhaps for a male bonding trip to a local strip club, and even this might not be divulged to a spouse, parent, or boss. Thus, the Internet is an ideal medium for the marketing of pornography of all sorts. It takes advantage of sophisticated targeting techniques as illustrated at the beginning of this chapter. It is convenient: no further away than one's computer, much to the dismay of employers who are finding that their employees' surfing of porn sites at work is increasing steadily. It is anonymous: participants can take on an entirely different persona when they enter chat group dialogues—children can pretend to be adults, adults can pretend to be children, men masquerade as women, straights as gay, and so forth. And it is private: one can access a wide range of porn sites without the awareness of others either at home or at work, unless the employer has invested in advanced software to monitor viewing of porn Web sites.

Privacy, of course, is a relative term. In mid-2002, the news media reported that terrorist scheming, both in this country and abroad, had been unearthed on captured computer hard drives. Crime dramas on television portray how criminals can sometimes be captured by the trails they leave by sending e-mail messages. But short of a criminal investigation, what a person says in e-mail and the sites that person visits on the Internet remain private and are probably not going to be discovered by friends and family.

As with magazines and movies, Internet pornography comes in different categories often described as soft-core or hard-core porn. Nudity by itself is usually considered in the first category. Explicit sexual coupling, group sex, and fetishes of a wide sort are likely to be considered hard-core porn.

Soft-Core Porn

Playboy Online is a major new venture for the magazine publisher into the world of cyberspace and the most well-known brand in the market of soft-core porn. As the magazine has struggled in recent years—never quite making it as a literary and sophisticated publication, yet rendered almost irrelevant as a sex magazine by its more explicit rivals—it was a natural move for Playboy Enterprises to extend its brand name to the Internet. A visit to the home page first shows the ubiquitous male voyeur bunny/ logo welcoming the viewer to the site, but another click or two brings onto the screen pictures of Playboy's specialty: nude, gorgeous, young women. Special sections describe and show just about all of Divini Rae, Playboy's Miss November, 2003; the Celebrities Club, which promises nude pictures of a bevy of celebrities; an announcement of an upcoming special edition featuring the "Women of Wal-Mart" and encouraging Wal-Mart women employees to send in nude pictures of themselves; and finally the Cyber Girl of the week in (almost) all her glory, Ms. Amy Currie, complete with her age, address, and vital statistics. For a monthly fee of $19.95 Playboy offers "a sexy new Cyber Girl every week" with "zoom technology" for focusing even more closely on the normally private parts of her bare body. Another $5 allows the browser to view "Girls With Girls, the sexiest women on the Web . . . give in to the temptation and explore forbidden lust." One more click of the mouse brings up the Playboy store, where a nearly nude model shows off her cotton briefs with "Kiss My" printed on the derriere, offered for sale at only $14.

Perhaps mindful of the magazine's experience competing with more explicit rivals such as *Hustler* or *Oui*, Playboy has launched another online site called SpiceTV.com, a subscription revenue operation offering "less edited" adult movies, video clips, and access to the SpiceTV store, where more than thirty-five hundred adult-oriented products, videos, and DVDs are available for purchase. At the beginning of this site is a very explicit photo of a young nude woman with her legs spread apart along with the now unnecessary warning that the site contains material for those over the age of eighteen. There is nothing to prevent younger viewers from progressing on to the rest of the site's erotic pages, however. Thus, if the visitor to the Playboy Web site is left unsatisfied with viewing only nudity, he is only one click away from the "harder" porn served up on SpiceTV.

The Playboy Web site illustrated once again the synergy between two or more of our subject industries that is often tapped by marketers. Playboy has started a separate venture, Playboy Casino.com, operating out of Gibralter, promotes it on its Web site, and offers hyperlinks to take the viewer there with just one click. There is also a sexy video clip advertising Bacardi Silver, the malt beverage jointly marketed by Bacardi and Anheuser-Busch, featuring line drawings of a stripped-down woman tantalizing a man spread out on a sofa and promising, "Your evening just got more interesting."

Demonstrating true gender diversity, the Playgirl Web site offers plenty of pictures of buffed young men, some in full frontal nudity. Once again, there is only a modest suggestion that anyone under the age of eighteen should not enter the site but no attempt to enforce this in any way. Offering up one's e-mail address connects the viewer to even more eroticism.

Hard-Core Porn

The nudity on Playboy, even after Amy Currie is fully exposed, is tame compared to the hard-core pornography available at literally thousands of sites on the Internet. Every possible combination of heterosexual and homosexual coupling, every conceivable erotic fetish is cataloged and waiting just one more mouse-click away.

While sampling is a tried-and-true sales promotion tactic for most consumer goods marketers from Procter & Gamble to PepsiCo, pornography purveyors on the Internet carry sampling to an extreme. The competition among the Web sites seems to require giving away more, showing more lurid, explicit frames than the competition, to keep the viewer on that particular Web site in the hopes that he will succumb to the enticements, enter his credit card number, and become a member with the privilege of viewing even wilder, more explicit material, if such is possible.

One marketing tactic on the Internet involves sending an unsolicited "messenger service" box that pops up on the viewer's screen with the following invitation: "Hi, my name is Jeni. I like to flirt with my webcam online. Check out this site. Webcamfantasies.org." This seems innocuous enough, but a visit to the Web site introduces the viewer to every XXX-rated online video imaginable, all available "4FREE" with only a registration of the viewer's e-mail address.

Two other amusing or not-so-amusing tactics are features of porn sites on the Internet. In "the old days," barkers outside striptease shows would actually take hold of prospective customers and not let them go until they had been directed inside the establishment. In the same vein, many of the porn sites are programmed so that when the viewer clicks the "x" box in the upper right hand corner of the computer screen to sign off, he is sent instead to another porn site. This game can go on sometimes interminably, so that logging off the Internet is the only solution.

The other tactic involves some Web sites finding clever ways to disguise their names, taking advantage of already well-established "brands." A middle school student might want to take a "virtual" tour of the White House for a civics class assignment, but if he types in whitehouse.com instead of whitehouse.gov, he will be connected and exposed to a very explicit porn site. For a number of years, another porn site used the barbiesplaypen.com address, trading on the enormous brand recognition of the famous Barbie doll.

If Playboy Enterprises is still struggling to make a profit from its venture into cyberspace, that is not the problem for the hard-core purveyors. It is often reported that the sex merchants were the first (and for a long while the only) marketers to show a profit from e-commerce. While Yahoo! and Lycos have struggled as "portals" to find the right combination of giving away their e-mail and search engine services to the public while generating revenue from advertisers eager to get their banners in front of the "eyeballs" of viewers, and while Amazon and other e-tailers have sought to balance slim margins and oversized marketing budgets, Web porn merchants have kept their focus on the bottom line from the beginning. No large investment required, no-frills operating budgets, no need to establish brand names, and *no marketing expenses* to speak of have allowed these thousands of porn Web sites to profit from their outset and have contributed to their proliferation.

The lure of easy profits, a sure demand, and differing cultural sensitivities have led certain Web firms to embrace pornography in some markets while shunning it in others. Microsoft's MSN network, for example, has no adult content in the United States, while its French version carries the full assortment of X-rated material between midnight and 3:00 a.m. French time. The French Lycos site carries pornographic content at all hours. A marketing manager at MSN France summed it up, "We're trying not to put our heads in the sand and ignore an entire swath of demand on the Internet. The demand for this type of content is there and we've chosen to address it."[18]

Still in its infancy, the Internet has already worked profound changes on our society. It has altered the way we work; it has brought changes in the way we entertain ourselves with the promise of much more to come. Because the rules of the Internet are still being written—both the formal rules as expressed in laws and regulations and the informal rules of a society as to what is acceptable and legitimate—all five of our subject industries have taken advantage of this new medium to greater or lesser degrees. Tobacco, alcoholic beverage, and firearms companies have used the Internet as a public relations tool primarily, because even though constrained, they have traditional media open to them for the major part of their marketing efforts. Gambling companies, because they are so limited in where they can actually do business, have been quick to embrace the Internet because of its ability to transcend geographic boundaries. Pornography, arguably the least legitimate of our five subjects, recognized the potential of the Internet from its inception and has taken advantage of its convenience, its privacy, and its anonymity.

More rules, both legal and social, are sure to come, but it is a certainty that the Internet will continue to play a special and important role in the marketing of socially unacceptable products. Because the firms and entire industries that produce these products are so constrained in their marketing activities, especially relative to their corporate counterparts that enjoy greater legitimacy, the unique features of the Internet will become increasingly valuable.

NOTES

1. Eric C. Newburger, "Current Population Reports, Home Computers and Internet Use in the United States: August 2000," U.S. Department of Commerce, Economics and Statistics Administration, U.S. Census Bureau, issued September 2001, http://www.census.gov/prod/2001pubs/p23–207.pdf (accessed May 22, 2002).

2. http://www.altria.com (accessed October 11, 2003).

3. http://www.bw.com (accessed May 24, 2002).

4. http://www.nationwidesmokes.com (accessed October 11, 2003).

5. David Williamson, "Research Finds Internet Cigarette Sales Present Potential Threat to Public Health," *UNC News Services*, December 7, 2001, No. 633.

6. Bruce Mohl, "Cigarette Shoppers Turn to the Internet," *Boston Globe*, February 16, 2001, as reported by Robert Weissman at http://www.lists.essential.org/pipermail/intl-tobacco/2001q1/000418.html (accessed May 14, 2002).

7. Reported by Covington & Burling, "U.S. District Court Strikes Down New York Ban on Internet Cigarette Sales," http://www.cov.com/new/pressreleases/136.html (accessed May 14, 2002).

8. http://www.lelnet.com/asg/dirs/1997–12–2/7831 (accessed May 25, 2002).

9. Center for Media Education, "Youth Access to Alcohol and Tobacco Web Marketing," October 1999, Chapter 1, An Overview. Available at http://www.cme.org.

10. Ibid.

11. http://www.ruger-firearms.com/news.html (accessed April 6, 2002).

12. http://www.nraila.org/LegislativeUpdate (accessed October 12, 2003).

13. http://www.bradycampaign.org/press/release (accessed October 12, 2003).

14. http://www.ascusc.org/jcmc/vol2/issue2/janower.html (accessed May 25, 2002).

15. Alex Wong, "Perfectas by Personal Computer," *Wall Street Journal*, August 27, 2001, B1.

16. http://www.internetcommission.com (accessed May 25, 2002).

17. http://www.americangaming.org/survey 2001/trends/trends.html (accessed April 19, 2002).

18. John Carreyrou and Rebecca Buckman, "U.S. Internet Portals That Shun Pornography Here Find It Very Lucrative in Europe," *Wall Street Journal*, December 10, 2001, B1.

CHAPTER 12

Problems in Pricing
and Distribution

PRICING ISSUES

From marketing textbooks we learn that pricing strategies and tactics can serve a number of purposes. They can help create a specific image for the product; for instance, a high price on Steuben crystal or Rolls Royce automobiles helps denote the ultimate in quality, while low prices at Wal-Mart reinforce the image of good value for the shopper's money. Pricing decisions will play a major role in determining the ultimate profitability of a product: other things being equal, a higher price will mean higher margins, higher profits, and a greater return on invested capital. Pricing will also help determine a firm's market share in its industry. A higher price, often referred to as a "skimming" strategy, is likely to result in higher profits per unit sold but a smaller market share. Conversely, a "penetration" or lower price strategy should mean just the opposite. Finally, lowering prices can be used to stimulate sales either in the short run by a temporary price reduction or over a longer period of time by reducing prices permanently.

For socially unacceptable products, these different pricing purposes meet with different reactions from society's critics. The image-creating purpose generates little or no criticism, nor does the market share purpose. On the other hand, lowering prices to stimulate overall or "primary" demand for products of questionable legitimacy—in other words, increasing sales by attracting new customers or encouraging present customers to consume more of the product, a perfectly common and accepted strategy for the marketers of breakfast cereals or detergents—will inevitably result in social protest. Even the profitability purpose—raising prices to increase profits—may lead to criticism from advocates on the grounds of "ill-gotten gains," that the manufacturer is reaping increased and "excessive" profits from the sale of these harmful and unacceptable products.

There are three factors that influence the setting of prices for some socially unacceptable products, factors that interfere with the normal, theoretical balancing of supply and demand forces. The first of these is taxes. We hear often enough of "sin taxes," and they are levied on the products of concern in this book: tobacco, alcoholic beverages, and gambling. As pointed out in the introduction, it is one of the defining elements of socially unacceptable products that government is likely to impose a tax on them. And so in the United States we have federal, state, and sometimes even local excise taxes on cigarettes and other tobacco products, on alcoholic beverages of all types, and on casino gambling.

In economic theory, the imposition of a tax on a product will result in less of the product being sold because the tax will increase the product's price, and fewer people will be willing or able to pay that higher price. This reduction in consumption satisfies one of the two purposes of imposing the tax in the first place, the other being to create a source of revenue for the government. There is an alternative possible result of the tax, however: that the producer will "absorb" the tax as a business expense, maintain the same price for the product, and realize less profit in the process. This limit on profitability means that only the more efficient firms can compete in the industry and will, therefore, limit the number of competitors.

It is not the purpose here to explore which of these alternative results of excise taxes is the more powerful. It is enough to say that they do serve as a constraint on prices and that they do enter into managerial consideration in the setting of prices.

The second "abnormal" factor that can influence pricing decisions in these socially unacceptable industries stems from the questionable legitimacy of the industry. The tobacco industry provides the clearest example. One might imagine, after only the briefest exposure to elementary economic principles, that because the manufacture and sale of cigarettes is so profitable, any number of firms would enter the business. Were this to happen, the increased number of suppliers and the heightened level of competition would tend to push prices lower. It is certainly true that to compete with Marlboro, Winston, or Camel, a potential competitor would need to invest great sums in plant and equipment to become an efficient producer and additional great sums in marketing expenses to establish the new brand as a viable competitor. Not many firms have both the resources and the will to take on Philip Morris, British American Tobacco (BAT), and Reynolds. But why wouldn't Procter & Gamble or PepsiCo want to enter this highly profitable business? Each firm has the skill and the resources to establish new brand names, each firm markets its products through the same retail outlets as cigarettes, and each firm already has quite diverse product lines. If Procter & Gamble already markets successfully such diverse products as soap, coffee, disposable diapers, and toothpaste, why not cigarettes?

The answer is, at least in part, that the cigarette business has too many other problems, as described in detail in chapter 2. Product liability lawsuits, increased government regulation, strong anti-smoking advocacy groups, and declining domestic demand are only a few of the factors that are part of the loss of legitimacy in this industry and a few of the reasons why new firms eschew the potential profits in the cigarette business and look elsewhere for new ventures.

The effects of this particular and peculiar factor are that competition is reduced, not by economic but by social and political forces, and this tends to put upward pressure on prices. Marketers of cigarettes, when they contemplate a price increase, have not had to worry for decades about attracting new competitors into the industry.

The third "abnormal" factor influencing pricing strategies and policies in three of our subject industries—tobacco, alcoholic beverages, and gambling—is that these products often lead to addiction. Certainly, not everyone who plays a slot machine or buys a lottery ticket is addicted to gambling and not everyone who drinks wine, beer, or hard liquor is an alcoholic. The question of smokers' addiction to the nicotine in cigarettes is the subject of a current public policy debate. But the fact that *some* consumers are addicted to these products—meaning that their buying decisions are not subject to the same trade-offs, and that other products will not be able to compete with the cigarettes, alcohol, or gambling for the consumers' disposable income—tends to put upward pressure on, or put a floor under, the prices of these socially unacceptable product categories.

Price Policies to Stimulate Consumption

In the marketing of rifles and shotguns, price reductions are seldom used to increase sales. The major manufacturers—such as Winchester and Remington—establish different price lines for their products, but seldom are price promotions used either at the manufacturers' or at the retail level to stimulate business. At the industry trade show, the Russian rifles imported to sell for $99.95 were an exception.

Handguns, however, are quite a different business. While the manufacturers like Colt with an important brand name, image, and equity to protect do not use price promotions, the lesser-known manufacturers rely heavily on price. Their targets are the inner-city markets, either the criminals themselves or those who are seeking protection. For these target customers, brand name and image are not important, only getting the most firepower for the cheapest price.

In the gambling industry, pricing is rather different than in the marketing of other products. The amount of a bet, whether a $1 lottery ticket, a pull of the handle on a $1 video poker machine, or a $100 roll of the dice at a craps table, must be related to the odds of winning to determine a true price. Prices in the true sense, therefore, are largely hidden from customers.

State lotteries sell most of their scratch-off tickets as well as chances on their lottery drawings for $1; that has become the standard, the common amount for a player to pay. But the state can increase the "price" by lowering the chances of winning, and the only indication of this, if there is any at all, will be in very small print on the back of the ticket where the extraordinarily small odds are spelled out in detail.

Gambling "prices" are higher at the MGM Grand, the Luxor, and the other exotic hotels on the Strip in Las Vegas than they are at the more plebian casinos in the downtown section of the city, presumably to pay for the fancier surroundings and the sometimes free entertainment that is provided. Certainly, one can find $1 video poker and slot machines at both locations. And a player can still bet whatever he or she chooses at blackjack, roulette, or craps. But the odds of winning at the Strip casinos are slightly lower than downtown: the "payback"—that is, the amount returned to customers in winnings—will probably be about 91 or 92 percent on the Strip, whereas downtown they will most likely be closer to 95 percent. In the gambling business, therefore, pricing is really quite different than in other industries and enters into the marketing mix in a rather unique way.

As noted, state lottery systems sell the majority of their tickets for $1. It is the most convenient price for retailers to collect, it is the standard and therefore expected price, and it is low enough that almost everyone can afford to buy at least an occasional ticket, thus attracting the broadest possible market. In late 1992, the state of Maryland experimented with an unusual pricing format with its "El Gordo" lottery, a concept imported from Spain. Only a limited number of tickets were sold at $5 each, but there was a guaranteed first prize of $10 million and as many as ten $1 million prizes, regardless of ticket sales. Theoretically, if ticket sales were lower than planned (which they were), the chances of winning would have been better, and this would have meant a better "buy" for the customer's five dollars: in other words, a better "price." Sales for "El Gordo" were quite disappointing despite massive television advertising and point-of-sale promotion; Maryland lottery officials were uncertain whether the failure was due to the $5 price for the tickets, unusually high for the time, or to the different lottery format.

Ten years later, in 2002, the majority of lottery tickets sold in Maryland are still at the $1 price line, but they represent only 26 percent of the total revenue. Tickets now range in price up to $10. To encourage the sales of its higher priced tickets, Maryland offers better odds on its $5 and $10 tickets than on those priced at $1 and $2.[1]

What we do not find in the marketing of either casino gambling or state lotteries is the use of price to stimulate business, that is, to encourage new customers to try the games or current customers to spend more money. No blue-light specials, no one-day sales, no "25 percent off this week only" promotions. Public opinion would run strongly against such a marketing tactic.[2]

Similarly, public opinion runs against price promotions in the marketing of wine and spirits. As noted in chapter 3, the sale of "brown goods" (whiskeys, dark rums, etc.) declined dramatically during the 1970s in favor of vodka, tequila, and light rums. In other industries, when such a change in taste and buying patterns occurs, we might expect to see a drop in the price of the category that is falling out of favor. This did not happen with whiskeys. Bars and cocktail lounges do promote "happy hours," usually an hour or two in the late afternoon after the normal workday when drinks are sold at a reduced price. The purpose is certainly transparent: to encourage customers to drop in for a drink when they might otherwise head straight home, or to stay for a second drink when they might otherwise have only one. While these promotions are popular with bar customers, they do stir up public reaction, and various local governments have begun to pass ordinances against the practice.

Pricing in the cigarette industry is a more complex story. For decades, the major manufacturers raised their prices about twice a year, usually an 8 to 10 percent increase each time, far outpacing inflation. These steady increases seemed to have little effect on demand, perhaps because a pack of cigarettes is a relatively low-cost item, perhaps because of the heavy advertising and promotion that helped keep demand high, and perhaps to some extent because of the addiction factor. As detailed in chapter 2, budget-priced cigarettes—that is, generics and private labels—did not pose much of a competitive threat to the premium brands prior to the early 1990s. By that time, however, the spread between the price of the premium brands and the discount cigarettes reached a point where many consumers could no longer resist the opportunity to save up to $1 or more on every pack or ten times that much on a carton. The premium brands, especially Marlboro, began to lose market share, Philip Morris reacted with a 20 percent price cut on "Marlboro Friday" in 1993, and the other premium brands followed along.

If we were to focus our attention only on the 1993 cigarette price cut, because of the heavy media coverage it received and because of its wide-ranging effects on premium brand pricing in all consumer goods industries, we might conclude that pricing was and is the dominant element in the marketing mix for cigarettes. A longer range view, however, including the years of uncontested price increases, shows that as with the marketing of other socially unacceptable products, pricing decisions in the tobacco industry must be made with great care and sensitivity as to how they will be perceived. Even though almost every observer recognized that the Marlboro price cut was to protect its market share, tobacco critics used it nevertheless as an opportunity to criticize the company, and the industry, for trying to increase sales especially to teenagers.

On the day the Master Settlement Agreement was signed, November 16, 1998, the average wholesale price for a pack of cigarettes jumped 45¢ (roughly 45 percent), as all the major producers moved quickly to cover the cost of the agreement. In the ensuing three years, it went up an additional 50 percent to approximately $2.25 per pack at the end of 2001. The price of cigarettes for smokers has increased even more because of tax hikes; the federal excise tax has increased by 39¢ a pack just since January 2000, and most states have increased their cigarette excise taxes during that time frame also.[3]

Although the Marlboro brand has been almost impervious to any adverse effects from these price increases—its market share has held steady over the past several years—some of the other premium brands have indeed lost market share to the lower-priced generics and store brands. Indeed, low-priced cigarette manufacturers have seen their market share grow from only 2.5 percent in 1997 to above 10 percent in 2003.[4] Another effect of these price increases has been the appearance of discount cigarette stores, which have become a significant factor in the retail distribution of cigarettes just in the past ten years.

Pricing strategies for socially unacceptable products, then, like product and promotion strategies, are seriously constrained by social pressures. Using price cuts to stimulate sales or to attract new segments of the market will invariably elicit public outcries from the industries' critics.

DISTRIBUTION STRATEGIES

Distribution strategies and policies involve, among other things, the *choice* of channels through which the product will move to get from the manufacturer's shipping dock to the ultimate consumer. Managers must decide whether the product will be sold through wholesalers, by agents or brokers, direct to retailers, or perhaps directly to the customer. But what if the choice is not there? In planning the distribution of socially unacceptable products, marketers are confronted almost always with a situation where certain channels are not available to them. These channels can be closed either by government, through laws and regulations, or less formally by social pressures. Both warrant some exploration.

Social Constraints on Distribution

Magazines, to use marketing language, are a true convenience good; it follows that they should be distributed as widely as possible through drugstores, supermarkets, convenience stores, gas stations, and kiosks at airports, train stations, and on downtown street corners. But no store could or would want to carry all of the hundreds of magazine titles available in this country. Choices must be made, and one of the choices that a store owner or merchandiser must make is whether or not to carry adult magazines. The more family-oriented the store (supermarkets are a good example), the more likely any magazines that might be objectionable to the store's customers will be screened out. The greater proportion of male customers a store has, the more likely that some adult magazines will be in stock. Convenience stores are more likely to carry *Playboy* than supermarkets. Liquor stores and train station kiosks are more likely to take the next step and offer magazines like *Penthouse* and *Hustler*. Street corner kiosks, with nothing at stake in terms of corporate reputation, are most likely to have an extended selection of adult magazines. But even these outlets exercise some discrimination. To find the hardest of the hard-core pornographic magazines, one must be willing to browse through the true specialty stores in the field, the shabby adult bookstores, usually located in a low-rent district, with their windows blacked out and the lights flashing around their "XXX" signs.

In the marketing of a pornographic magazine—whether hard-core, soft porn, or even an unusually sexy cover on an otherwise mainstream women's fashion magazine—the marketer does not have the freedom of choice that we normally ascribe to distribution decisions; the distribution of the product is significantly constrained by social pressures as interpreted by retailers.

Social pressures are also beginning to affect the distribution of cigarettes, the quintessential convenience good sold through more stores than any other product category. More than one-third of the drugstores in the United States no longer sell cigarettes. Perhaps belatedly, many drug store merchandisers have come to realize that there is a fundamental conflict in selling a product with such adverse health consequences in stores founded on the principle of keeping their customers healthy. Wal-Mart, under pressure from various stakeholder groups, has discontinued selling cigarettes in its Canadian stores, where government action to limit tobacco sales and public awareness of the health hazards of smoking are greater than in the United States. The Wal-Mart Board of Directors has discussed the issue and to date the firm continues to sell cigarettes in this country, albeit under restricted conditions and with no in-store promotions or displays.

Gun marketers also are feeling these same constricting pressures as anti-gun groups continue their campaigns of making the public aware of the dangers associated with the sale and ownership of guns in general, and handguns specifically. Wal-Mart gave up selling handguns in its stores in 1993, bowing to social pressure and also no longer willing to risk its name and reputation as being the seller of a gun used in a crime. The company was sued by the family of a couple slain by their schizophrenic son who allegedly used a handgun purchased at Wal-Mart. Montgomery Ward discontinued handgun sales in 1981. "We just looked at it and said we don't really want to be in this business, because the potential for problems was significant," according to a company spokesman. Sears, Roebuck had stopped selling all firearms by the early 1980s.[5] Handguns, especially cheap handguns, are going the way of hard-core pornographic magazines: their sale is increasingly limited to small dealers with little equity in name or reputation to risk.

Legal Constraints

The distribution of firearms is constrained not only by social pressures and retailers' choices, but by legal restrictions as well. No individual or company can "trade" in firearms of any type unless licensed to do so by the federal government through the Bureau of Alcohol, Tobacco, and Firearms. While it is a simple matter for any legitimate business to obtain such a license, this government control acts as a constraint on the distribution decisions of gun manufacturers.

The distribution channel in the marketing of guns often includes an element not common in the distribution of most other products: temporary gun "shows" or even flea markets. This has led to a major battle between gun control advocates and the firearms industry. To prevent criminals and ex-felons from purchasing handguns, the government now requires a waiting period between the purchase of the weapon and actually taking delivery of it—time for the purchaser's identity to be checked against FBI files to uncover if he or she has a past criminal record. Currently, however, sales of handguns at gun shows and flea markets are not covered by this restriction, and so felons and ex-felons can buy weapons through this channel with no restrictions.

Certain forms of pornography may also be constrained as to their distribution. In New York City, Mayor Rudolph Giuliani, concerned about a deteriorating "quality of life" in the city, proposed a one-year moratorium on any new or expanded topless bars, X-rated theaters, and sex-oriented video stores. In the future, such stores could not open in residential neighborhoods or within five hundred feet of schools or places of worship, and would be relegated eventually to the fringes of the city through broad new zoning regulations.[6] During Giuliani's term in the mayor's office, he was given much credit for the renaissance of the Times Square area of

Manhattan, which included ridding the neighborhood of its proliferation of porn shops.

Blockbuster Entertainment, the country's largest chain of video rental stores, refuses to carry NC-17-rated movies, nor will it carry *Playboy* and *Penthouse* videocassettes. Mass merchandisers such as Kmart, drugstores, and supermarket chains have the same policy. "They won't even try a test," according to an executive at Playboy Home Video. "We think they are leaving a lot of money on the table. Our sell-through business could be double or triple if we could break through to some of those accounts which are capable of doing huge volume."[7]

Most mainstream movie theaters draw the line at R-rated films and will not screen movies carrying an NC-17 rating. This creates a serious distribution problem for legitimate (as opposed to hard-core) movie producers, as discussed in chapter 6.

At the insistence of the federal government in 1917 when the United States entered the First World War, Storyville, the New Orleans brothel district, which had been legalized by Louisiana in 1888, was shut down. The government worried that the temptations would prove too great for the anticipated influx of its sailors.[8] Since that time, prostitution has been illegal throughout the United States with the exception of Nevada, where it is allowed only in certain counties. Many cities, however, are either unable or unwilling to get rid of prostitution entirely and so settle for limiting the trade to certain areas, sometimes even to specific blocks. "Red-light districts" have been a common phenomenon in many major U.S. cities for decades. Either officially or unofficially, the "distribution" of prostitution is definitely limited and controlled.

Until the recent mushrooming of state lottery systems, gambling of all forms was tightly restricted by law. Racetracks for horses or dogs were allowed only under license in certain communities. Casinos, which have recently spread beyond Nevada and Atlantic City to New Orleans, to riverboats up and down the Mississippi, and to Indian reservations, still must be licensed and state and local governments tightly control their locations.

The sale of alcoholic beverages is controlled in one way or another in every one of the fifty states. Whether sold through state-owned liquor stores, state-licensed liquor stores, or even through supermarkets, drugstores, and convenience stores, every outlet must be licensed by the state. The pattern and intensity of distribution can vary dramatically. In the District of Columbia, nearly eight hundred businesses are licensed to sell carryout liquor, wine, and beer. By contrast, neighboring Montgomery County, Maryland, which spreads across four hundred fifty square miles, has only nineteen county-owned stores that can sell carryout liquor to a population of more than eight hundred thousand.[9]

Recently, where neighborhood residents believe that licenses have been granted too liberally, groups have been organized to curtail the prevalence of liquor shops in their areas. Civic groups—sometimes minority or immigrant communities—are waging battles to control the number of liquor stores and alter the way they do business. Their threat is to bring pressure on the alcoholic beverage commissions when it is time for license renewal.

Among our five subject industries, cigarettes over the years have enjoyed the most freedom in terms of distribution and as noted above, are the most widely distributed product category in the United States. That near-total freedom has come under serious challenge in recent years. Cigarette vending machines are now permitted only in areas limited to adults, such as bars. Stores that sell cigarettes, such as convenience stores and supermarkets, must keep them in locked fixtures. Advocacy groups feel these restrictions do not go far enough and would like to see cigarettes sold only through licensed outlets, as with alcoholic beverages.

Constraints, limitations, roadblocks—these are the operative words to describe the distribution of socially unacceptable products. Marketers in these industries cannot base their distribution strategies and decisions solely on economic factors, in other words, what will be the most efficient outlets and channels given their target markets and their other marketing mix decisions. The business world for them is not so simple. Certain channels will be closed to them, and social, political, and regulatory constraints may outweigh strictly economic considerations.

NOTES

1. From information supplied by Gary J. Smith, Instant Ticket Product Manager, Maryland State Lottery, personal communication May 21, 2002.

2. Occasionally, retailers print and redeem "cents-off" coupons for lottery tickets (e.g., a $1 ticket for 39¢), but it is the retailer, not the state, making this decision, and the purpose is to stimulate traffic and business for the store, not to sell more lottery tickets.

3. Thomas C. Capehart, Jr., "Trends in the Cigarette Industry after the Master Settlement Agreement," U.S. Department of Agriculture, TBS-250–01, October 2001, http://www.ers.usda.gov (accessed September 24, 2003).

4. Anne D'Innocenzio, "Report: Top Four U.S. Tobacco Companies Face More Pricing Pressure," *Kansas City Star*, July 11, 2003. From www.kansascity.com/mld/kansascity/business/6284197 (accessed September 20, 2003).

5. Andrea Geblin, "Wal-Mart Stops Handgun Sales Inside Its Stores," *Wall Street Journal*, December 23, 1993, B1.

6. Steven Lee Myers, "Giuliani Proposes Toughening Laws on X-Rated Shops," *New York Times*, September 11, 1994, 1. See also Jonathan P. Hicks, "City Council Supports Mayor on a Sex-Store Moratorium," *New York Times*, A1.

7. "*Playboy, Penthouse* Leveled," *Billboard*, June 19, 1993, 1.

8. "When Brothels Closed, All That Jazz Migrated," *Wall Street Journal*, February 3, 1995, Letters to the Editor.

9. Rene Sanchez, "In Parts of D.C., Alcohol Is Everywhere," *Washington Post*, March 20, 1994, A1.

CHAPTER 13

Public Affairs Strategies

Opposition, criticism, controversy, constraints—this is the environment in which the marketers of socially unacceptable products are forced to operate. Whether the issue concerns what segments of the market to target, how to manage a product line, what pricing or promotional strategies to use, or how to distribute the products, marketers in these socially suspect industries are certain to butt up against some form of societal or governmental opposition.

It comes as no surprise, therefore, that for firms in the industries we have been analyzing, managing this opposition becomes an important feature of their business strategy. For a typical firm in a mainstream industry, a public affairs program is designed to create some positive regard. For firms marketing socially unacceptable products, however, the goal is more likely to be a form of damage control: the minimizing of adversarial government and social pressures that stand in the way of the firm's success.

Because we are concerned with marketing in the broadest sense—that is, not simply selling a product, but marketing the whole firm or even the entire industry—it is clear that this public affairs responsibility is very much a part of the overall marketing function. Therefore, it is important that these two responsibilities—the marketing of the firm's products and managing social and governmental constraints—be very closely coordinated, even if they are handled by different individuals or different divisions in the firm.

The companies in all five of the industries under examination in this book use some sort of public relations methods to deal with the social and political opposition they encounter. But there is an enormously wide variance as to the extent or degree of their efforts, the methods they use (for example, individual firm activity or reliance on industry associations), and the nature of their activity (adversarial or accommodative).

FIREARMS, PORNOGRAPHY, AND GAMBLING

Firearms

For the firearms industry, gun control is really the only public policy issue on the table. And because the National Rifle Association (NRA) has been so aggressive and dominant—and generally so successful—in opposing gun control in almost any form, the individual manufacturers and the industry-wide National Shooting Sports Foundation have been content to sit back and let the NRA carry the ball.

This is for good reason. The NRA, working through its lobbying arm, the Institute for Legislative Action, has established a reputation for political power and influence second to none in Washington, D.C., as well as in many of the state capitals. Its ability to flood a legislator's office with grassroots messages opposing some aspect of gun control and its willingness to spend heavily on political campaigns—$20 million in the 2000 elections on "direct campaign donations, independent campaign expenditures, and on mobilizing the most aggressive grassroots operation in NRA history"[1]—have established the NRA as a political force of almost mythic proportions.

The NRA's lobbyists have been effective in the halls, offices, and cloakrooms of Congress, making sure that their facts, figures, messages, and interpretations are in front of the appropriate legislators. The NRA rewards its friends with campaign contributions, and it punishes its enemies by supporting their opponents. It claims to have won in 237 out of the 275 House and Senate races in which it was involved in the 2000 elections, it claims an 82 percent success rate among the "thousands" of state legislative candidates it supported, and it boasts that it also "played an important part in helping George W. Bush and Dick Cheney win the White House by activating gun owners in crucial states such as Arkansas, Tennessee, West Virginia, and, of course, Florida."[2]

The NRA is never shy about attacking its opponents. In one publication concerning Handgun Control, Inc., it shouted, "Don't Buy HCI Lies." "Guns, Bias and the Evening News" criticized the media in 1994 for what the NRA considered the networks' slant toward support for the Brady Bill.

But more than anything else, the NRA promotes the right of U.S. citizens "to keep and bear arms" as guaranteed by the Second Amendment to the Constitution. Too frequently these five words are taken out of the

context of the full sentence from the Bill of Rights: "A well-regulated militia, being necessary to the security of a free State, the right of the People
to keep and bear Arms, shall not be infringed." This full context of the
amendment has spawned a debate that ranges across the entire spectrum
of American life: from a battle of bumper stickers to public policy confron-
tations between the NRA and gun control advocates to scholarly debate
between constitutional law experts. Does the amendment give *individuals*
the right to bear arms or only members of a militia? Is it a *collective* right?
Are individuals de facto members of a state militia? Was it "the clear
intention of the Framers of our Constitution that the citizenry possess
arms equal or superior to those held by the government," as the NRA
claims?[3] Invariably, the NRA arguments rest heavily on quotes from the
Founding Fathers: Thomas Jefferson, James Madison, John Adams,
Thomas Paine, and others. Opponents question if the wisdom of these
eighteenth-century leaders regarding the ownership of weapons is still
appropriate, word for word, at the beginning of the twenty-first century.

In promoting its unequivocating answers to these questions, the NRA
has the support of some less well known and perhaps more radical fringe
groups. The Not-for-Profit Second Amendment Foundation and the Citizens Committee for the Right to Keep and Bear Arms (CCRKBA) have
offices on opposite sides of the country, but they are directed by the same
individuals, and their publications, *Gun News Digest, The Gottlieb-Tartarro
Report,* and *Point Blank,* all carry similar messages and warnings. These
groups and the NRA oppose *any* effort at gun control—outlawing assault
weapons, gun registration, waiting periods for the issuance of handgun
licenses, and so forth—as only the beginning of a long slide down the
"slippery slope" toward total gun control and an outright ban on the
personal ownership of firearms.

This debate has become so heated and contentious at times that it has
taken on a political and social life of its own, removed from the marketing
problems of the firearms manufacturers and retailers. It is certainly questionable whether effectively turning over the activity and control of the
public affairs functions of the industry to these external groups is wise
and helpful in the long run to the industry members.

Pornography

The pornography industry's public policy agenda focuses on the First
Amendment's right to free speech. The Free Speech Coalition in Los Angeles serves in the capacity of an industry association for the producers
and distributors of pornographic films, videos, magazines, books, and
paraphernalia as well as for "exotic dance emporiums," its euphemism
for striptease parlors, and for the "talent" of the industry, the actors, actresses, and dancers who perform in the films and onstage.

The coalition publishes a bimonthly newsletter, *The Free Speaker*, which advises members on issues across a broad spectrum: piracy and bootlegging problems for films and videos, film and video labeling laws, and even sexually transmitted diseases and how the talent can avoid them. It maintains a database of what specific films or videos are challenged and seized by local prosecutors, an aid to distributors and retailers, and will offer legal advice to adult entertainment stores facing zoning restrictions or producers facing censorship problems. In the 1994 elections, it contributed money and technical assistance toward defeating an initiative in Oregon that would have established an obscenity law (there is none currently) and in Colorado toward defeating an initiative calling for a more restrictive definition of obscenity and stricter enforcement.

Gambling

Because the gambling industry is split into two quite disparate divisions—state lotteries and casinos—there is not one umbrella organization or industry association that represents the two groups. As indicated in chapter 5, there are issues that affect both divisions—moral questions related to gambling, gambling addiction, underage gambling, relationship with criminal groups, economic issues related to gambling taxes, and so forth—but these issues have been dealt with, to the extent they have been addressed at all, by the individual state lottery administrations and by the individual casinos. For both groups, major public relations efforts are required during the debate and approval process when gambling is being considered. When a state goes through the sometimes bitter, always prolonged and difficult dispute over whether or not to establish a state lottery, and when a state, county, or municipality debates whether or not to permit casino gambling, either on land or on riverboats, the public relations experts are in greatest demand. Once the lottery or casino has been approved, however, the public policy issue either disappears completely or is greatly diminished, and with it goes much of the need for public relations or public affairs expertise.

Because of the rapid growth in land-based casino gambling, however, an industry association was formed in June 1995: the American Gaming Association (AGA), headquartered in Washington, D.C., and headed by political pro Frank Fahrenkopf, Jr., former chairman of the Republican National Party. The AGA's stated goal is "to create a better understanding and appreciation of gaming-entertainment by bringing the facts about the industry to elected officials, other decision makers and the media." It plans and implements an aggressive public education program, monitors and influences federal issues related to gambling, acts as an information clearinghouse, and plays a leadership role in addressing industry-wide issues. It also develops "industry-wide programs on critical issues such as problem and underage gaming."[4]

The organization emphasizes strongly the positive economic impact that casino gambling can offer a community or a state. Its promotional literature and its Web site are crammed full of facts and figures on the number of people who now visit casinos, the revenues and tax contributions produced, and the one million people employed (directly or indirectly) by the gaming-entertainment industry. The AGA also tries to head off the formation of any congressional or federal control or review board, preferring instead for each state to debate the merits and demerits of casino gambling.[5]

ALCOHOLIC BEVERAGE INDUSTRIES

Because of the ongoing battle for legitimacy waged by the beer, wine, and distilled spirits industries, the importance of an effective public affairs strategy is not new to these industries and to their member firms. Over the past few decades, the thrust of this strategy has been focused on two major issues: drunk driving and underage drinking. Since the mid-1990s, attention has also been focused on so-called binge drinking, which has become an increasingly difficult problem on college campuses. So while the alcoholic beverage firms are busy marketing their own brands of beer, wine, or spirits, they also must market their corporate images, the economic contributions of the industries, and even the legitimacy of consuming alcoholic beverages in moderation.

They have an uphill fight. A 1991 survey conducted by the industry itself revealed that the general public, not just advocacy groups, think that alcoholic beverage marketers are unethical and that the industry's ads encourage teenage drinking.[6]

The beer industry faces a special dilemma. It is big and mature, and dominated by a handful of powerful firms. Under these oligopolistic conditions, it is axiomatic that the firms will spend heavily on advertising and marketing to promote their individual brands, to carve out small gains in market share, or at the very least to defend their positions and avoid losing market share to their competitors. With no shortage of anti-alcohol advocates looking for a fight to pick, it is not surprising that this heavy advertising will be perceived as, and criticized for, encouraging nondrinkers to become drinkers. Marketers' tools for the evaluation of the effectiveness of ads are blunt instruments at best; they certainly are not up to the task of determining whether a series of beer ads will lead only to brand switching or whether new beer drinkers will be recruited.

The industries have tackled this dilemma on two levels: some individual companies, especially Anheuser-Busch and also Seagram (to a lesser extent), have developed expensive and sophisticated programs to promote moderation in drinking in a variety of ways. And all three industries have contributed to the formation of the Century Council, a nonprofit group "dedicated to reducing alcohol abuse across the United States."[7]

Individual Corporate Efforts

Anheuser-Busch

The leading brewer in the United States has taken the leading role in promoting moderation in drinking. In Anheuser-Busch's 2000 annual report, Chairman August A. Busch III states in his letter to shareholders under the heading "Delivering Responsibility":

Anheuser-Busch and its wholesaler family have invested nearly $350 million in efforts designed to eliminate underage drinking and drunk driving and to promote the moderate consumption of alcohol by adults of legal drinking age. Our "We All Make a Difference" campaign, which was launched in 1999, continues to salute Americans for their efforts to reduce drunk driving and underage drinking—and for the positive results they have achieved.[8]

The company has included similar passages in its annual reports for at least the past six or seven years. It has also published a full-color brochure, "Our Commitment," detailing the many ways in which Anheuser-Busch has been attacking the problems, including: youth education, offering free "Family Talk about Drinking" guidebooks; college awareness programs, including the "Buddy System" brochure and "Your Alcohol IQ" video; "Alert Cab," "O'Doul's Designated Driver," and other safe-driving programs under which the appointment of designated drivers is encouraged by offering them free or reduced-price food and non-alcoholic drinks; the "T.I.P.S." program (Training for Intervention Procedures by Servers), which trains bartenders, waiters, waitresses, and liquor store employees how to recognize and deal with intoxicated customers; and various other community awareness programs.

Anheuser-Busch traces its promotion of moderation in drinking back to the turn of the century, and it is making an aggressive and impressive effort to let the public know about it. This is not the only tune the company's public affairs department plays, however. Along with the material on responsible drinking, the company also sent me five pages of "literature cites" that purport to show that advertising alcoholic beverages does not lead to increased consumption or to encouraging young people to start drinking.

In sum, Anheuser-Busch has made a serious effort to promote responsible drinking, and this has become an important part of its public affairs and overall marketing strategies.

Miller Brewing

Miller Brewing has also taken an active role in promoting responsible drinking, but its role as a relatively small division of parent Philip Morris influences the extent to which Miller publicizes its activities. In contrast to Anheuser-Busch, Philip Morris only recently has focused on social responsibility in its annual report. As recently as 1994, Chairman Geoffrey Bible's letter to the company's shareholders mentioned not a word about the responsible drinking programs its brewing division had instigated. But Philip Morris's *2000 Annual Report* includes a section headed "Addressing Societal Concerns" for its report on each division's accomplishments: tobacco, food, and beer. Miller, according to the report, "worked with legislators and led a coalition . . . to champion the passage of landmark legislation that toughens drunk-driving laws against repeat offenders and underage drinkers . . . developed and launched a comprehensive Responsibility Initiative . . . and broadened the availability and distribution of 'Let's Talk,' a guide for parents on how to talk to their children about drinking and responsible decision making."[9]

Miller has developed a "Think When You Drink" program, a coordinated effort including television and radio spots plus some billboard advertising. With its distributors, Miller sponsors a "safe ride home" via taxi or bus from a bar where a patron has drunk too much to drive safely. It sponsors designated driver booths at sports stadiums, it supports Bacchus (Boost Alcohol Consciousness Concerning the Health of University Students), and it helps fund the efforts of the Beer Institute.

Coors

Coors's 2002 annual report is all about the acquisition of the United Kingdom's number-two brewer, cutting costs, transformation, and revitalizing advertising in the United States, all to hide as politely as possible the somewhat disappointing financial results for the year.[10] Although sales and profits were up sharply due to the acquisition, return on invested capital was the lowest in five years. Nowhere in his letter to the shareholders does CEO Peter Coors tell of the company's very significant efforts over the years to promote responsible drinking, including: support for student assistance programs, teen driving safety, Bacchus, and even alcohol abuse and the elderly. In some of its literature, Coors manages to mix its messages. Along with warnings about drunk driving and underage drinking, the company includes arguments against putting warning labels on beer, restricting advertising, and considering alcohol as a drug.

Among the distilled spirits makers, Diageo's annual report for 2003 contained a strong statement on the subject of social responsibility. Chairman Lord Blyth of Rowington's letter to the company's shareholders contained the following paragraphs:

[O]ur industry is controversial. We are experiencing a growing focus on the role of alcohol in society. Although governments welcome the revenue from taxes on drinks, they are increasingly concerned about its social impact when it is misused. Enjoyed responsibly, our products have unrivalled potential to bring pleasure to millions of adult consumers, and for the vast majority that is exactly what they do. But there are legitimate concerns about misuse of alcohol and the health, social, and behavioral problems which can result. We have engaged in active cooperation with ministers, officials, and administrators in many parts of the world but we need to do more.

We are investing significantly in a range of initiatives including advertising focusing on intelligent drinking, education programmes to explain the dangers of underage and binge drinking, and server training to ensure that those who run bars have the expertise to stop misuse before it starts.

Seagram, when it was an independent company, included in its annual report a foldout section under the heading "Integrity—Responsibility— Some Things Don't Change." The section reproduced print ads from as far back as 1934, when the company urged, "We who make whiskey say: 'Drink Moderately.'" During the depths of the Depression in 1937, the company's message was: "We Don't Want Bread Money. Liquor is one of the luxuries of life, to be bought and enjoyed only after the necessities are provided. Whoever needs bread for himself or his family, should not buy whiskey." In 1945 near the end of the Second World War, the public service ad was headlined, "We Don't Want Bond Money," advising that the purchase of war bonds should come before the purchase of liquor. Throughout the 1980s and 1990s, the company's message was to avoid driving while drinking. "We're not anti-drinking. We're anti-dying. Designate a driver. Sometimes Drinking Responsibly Means Not Drinking At All."[11]

The Century Council and Industry Associations

The Century Council

Formed in 1991 by seventeen concerned members of the alcoholic beverage industries, this national, nonprofit organization now is funded by the leading distillers in the United States that have invested more than $110 million to tackle the problems of alcohol abuse, underage drinking, and drunk driving. The council has developed innovative education programs for middle schools through colleges, such as:

"Ready or Not: Talking with Kids about Alcohol" developed with Boys & Girls Clubs of America.

"Full House at Prom Night," a partnership with the National Commission Against Drunk Driving.

"Alcohol 101," an educational CD-ROM developed in collaboration with the University of Illinois for use on college campuses.

"Si Toma, No Maneje" ("If You Drink, Don't Drive") and other bilingual programs aimed at Hispanic Americans.

The council also gets involved in lobbying and political activity related to these concerns, such as working for passage of administrative license revocation laws at the state government level, but it leaves to the other associations economic issues such as taxes, prices, advertising, and labeling.

Industry Associations

The Wine Institute, which represents primarily the California wineries, works on such issues as minimizing state and federal excise taxes, franchise security laws under which a winery must contract with one specific distributor when shipping out of its own state and effectively gets locked into doing business with that distributor whether the winery wants to continue or not, problems arising from the three-tier system, and slotting fees, which are charges imposed by supermarkets on manufacturers for granting shelf space in their stores. On occasion, the Wine Institute will file amicus briefs where wineries will be affected by the outcome of cases, such as a challenge to Rhode Island's attempt to control the pricing of wine. The institute's one effort at product promotion—advertising California wines to the Texas market—was deemed an abject failure.

The Beer Institute, organized in 1986, "is proud to be the voice of the U.S. brewing industry and of millions of Americans who brew, sell, and enjoy the beverage of moderation."[12] It acts as the industry's public policy representative, working with Congress on regulatory and economic issues, and it promotes and publicizes the responsible drinking campaigns of the major brewers. Through the Beer Industry Community Assistance Fund it also helps finance community groups across the country in a wide variety of programs (youth groups, women's centers, museums, arts programs, etc.) that contribute in any way toward curbing alcohol and drug abuse.

Predictably, in its lobbying efforts, the Beer Institute leans heavily on two supports. Beer drinking is an American tradition: "The Pilgrims aboard the Mayflower landed at Plymouth Rock in part because, as one colonist wrote in his diary, 'We could not take time for further search ... our victuals being much spent, especially our bere [sic].' Later, George Washington, an accomplished brewmaster, demanded that the Continental Congress meet its promise of supplying his soldiers a quart of beer daily."[13]

The second support is that the beer industry is a mainstay for the U.S. economy: 2.7 million American jobs depend directly or indirectly on beer; almost $1 billion goes to buy corn, rice, hops, and malt barley from American farmers; and the industry pays $8.8 billion in federal, state, and local taxes.[14]

The Beer Institute's efforts are not all easygoing, public relations flack, however. Its president has described its goal as putting "a more appealing face on the beer industry while drawing a line in the sand with regard to our priorities in Congress and with the executive branch." And its chairman lists as primary issues "challenging the threat of new government restrictions," such as any limitations on the sale and advertising of alcoholic beverages, and "Confronting the critics who question the legitimacy of our business . . . who would like nothing better than a return to Prohibition. . . . We must make a renewed commitment to promoting the positive efforts of our industry and challenging [the critics'] unfounded charges. We cannot tolerate the misperceptions they create."[15]

Critical Response

In spite of the hundreds of millions of dollars spent by the three divisions of the alcoholic beverage industry in recent years on promoting responsible drinking and on working to eliminate drunk driving and underage drinking, the industry's critics have not been won over. Lawrence Wallack of the School of Public Health at the University of California at Berkeley has written that the vague messages such as "Know when to say when" and "Think when you drink" "are more public relations efforts than public interest campaigns." His research shows that even in the moderation ads:

a pro-drinking message often dominated and good times, good friends, and fast paced lifestyles were associated with drinking. The prevention or health message was overwhelmed by the pro-drinking emphasis. In addition there was a failure to separate the activities of drinking and driving. In one spot promoting a designated driver it is unclear whether the designated driver abstains, drinks less than the others, or is just not as intoxicated.[16]

Wallack's research team interviewed more than three hundred high school and college students and found "that 38% of the young adults thought that the Anheuser-Busch message, 'Know when to say when,' meant stopping after 4 or more beers," that a majority of the students thought the message of the Anheuser-Busch and Coors ads was "It's OK for teens to drink in moderation," and approximately 40 percent thought the message was, "It's OK for older teens to get drunk on occasion."

Wallack concluded, "At best the youth in this study received a mixed message about moderation and the prevention of alcohol related problems. This serves as an illustration of the need for public health educators, not alcohol marketers, to develop educational campaigns."[17]

In addition, alcohol critics claim that even if the messages of the moderation ads were not mixed, these ads represent only a drop in the bucket

compared with the $2 billion spent each year[18] in advertising and pro-
moting the consumption of all forms of alcohol. However, there is serious
dispute as to whether increased levels of advertising of alcoholic beverages actually cause increased sales. Some scholars have argued that the
evidence is inconclusive and that it may be equally valid to argue that
higher sales lead to increased advertising, because many marketers base
their advertising budgets on projected sales figures.[19]

Other critics are more concerned that the preponderance of alcohol
advertising and the nature of some of the advertising (88 percent of fifth-
and sixth-grade children were able to match Spuds Mackenzie, the original party animal, with Bud Light) increase children's awareness of alcohol
and especially of beer. Furthermore, children who are more aware of beer
advertising hold "more favorable beliefs about drinking, [and intend] to
drink more frequently as adults."[20]

The Center for Science in the Public Interest continues to criticize all
segments of the alcoholic beverage industry for selling "the notion that
drinking is an essential part of daily life and is inextricably linked to social,
athletic, and sexual success" and for targeting heavy drinkers, minorities,
and women as part of their marketing strategies.[21]

Even charitable donations and cause-related marketing are unacceptable to the industry's critics. Over more than a decade, Anheuser-Busch
raised in excess of $47 million for the Muscular Dystrophy Association,
in part through its "Shamrocks for MDA" promotions around St. Patrick's
Day. Seagram sponsored a 900-number, $2 call-in contest to name your
favorite quarterback and enter a drawing for Super Bowl tickets, which
raised $20,000 for the National Multiple Sclerosis Society, and Heublein
contributed another $12,000 to the same charity through its "Ugliest Bar-
tender" contest. Over ten years, Miller has helped raise $8 million for the
Cerebral Palsy Association, and Absolut vodka has contributed to the
Multiple Sclerosis Society. The counterarguments from the critics, however, are that donations to health-related charities are "a conscious effort
to shift the blame for the alcohol problem in this country, to neutralize
people who might demand higher taxes on alcohol to pay for its costs to
society." Or, "the alcohol companies are showing how enlightened and
wonderful they are by donating to the charities to make up for the damage
their product does. There is no way a health organization can accept profits from that industry without it being a conflict of interest."[22]

THE TOBACCO INDUSTRY

During the 1990s, the tobacco industry was subject to more social and
governmental criticism than any other industry in the United States—
perhaps in the country's history. For tobacco, therefore, the public or governmental affairs function has been extremely important and also very

visible. It has been carried out on two levels: by the individual firms with Philip Morris and Reynolds in the vanguard, and until 1998 by the Tobacco Institute.

The Iron Fist

There has been a decided shift in emphasis in the public affairs strategy of the tobacco industry beginning in the mid-1990s. Prior to that time, the strategy might have been described as an iron fist. With their avowed adversaries, the firms and the industry were fiercely tough. They gave no quarter; they took no prisoners; they made no compromises. This was not just an "eye for an eye" principle. Attack the tobacco industry with a blow of some sort and expect two or three or four blows in return.

This combative—and some would say arrogant—approach to dealing with external threats to the tobacco industry was exemplified in Philip Morris's chairman Geoffrey Bible's letter to shareholders in the company's 1994 annual report. Under the heading "Defending Our Company" Bible wrote:

Protecting your investment, our business and employees, and the rights of consumers to enjoy our products are all top priorities for this management team. No doubt you're aware of the many pressures facing the U.S. tobacco industry: public smoking restrictions, possible excise tax hikes, the threat of FDA regulation, congressional hearings, negative media coverage, litigation. Still, you should remember that our U.S. tobacco company has faced similar threats before and has overcome them. I want to make this crystal clear: We believe these issues remain manageable. . . . In the legal arena, we are committing all the resources necessary to defend the company from new forms of litigation, making sure we have better firepower than our foes, no matter how formidable. . . . [W]e should prevail in [these new class-action suits], just as we have been successful in other types of cases over the last 40 years. It is important to note here that the tobacco industry has never lost or paid to settle a case. . . . We are going on the offensive. . . . We're suing the EPA . . . suing state and local governments . . . and suing ABC. . . . We believe that we are absolutely right in all of the positions we take on these issues.[23]

Nowhere is this fierceness of the tobacco companies' retaliation more apparent than in the courtroom. For a product that is responsible for more than four hundred thousand deaths each year in the United States alone, according to industry critics, not to mention serious health problems, fires, and the rest of the long list of social ills attributable to cigarettes, it was an extraordinary achievement that until the late 1990s no firm in the industry had been forced to pay out a penny in damages, just as Bible claimed. The industry took considerable pride in this fact and offered it as proof that the firms carried out their operations in a legal and socially respectable manner. Anti-tobacco critics and those who brought suit against one or more tobacco firms claimed that the companies' all-wins-and-no-loss record was due to the overwhelming power they brought to the court-room. The cigarette companies were notorious for committing seemingly limitless resources to the winning of any product liability lawsuit that was brought against them. Teams of highly paid and very talented attorneys, both in-house and hired, were available to defend against any claim. The suits predictably stretched out over years; the companies seemed not to mind, but inevitably it helped defeat the plaintiffs' lawyers who were gambling on a contingency fee. Ironically, the cigarette package warning labels against which the industry fought so hard turned out to be its sal-vation. In the product liability suits decided before 1998, the companies were able to convince a jury that the smokers were adequately warned of any dangers inherent in cigarettes and willingly accepted the risk of those dangers.

The ABC suit, to which Bible referred, is also an interesting example of the company's strategy. In 1994, the debate over nicotine in cigarettes became more intense, focusing on several key questions. Is nicotine ad-dictive? Did the cigarette companies know that it is addictive? Do the cigarette manufacturers control the level of nicotine in cigarettes? ABC television ran a news special on the industry, including an interview with an unnamed and disguised former Philip Morris scientist, in which ABC accused the company of manipulating or "spiking" the level of nicotine in its cigarettes. Philip Morris, choosing the "iron fist" response, imme-diately slapped ABC with a $10 *billion* libel suit, the largest in history. Along with the size and swiftness of the lawsuit went a message to all industry critics: if you make any mistake in your criticism, the price you will pay will be not just a severe fine, but financial ruin.

The suit was settled in 1995, after the argument had devolved into one of semantics. There seemed to be no question that the manufacturers, through the use of various tobacco blending techniques and chemical pro-cesses, control the level of nicotine and put back into the cigarette at least as much nicotine as is lost in the normal manufacturing process. But does this constitute "spiking"? And just what does "addictive" mean? The cig-arette companies compared their product to Twinkies and claimed, in spite of uncovered company documents to the contrary, that their sole interest in the nicotine content was to improve the taste of their cigarettes. By 1995, ABC was in the process of being acquired by Disney and was unwilling to go through a lengthy trial with a $10 billion sword hanging over its head. So the broadcaster caved in, agreed that "spiking" the nic-otine content had been an improper description of the manufacturing pro-cess, and paid $15 million to Philip Morris for its legal troubles.

Philip Morris's lawsuit and ABC's reluctant apology seem to have had a ripple effect. Late in 1995, CBS' usually gutsy and hard-hitting *60 Min-utes* declined to air a segment in which a former Brown & Williamson employee revealed information damaging to the company. At the time, CBS admitted that although Brown & Williamson had not even threatened to sue, the network, also in the midst of an acquisition by Westinghouse, was unwilling to risk the disruption and the financial impact of a potential lawsuit.

The cigarette companies are no less tough and just as willing to spend money freely in their relations with various governmental bodies. In 1994, Brown & Williamson subpoenaed two prominent congressmen, representatives Henry Waxman (D-CA) and Ron Wyden (D-OR), to force them to turn over documents allegedly showing that the company and other cigarette manufacturers had conspired to jeopardize the health of Americans.[24] That same year, Philip Morris spent $20 million in an unsuccessful attempt to pass a proposal in California that would have overturned tough local anti-smoking ordinances.[25] Shortly after Florida's governor Lawton Chiles had succeeded in tacking onto an otherwise uncontroversial measure an amendment that would pave the way for the state to sue the tobacco companies for the recovery of billions of dollars in smoking-related health costs, the industry put together a high-powered team of lobbyists to organize business, government, and grassroots opposition to the plan. The team recruited "the cream of the Tallahassee lobbying crop—including Jim Krog, the Governor's former campaign manager. Signing up new troops from across Florida and as far away as Washington, a contingent of more than 50 strong descended on lawmakers and editorial boards." At least $750,000 was spent by the industry, including more than $120,000 in campaign fund gifts to the Republican-dominated lawmakers. With the help of the Associated Industries of Florida—a six thousand-member trade group, which was told that what was happening to tobacco then could happen to some other industry in the future—the amendment was overwhelmingly repealed.[26]

The speed and willingness of the industry to go to court is legendary. On the very same day that the Clinton administration announced its proposals for the FDA to control more effectively the sale of cigarettes to minors, the major tobacco companies filed suit in a federal court in Virginia to halt the program.

When New York City threatened to pass a tough ordinance severely restricting smoking in workplaces, Philip Morris threatened to move its corporate headquarters and two thousand employees out of the city and to cut off its support for the arts in that city as well.[27] The ordinance was passed, after long debate, in spite of the threat. The industry had better luck contesting a Maryland proposal to ban smoking in just about all workplaces. After heavy lobbying and suing the state before a friendly judge over the constitutionality of the ban, the bill was eventually changed to exclude bars and restaurants.

Tobacco companies have been ready and willing to use their economic muscle in other ways. As their advertising budgets have grown over the years and because so much of that money now is channeled into magazines, the companies now have some influence over the editorial content of those magazines. This is especially important when it comes down to the question of how well or how completely a magazine reports on issues involving health and smoking. Kenneth Warner at the University of Michigan compiled data over a thirty-year period to show that media dependant on cigarette advertising revenues tended to limit their coverage of smoking and health issues. He reported that *Harper's Bazaar* and *Family Circle* rejected articles on the tobacco and health issue for fear of losing cigarette ads. Philip Morris pulled its ads from *Connoisseur* magazine in 1988 because of remarks made about the tobacco industry by its publisher, Thomas Hoving.

Perhaps the most widely reported use of advertising clout was Philip Morris's abrupt firing of Saatchi & Saatchi from one of its General Foods accounts, worth some $70–80 million, because of that agency's creation of television ads for Northwest Airlines promoting its nonsmoking flights. Philip Morris attacked the airline as well, sending thousands of letters to its direct mail lists of smokers denigrating Northwest for "its poor on-time performance and . . . 139 transgressions of Federal Aviation Administration standards." Guy Smith of Philip Morris warned, "I would suggest that organizations that discriminate against one-third of the adult population [smokers] do so at their economic or political peril." Walker Merryman of the Tobacco Institute backed this hardball approach, "If we're attacked, we're not going to roll over and play dead. The sooner our adversaries, friendly or otherwise, learn that, the less difficulty they're going to find themselves in."[28]

As described in chapter 2, the Environmental Protection Administration (EPA) issued its long-awaited report on the health consequences of environmental tobacco smoke in early 1993. Philip Morris alone spent millions of dollars on a series of full-page ads (some were three consecutive pages) in major newspapers across the country refuting the statistical evidence used to justify the EPA report. This particular barrage of ads from Philip Morris was also attributed to the company's change in top management. Michael Miles had left as chief executive officer, and part of the criticism of Miles was that he had been too soft in the face of criticism, too reluctant to strike back. Geoffrey Bible, who had come up through the tobacco ranks, succeeded Miles and pushed the company to be just as aggressive in its public affairs role as it was in defending its enviable market share against all its competitors.

Reynolds Tobacco was equally aggressive in its own way, adamantly refusing under government and advocacy group pressure to back away from the use of its Joe Camel advertising campaign. In fact, while criticism of Smokin' Joe was at its peak, Reynolds continued to increase Joe's public exposure and the company's ad budget in open defiance of his critics, at least until the campaign began to fade due to old age.

RJR Nabisco's 1994 Annual Report took a somewhat less pugnacious stand regarding the social and political issues facing the industry than did Philip Morris's report. The chairman's letter characterized the difficult political environment problems as "short-term obstacles" and noted that the company's future was tied to how well it managed "a policy environment that at times has been hostile to tobacco." This was something of an understatement compared to the rhetoric of its chief competitor! The tobacco division's chief did promise, however, that the company's "commitment to vigorously defend the rights of adults to choose to smoke does not waver. We work for smokers."[29]

The Velvet Glove

While projecting this tough—sometimes even merciless—image of an industry that would brook no opposition, the tobacco companies were trying to hide the iron fist with a velvet glove of philanthropy. Using their billions of dollars of profits from selling cigarettes, they could afford to be generous to cultural and social causes. Philip Morris has been called "a 20th century corporate Medici, probably the art world's favorite company." The cigarette manufacturer's "strategic philanthropy" enriched in one year such venerable institutions as New York's Lincoln Center, Whitney Museum, and Carnegie Hall, Washington's Kennedy Center, the Joffrey Ballet, and the Alvin Ailey American Dance Theater to the tune of $13 million. Reynolds's donations were aimed more at community arts organizations, and BAT (British American Tobacco) sponsored the Kool Jazz Festival for more than a decade. Of course, even generous contributions do not guarantee some sort of quid pro quo. When Philip Morris sent a letter to museum directors trying to get their support in fighting an anti-smoking bill being considered by the New York City Council, the director of the Whitney Museum, Thomas N. Armstrong III, said simply, "I threw it in the trash."[30]

Tobacco support can be important for social causes as well, and the list of recipients would be a long one indeed. Both Philip Morris and UST, the smokeless tobacco giant, have been significant contributors to Students in Free Enterprise (SIFE), which is enough to raise some eyebrows because tobacco involvement with any student group tends to be suspect. Some organizations, notably certain colleges and universities, have begun to turn down charitable contributions from tobacco companies as the industry's legitimacy continues to wane.

In the late 1980s, Philip Morris sponsored an expensive campaign to call public attention to the bicentennial anniversary of the U.S. Bill of Rights. On the surface, this was a selfless effort to honor this country's history, offer a modest but badly needed civics lesson, and promote some good, old-fashioned patriotism. There was a convenient subliminal message, however: that as more and more communities and states limited the areas in which smoking was allowed, smokers were losing their "rights."

The industry's concern over rights continued as part of the public persona of reasonableness and compromise it hoped to project. In 1995, the National Smokers Alliance, an industry-supported organization, ran an equally impressive series of full-page ads reminding the country again that smokers were in danger of losing their rights. According to these ads, a handful of so-called "lifestyle police," evil-looking cartoon-style characters, were threatening smokers today, but tomorrow, the ads warned darkly, they might target "the right to speak your mind," "the right to think for yourself," even "the right to eat bacon and eggs." Under headlines such as "How can the opinion of so few outweigh the rights of so many?" the ads went on to state,

Most Americans want Big Government off their backs and out of their private lives. But a group of extremists isn't getting the message. These self-appointed lifestyle police believe they know what's best for all of us and they're pushing to control many aspects of our daily lives. If they succeed, we lose our basic right to free choice.

Today, the "lifestyle police" are targeting smokers. But who's next? If 50 million smokers can lose their rights, anyone can.

At the very same time, Philip Morris was promoting its Accommodation Program and Reynolds was pushing its plea for peaceful coexistence. Both programs were advertised to the public but were aimed especially at the hospitality industry. Reynolds published a "Peaceful Coexistence Directory," listing the names, addresses, and telephone numbers of restaurants and taverns across the country that welcomed both smokers and nonsmokers. This was followed by a dual "Guide" for smokers (and nonsmokers), which had advice on how to be a "polite smoker" (or polite nonsmoker) and suggested that peaceful coexistence is the responsibility of both groups.

Meanwhile, Philip Morris claimed to have signed up more than sixteen thousand hotels, restaurants, shopping malls, bowling alleys, and other hospitality businesses that were pledged to support "Accommodation [as] the reasonable way for smokers and non-smokers to work out their differences." The velvet glove was all about working together, reasonableness, accommodation; the iron fist was all about using the billions of dollars of tobacco profits to intimidate industry critics.

By the late 1990s, the legal environment had changed dramatically for the tobacco companies, and this necessitated a public affairs strategy shift. As noted in chapter 2, the combined power of several states' lawsuits to recover years of health-care costs led to the companies' willingness to sign the Master Settlement Agreement in 1998. In gathering material in preparation for trial, the states had uncovered internal documents allegedly showing that decades ago the tobacco companies had evidence that cigarette smoking was addictive and harmful and that they conspired to cover up that evidence. Such documents, and the possibility of even more incriminating material, brought an end to the companies' perfect record with liability suits. A Florida smoker won a multimillion suit against Brown & Williamson, and Philip Morris lost a string of five decisions in California and Oregon. Suddenly, there was a real possibility, albeit remote, that courts in other states might also find reason to award multi-million and even billion dollar sums to plaintiffs, to the point of forcing the companies into bankruptcy. It should be noted that all of these verdicts against the tobacco companies are under appeal.

The companies in recent years have taken seriously the bankruptcy possibility. In the 1996–97 period, they entered into serious negotiations with a group of anti-smoking organizations, hoping that if they agreed to serious marketing restrictions and FDA regulation, Congress would agree to put limits on their liability for health claims. The negotiations foundered when some of the anti-smoking advocates refused to countenance any limits to the companies' liability.[31]

While the tobacco companies are still formidable opponents in a courtroom, they are far less combative in their public statements. The velvet glove is all that the public has seen in recent years. Philip Morris and most of the other companies now admit "that smoking is addictive and can cause lung cancer and other diseases."[32] Louis Camilleri, Geoffrey Bible's replacement as chief executive officer of Philip Morris, is seen as more "soft-spoken" and less "pugnacious."[33] Michael Pertschuk, former chairman of the Federal Trade Commission, has written in his book, *Smoke in Their Eyes:*

the industry, led by a $100 million Philip Morris public relations campaign, has sought skillfully to reposition itself in the public mind as a chastened, reformed sinner. The essence of their message: "Oh, that was then; this is now. Those were bad guys that ran the companies back then; we're reformers. We've paid our debt to society. And now we *really* don't want kids to smoke, and we're funding programs—approved by public health authorities—to help keep them from smoking."[34]

Has this change in strategy been successful? Pertschuk reports that though the industry is still scorned, in a recent survey "the percentage who gave the companies a strong rating for supporting 'good causes' leapt from 10 percent in 1999 to 40 percent in 2000."[35]

The Public Affairs Professionals

Behind both of these images—the iron fist and the velvet glove—is yet a third view of the tobacco industry's public affairs managers: a group of experienced, intelligent professionals who know that the direction of scientific, social, and governmental criticism has been running against the industry for years and who are dedicated to giving ground as slowly and as grudgingly as possible. With their strong financial resources, these public affairs managers have carved out a presence in Washington and the fifty state capitals that is second to no other industry.

These public affairs people have been adept at building coalitions to provide added muscle to their lobbying efforts. Whenever there are threats to limit, tax, or ban the advertising of tobacco products, the industry can gather support from almost all areas of the advertising and media industries as well as from those elements of the civil rights organizations who worry about encroachments on the First Amendment. In spite of African Americans suffering more from the adverse health effects of smoking, the tobacco industry has done a good job of maintaining the support of black and Hispanic communities by heavy advertising in minority-oriented media. The industry has reached out for support even from organized labor. A booklet, financed by the Tobacco Institute, warned workers that restrictive smoking rules are a "smoke screen" allowing management to avoid safety improvements and liability for industrial health problems.[36]

Over the past thirty to forty years, however, it has been the skillful, professional, and generally successful lobbying efforts of the industry's public affairs managers that have prevented the tobacco control groups from making more inroads than they have and that have kept the industry viable and so very profitable. In a 1993 speech to a conference of tobacco control groups, Michael Pertschuk, codirector of the Advocacy Institute, paid tribute of a sort to his foes, "[T]he tobacco industry never sleeps. While their moral resources erode, their financial resources are inexhaustible. And they continue to be able to buy a vast army of lobbyists, propagandists, and lawyers—among them, alas, otherwise worthy community leaders and vanguard community organizations."[37]

The industry's clever lobbying started early. Thanks in part to this effective lobbying, tobacco is specifically exempted from coverage under the Consumer Product Safety Act, the Toxic Substances Act, the Fair Labelling and Packaging Act, the Federal Hazardous Substances Act, and the Controlled Substances Act.

During the 1960s, after the publication of the surgeon general's report, the Federal Trade Commission (FTC) was eager to take some important steps in controlling the packaging and promoting of cigarettes. Sensing that Congress was a far friendlier environment than the hostile FTC, the industry pressured Congress through its oversight powers to take control of the smoking issue, thus neutralizing the FTC. A. Lee Fritschler, in his book *Smoking and Politics*, claims that the original "Cigarette Labelling and Advertising Act passed by Congress in 1965 was more of a victory for cigarettes than it was for health."[38] The manufacturers won on the size and positioning of the warning labels on the packages, there would be no warnings (at that time) in cigarette ads, state and local governments were preempted from any regulations on packaging or advertising, and the FTC was banned for four years from even considering more restrictive regulations.

More recently, in 1995, there were two examples of how the industry will compromise and give ground, but only slowly and grudgingly. On the issue of cigarette advertising on billboards in sports stadiums, which anti-smoking activists have complained for years was simply exploiting a loophole in the law banning television advertising, after six months of negotiations with the Justice Department, Philip Morris agreed to stop using those billboards that were in prominent view of the television cameras. The company claimed that it had already begun to reposition its signs voluntarily, and the agreement with the government was "consistent with our ongoing efforts to place signage where it remains visible to stadium attendees but doesn't generate television coverage."[39] Left unresolved by the agreement, however, was the much bigger question of tobacco sponsorship of auto racing, where cigarette logos on cars and drivers' racing suits result in far more television exposure than the occasional shot of a billboard at a baseball, football, or hockey arena. Only in 1998 in the Master Settlement Agreement did the industry agree to reduce such sponsorship.

Another example of Philip Morris's grudging compromises occurred in 1995. Just days before the Clinton administration issued its proposals to keep cigarettes out of the hands of underage teens, Philip Morris attempted a preemptive strike and unveiled its own program to curb smoking by minors. Although the company and the industry for years have opposed aggressively states' efforts to limit children's access to tobacco, suddenly Philip Morris announced in double-truck ads its "Action against Access." The company agreed to put notices on its packages saying "Underage sale prohibited," to stop giving away free samples, to stop distributing cigarettes through the mail, to support laws requiring cigarette retailers to be licensed, to help prevent minors' access to cigarette vending machines, to increase efforts to prevent the use of cigarette logos on video games, and through signage and other point-of-sale methods to help retailers do a better job of preventing cigarette sales to minors. Sounding to all the world like its anti-smoking adversaries, Philip Morris tagged these ads with the slogan, "The best way to keep kids away from cigarettes is to keep cigarettes away from kids."

This last-minute program of compromise had two purposes. First, it suggested a far less rigorous set of proposals than what the administration announced; the FDA proposals would ban *all* vending machine sales of cigarettes and would impose serious restrictions on outdoor and magazine tobacco advertising. Second, it laid the groundwork for the argument that industry self-regulation should be given a chance to work before the imposition of draconian governmental regulations.

For forty years, the tobacco industry has been able to avoid regulation by the Food and Drug Administration. However, in the negotiations of 1996–97 with the anti-tobacco groups, which would have culminated in the McCain Bill, the industry was ready to give in even on this issue and accept FDA regulation on most matters if only the cigarette companies could shield themselves from unlimited liability claims. With the collapse of those negotiations, the FDA still has no authority to regulate the nicotine and toxic chemical ingredients of cigarettes.

Now, the wheel seems to have come full circle. Steven Parrish, senior vice president for corporate affairs of Altria and longtime chief apologist not only for his company's tough-as-nails stand but for the entire tobacco industry, described in the *Yale Journal of Health Policy, Law, and Ethics* a policy shift that would seem to be an abrupt U-turn for the world's biggest, strongest, and some would say meanest tobacco company. Parrish begins with a mea culpa. "Put simply, ours was a culture of arrogance. . . . There was a bunker mentality, an 'us against them' attitude, a belief that anyone who disagreed with us was an enemy out to destroy us. . . . The industry did not have sufficient appreciation that, from society's perspective, the unique dangers posed by cigarettes call for both rigorous regulation and significant voluntary restraints, regardless of the protection that the First Amendment guarantees commercial speech."[40] He then goes on to lay out a new policy of accommodation, including assurances that even FDA regulation can be countenanced, including the regulation of nicotine, which Altria and the other cigarette makers have for years said was totally unacceptable.

This dramatic shift in public relations strategy was not immediately embraced by Altria's competitors. Indeed, they saw it as a not-so-subtle way for Altria to maintain its dominant position. If there were further restrictions on cigarette promotion, how could any brand ever hope to dethrone Marlboro?

Finally, another example of the tobacco industry's very clever, very professional public affairs strategies is the attempt to control the essence and the wording of whatever issue comes to the public's attention. Questions pertaining to health issues are moved aside subtly by the cigarette companies, and attention is focused instead on individuals' rights to make informed decisions for themselves. Bans on smoking in the workplace become issues not of workers' health but of workers' rights in collective bargaining. Any effort to limit cigarette advertising to children—for example, a ban on cartoon characters—was, until the MSA, an issue of freedom of speech. The EPA's findings on environmental tobacco smoke became an issue of statistical standards. The tobacco companies know that the public strongly supports efforts to limit smoking by minors. The spin from the tobacco industry shifts the focus away from children and smoking by claiming that what the critics *really* want is to ban smoking entirely, a position strongly opposed by the public. Parallel industry tactics cast the proposals as a vast expansion of the bureaucratic reach of a federal agency (at a time when public opinion and the political tide are running in the opposite direction), and, in an ad hominem attack, as a power-grab by then FDA chief, Dr. David Kessler.

CONCLUSIONS

Perhaps the only common thread that ties together the public affairs strategies of these five industries is that because of the opposition and criticism that they all face, the public affairs function becomes vital to their marketing and overall business strategies. Fending off social and political critics is a far cry from marketing the organization's products, but the two tasks must be carefully coordinated if the organization hopes to continue to prosper.

Beyond that, there is great diversity both in choice of strategy and in implementation. As to strategies, all three segments of the alcoholic beverage industries have taken basically an accommodative position on the issues of underage drinking and drunk driving, even while they resist higher taxes and other regulations on the sale of their products. At the other end of the spectrum, the cigarette companies over four decades showed little willingness to bow to any social or political pressures. This has had the predictable result of strengthening the opposition and hardening the battle lines.

As to implementation, the larger companies in the more structured industries, especially beer and tobacco, have well-developed public affairs offices and strategies of their own as well as participating in industry-wide efforts. Public relations and governmental affairs for the casino gambling industry are now in the hands of the American Gaming Association, a well-connected Washington, D.C., office. The NRA does not officially represent the firearms industry, but it certainly has shouldered the responsibility for confronting all of the industry's critics. And the various participants in the business of pornography rely on a loose association with the Free Speech Coalition to represent their interests, at least in defending their First Amendment rights.

The variety of implementation arrangements suits the peculiarities and differences of the five industries. What about the strategies? Are there conclusions to be drawn as to what works and what doesn't work? It seems reasonable to conclude that the more accommodative positions of the alcoholic beverage groups and of the casino gambling interests have bought some "slack" for these industries. Certainly there are still advocacy groups that would like to ban gambling of all kinds, and presumably there are those who really *would* like to return to Prohibition. But these are extreme positions, and it appears that the mainstream of American thought is relatively tolerant of these two consumer preferences. Accommodative efforts, genuinely undertaken, have tended to reduce the numbers of the opposition and softened their positions.

The opposite approach, a consistently adversarial strategy, appears to have had little in the way of positive consequences for tobacco. Throughout much of the 1990s and the early years of the twenty-first century, the tide has been running against this industry; and its opponents, both in advocacy groups and in governmental bureaus and legislatures, have definitely grown in number and in influence. To what extent an adversarial public affairs strategy has caused this continued drain on the legitimacy of cigarettes is difficult to say; it is reasonable to conclude that it has been a contributing factor.

NOTES

1. "About the NRA-ILA," http://www.nraila.org (accessed May 18, 2002).

2. Ibid.

3. NRA Institute for Legislative Action, *Ten Myths about Gun Control*, October 1994, 17.

4. American Gaming Association brochure, October 1995.

5. Letter from Frank Fahrenkopf, Jr. to Congressman Frank R. Wolf, dated August 9, 1995.

6. Joanne Lipman, "Sobering View: Alcohol Firms Put Off Public," *Wall Street Journal*, August 21, 1991, B1.

7. The Century Council, press kit.

8. Anheuser-Busch Companies, Inc., *Annual Report 2000*, 5.

9. Philip Morris Companies, Inc., *2000 Annual Report*, 12–13.

10. Adolph Coors Company, *2002 Annual Report*, www.coors.com/2002_annrpt/ shareholder (accessed October 13, 2003).

11. The Seagram Company Ltd., *Report for the Fiscal Year Ended January 31, 1995*.

12. Beer Institute brochure, "Advancing a Great American Tradition."

13. Ibid.

14. Ibid.; and Beer Institute, *Safeguarding an American Tradition, Beer Institute Annual Report 1994–95*, Washington, DC. See also Beer Institute, *Annual Report, 2000–2001*, 1.

15. *Beer Institute Annual Report 1994–95*.

16. Lawrence Wallack, in testimony in support of Senate bill S. 674, The Sensible Advertising and Family Education Act of 1993.

17. Ibid.

18. Center for Science in the Public Interest, "Alcohol Advertising Facts," October 1994.

19. George Franke and Gary Wilcox, "Alcohol Beverage Advertising and Consumption in the United States, 1964–1984," *Journal of Advertising* 16, no. 3 (1987): 22–30.

20. Joel W. Grube and Lawrence Wallack, "Television Beer Advertising and Drinking Knowledge, Beliefs, and Intentions among Schoolchildren," *American Journal of Public Health* 84, no. 2 (February 1994): 254–59.

21. Center for Science in the Public Interest, "Alcohol Advertising Facts," October 1994.

22. The Marin Institute for the Prevention of Alcohol and Other Drug Problems, "Sell a Case, Save a Kid? Activists Knock Health Charities for Taking Alcohol $," Newsletter, Winter 1993, 3–5.

23. Philip Morris Companies, Inc., *1994 Annual Report*, 4–5.

24. Lauren Neergaard, "Tobacco Firm on Offensive," *Monterey Herald*, May 17, 1994, 2A.

25. Barbara Rosewicz, "Voters Break New Ground with Oregon's Suicide Law," *Wall Street Journal*, November 10, 1994, A9.

26. Maria Mallory, "Full-Flavored, Unfiltered Statehouse Shenanigans," *Business Week*, May 22, 1995, 52.

27. "Call from Philip Morris," *Washington Times*, October 1, 1994, D4, as reported in Katherine Dahlmeier, *Philip Morris Companies, Inc. and the Issue of Secondhand Smoke* (unpublished paper).

28. Steve Coll, "Tobacco Companies Turn Up Heat on Firms Pushing Smoking Bans," *Washington Post*, April 7, 1988, E1.

29. RJR Nabisco, *Annual Report*, 1994.

30. Alix M. Freedman, "Tobacco Firms, Pariahs to Many People, Still Are Angels to the Arts," *Wall Street Journal*, June 8, 1988, 1.

31. See Michael Pertschuk, *Smoke in Their Eyes* (Nashville, TN: Vanderbilt University Press, 2001).

32. Gordon Fairclough, "Philip Morris Is Hit with $3 Billion Verdict," *Wall Street Journal*, June 7, 2001, A3.

33. Gordon Fairclough, "Philip Morris to Pick Insider Camilleri as Next CEO," *Wall Street Journal*, January 30, 2002, B1.

34. Pertschuk, *Smoke in Their Eyes*, 247.

35. Ibid.

36. Myron Levin, "The Tobacco Industry's Strange Bedfellows," *Business & Society Review* (Spring 1988): 11–17.

37. Thomas P. Houston, M.D., ed., *Tobacco Use: An American Crisis, Final Report of the Conference* (American Medical Association, 1993).

38. A. Lee Fritschler, *Smoking and Politics: Policymaking and the Federal Bureaucracy* (Englewood Cliffs, NJ: Prentice-Hall Inc., 1983), 110, 112.

39. Suein L. Hwang, "Philip Morris Agrees to Stop Placing Ads in View of TV," *Wall Street Journal*, June 7, 1995, B1.

40. Steven C. Parrish, "Bridging the Divide: A Shared Interest in a Coherent National Tobacco Policy," *Yale Journal of Health Policy, Law, and Ethics* 3, no. 1 (winter 2002): 111.

CHAPTER 14

Summing Up

In the long run, a company's right to continue in business is granted by society, not by its profitability. If an organization is to maximize its return to its shareholders, it must maximize its contribution to the society in which it operates. This means earning and maintaining the trust of that society—in other words, establishing the firm's legitimacy—and marketers have a critical role to play in this.

The marketing questions we have explored in this book are extraordinary ones. They are different than the problems discussed in most marketing texts because these deal with the fundamental relationship between business and society. This is an interactive relationship. It is clear that the decisions made by marketers will affect how society accepts the firm and its products. Equally clear is that the extent to which society grants its approval—grants legitimacy—will have a major impact on the firm and especially on its marketing function.

All of the foregoing material has been focused on five specific industries because they are good examples for illustrating what happens when an industry begins to lose its legitimacy. At this time in the United States, tobacco, alcoholic beverages, firearms, gambling, and pornography all face the challenges of a hostile environment and significant opposition by various groups for a variety of reasons.

In other industries, under other circumstances, similar marketing challenges can arise due to specific products, even though the company and the industry are given a relatively clean bill of health by society. For example, there is little criticism of the chemical industry in its entirety, although specific products such as certain agricultural chemicals and napalm for military use have encountered severe opposition. No one finds the athletic shoe industry qua industry unacceptable, although there has been sharp criticism of the employment practices of the contractors who manufacture the shoes and of the marketing of very expensive shoes in low-income neighborhoods. There is general acceptance now of biotechnology products used for medical purposes, although genetically engineered bovine growth hormone to stimulate milk production in the dairy industry, along with other biotech products used in the food industry, still encounter severe opposition. In other words, problems of legitimacy and social unacceptability can crop up in specific areas of otherwise perfectly respected and accepted product lines, companies, and industries.

Marketers across all industries can therefore benefit from studying the lessons, experiences, and challenges described in this book. Of course, there are no universally applicable solutions. More precisely, there are no "solutions" at all. Even amongst the five industries studied here there are no tactics or strategies that can be considered applicable across the board. Just as one product's marketing strategy, no matter how successful, cannot be replicated and used with any guarantee of similar success for a different product, or in a different industry, so too one company's approach to dealing with problems of social unacceptability cannot be prescribed across product lines or across industries. In marketing, as in all social science fields, there are simply too many variables—too many differences in products, markets, company cultures, and surrounding environments.

Therefore, as with any case analysis work, the benefits for marketers will come from the generation of ideas, from seeing what has or has not worked under a particular set of circumstances, and from using that knowledge to tailor a strategy to the marketer's unique needs and conditions.

What are some of the lessons we as marketers can learn from the material collected in this book?

EXPANSION OF MARKET

Perhaps the first lesson to be learned is that the most basic objectives of marketing—to expand the business, to attract new customers, and to increase usage of the product—all must be reconsidered if the product category or the industry faces questions of social acceptability. Critics may tolerate continued consumption or usage of the product by current customers, but the degree of opposition will increase dramatically when manufacturers are perceived as going after new markets, recruiting new customers, or even trying to increase usage. To encourage people to gamble more, to drink more alcoholic beverages, or certainly to smoke more would be totally unacceptable and would be like pouring fuel on the opposition's fire. To give the appearance of encouraging non-gamblers to begin buying lottery tickets (as with the slogan "You can't win if you don't play") or to encourage nonsmokers to take up the habit (you can be cool like Joe Camel or rugged and individualistic like the Marlboro Man) is a dangerous message in terms of inflaming the critics. Even the tobacco companies, in their public relations utterances if not in their actions, eschew recruiting new smokers. After five decades of mounting evidence about the health problems associated with smoking, the firms now acknowledge some risks, but counter that many products, even Twinkies, present risks and insist that adults should make their own individual choices.

The firearms industry presents a definite exception to this rule. To the extent that the National Rifle Association (NRA) represents the views and furthers the strategy of the industry's member firms, the message that it projects is that more and more people who do not now own guns should acquire them! In spite of a high level of social protest, in spite of very active and vocal advocacy groups working to limit the spread of guns, especially handguns, the NRA and the industry are not backing down or softening in any way their marketing efforts to increase the size of the market by recruiting new customers.

The marketers of cigarettes and beer, on the other hand, claim that all of their formidable marketing budgets and efforts are aimed only at current consumers. They claim not to be trying to attract new customers, only to defend, or better yet to increase, their current market share. In other words, they say they are not trying to increase the size of the pie, only to get a larger slice of the present pie. In previous chapters, we have shown that these claims are widely disputed by the industries' opponents.

This battle of words—of claims and counterclaims—can never be won. Inevitably, consumer advertising that a manufacturer insists is meant to defend or increase its brand's market share will be perceived by critics as meant to entice new users. Circumstantial evidence can be gathered—for example, that 75 percent of underage smokers smoke the three most heavily advertised brands—yet the cigarette companies will insist that the intent of their ads is not to attract new, young smokers. By extension, all consumer advertising for socially unacceptable industries or products becomes suspect because it would seem to legitimate the use of that product in our society.

Under these conditions, an argument can be advanced that a manufacturer should emphasize a "push" rather than "pull" strategy. Promotion budget dollars should be shifted away from consumer advertising and consumer-oriented sales promotion tactics, which are the most visible elements of the entire marketing mix and the most subject to public scrutiny, into increased marketing efforts directed at the trade channels, which are less obvious and less likely to incite the product's critics. Larger and more active sales organizations making more calls on retailers and increased dealer incentives should result in increased sales and market share without triggering the level of opposition that consumer advertising is certain to initiate.

It would be naive to suppose that in a mature industry such as cigarettes or beer, dominated by a few large, powerful competitors, that any one company could unilaterally reduce its consumer advertising dramatically. Even though the benefits of advertising are notoriously difficult to measure, very few marketing executives are daring enough to cut back on advertising their brands and risk losing some market share that would be very expensive to regain. The threat is simply too great. Nevertheless, there can be important shifts, especially when an entire industry moves in the same direction. Between 1996 and 2001 the tobacco industry more than doubled the amount it spent on coupons and "retain value added" (promotions such as buy one, get one free, for example) while media advertising (newspapers, magazines, outdoor and transit) has been cut drastically in large measure due to the MSA restrictions. What is suggested here is that in the planning of an overall marketing strategy, in the budget allocation process, the avoidance of social criticism is an additional factor to consider in weighing the relative merits of consumer advertising versus trade promotions.

THE WOES OF TARGETING; PRICING AND DISTRIBUTION ISSUES

As important as precise, careful targeting is in the marketing of most products, it is almost certain to backfire in the marketing of socially unacceptable goods. As we have seen, targeting is meant to identify segments of the market with some common characteristics so that a specific marketing strategy can be developed that will be especially effective with that defined group. Critics of the product can readily paint this as a picture of exploitation: a large, billion-dollar corporation zeroing in on a small segment of our society, employing all of its marketing muscle and persuasive powers to increase the sales of its product. When the product carries some risk or danger—as do all socially unacceptable products— and when the targeted segment is perceived as being vulnerable in any way, this creates an exploitative situation that simply is intolerable in our society.

Problems can surface as a result of targeting with a wide variety of groups: women, racial or ethnic minorities, the elderly, or lower income groups. But no targeted group arouses more sympathy and protection than do children. Remember that the five product categories studied in this book have been defined by our society as adult products, and so there is a natural inclination for young people, especially teens, to be attracted to the products as a way of assuming adulthood. When cigarette manufacturers, brewers, or pornography merchants are perceived as targeting children, therefore, a strong backlash of social pressure and criticism is unleashed. Many possible measures have been suggested to constrain the marketing of tobacco products, including higher excise taxes and the disallowance of advertising as a tax-deductible expense, but the tobacco control program brought forward by the FDA in 1995, and many of the Master Settlement Agreement terms of 1998, were all about protecting children because the Clinton administration recognized this would have the widest popular appeal. In a similar vein, it is the protection of children from the pornography to be found in popular music lyrics, in 900-number telephone messages, and in cyberspace that engenders the most widespread attention and support.

The lesson or message to marketers, then, is obvious. If your product is socially unacceptable to some degree, choose targets with the greatest of caution. Targeting almost any group other than well-to-do white males will be criticized. And by all means, avoid even the perception of targeting children.

Just as with targeting, pricing decisions must be made with an eye as to how they will be perceived by the market, especially by the product's critics. With mainstream products, low prices are not only accepted but welcomed as an introductory tactic or as a way to move potential customers to the trial or adoption stages of the product adoption process, but this is not so with socially unacceptable products. Special prices on cigarettes or alcoholic beverages for the purpose of attracting new consumers or encouraging present customers to consume more are certain to ignite a storm of protest.

The price lining of the major brewers—Anheuser-Busch's Michelob in the super premium category, Budweiser at the premium level, and Busch at popular prices, for example—must be administered as simply catering to the needs of beer drinkers in different income brackets. This is also true with regard to the premium, value, and generic or private-label cigarette brands. Philip Morris's fateful price cut on Marlboro and its other premium brands in 1993 had to be explained as a desperate measure to regain market share from the generics and private labels, which it indeed was. Handgun control advocates are especially critical of cheap "Saturday-night specials" because they are purposely priced low to encourage increased sales.

Casinos have an advantage in that they can disguise their price promotions. Traditionally they have offered their hotel rooms and meals—and sometimes even their Hollywood extravaganza shows—at quite reasonable prices, not to mention free drinks for those gambling at the tables. A thin disguise, perhaps, but the low prices are associated with the rooms, food, and drinks rather than directly with the gambling.

Distribution strategies used by producers of socially unacceptable products have received less attention than targeting, pricing, promotion, and product line management decisions. If a product, such as any one of our five, is subject to a significant degree of social criticism, it would seem to make sense to *shorten* to whatever extent possible the channel of distribution. The longer the product is in the stream of commerce and the more hands it passes through, the more public exposure it receives and the more likely it is that it will be criticized.

From the producer's viewpoint, the ideal form of distribution is direct to the consumer. This entails the least amount of public exposure. For convenience goods such as beer and cigarettes, which in theory and in practice require the longest channels and the widest distribution, this would be impossible. However, it is widely accepted that the major cigarette manufacturers are building enormous databases of their customers in the hopes of being able to turn this information at some point into a direct marketing program. Pornographic conversations through 900 telephone numbers are a form of direct distribution, as are the various pornography sites on the Internet.

Public policy interests point in the opposite direction. Whether the product is guns, alcoholic beverages, cigarettes, lottery tickets, or slot machine bets, whatever social and regulatory controls are to be exercised—and whatever taxes are to be collected—require that these products be distributed through a totally open and transparent system. There are already prohibitions against distributing guns and alcoholic beverages through the mail. Cigarette companies have been stymied so far in selling by mail due to the problem of verifying minimum age requirements. But there are still plenty of proposals being floated for at-home betting on horse races, lotteries, or even casinos in cyberspace, and the prospect of five hundred channels being available for television viewing raises the prospects of direct access to more X-rated movies and more pornography channels.

ADDRESSING THE ISSUES

There comes a time for every firm facing social pressures, criticism, and disapproval when the issues on which that disapproval is based must be addressed. How will the firm defend itself, its products, and its right to continue in business? Making adjustments to the firm's marketing strategy—promotion mix, product line management, pricing decisions, choice of targets, and so on—while necessary and helpful, does not deal with the underlying problem. Can the criticism at least be blunted, if not silenced? Can the critics be isolated and industry supporters be organized and energized? Can some degree of legitimacy be restored?

Accomplishing these tasks goes well beyond the normal duties of the firm's public relations department and beyond the traditional scope of marketing strategy. But we have considered them in this book because they are in fact public relations issues, they must be coordinated carefully with the everyday marketing activities of the firm, and because they are absolutely crucial to the success of the firm over the long run.

In reviewing the five industries that we have studied in this book several common themes emerge.

Deflect the Criticism

Perhaps the most common ploy in attempting to deal with social criticism is to deflect the criticism away from the firm's core products. The alcoholic beverage and gambling industries have been rather successful in doing this; the National Rifle Association, as a stand-in for the firearms industry, has also used this tactic with somewhat less success.

Alcoholic beverages are not the problem, insist the industry representatives, certainly not as they are normally used and as they should be used. The problems lie with the users' behavior: excessive drinking, underage drinking, and drunk driving. The industry strives to focus social attention on these limited issues and works *with* its critics on developing and financing programs to deal with them. The hope, of course, is that this will leave the industry relatively free to produce and market wine, beer, and spirits with a minimum of controversy.

"Guns don't commit murders; people do," is the message from the NRA. Firearms themselves are simply tools, essential for various sports and personal protection. It is the criminal use or careless use of guns that must be curbed. To this end, the NRA and the industry sponsor training classes for the proper use of guns and safe shooting for both children and adults.

The gambling industry has followed the same course. Gambling per se is not the problem; it is excessive gambling that society must prevent, and the industry demonstrates its concern by providing money and initiative to ameliorate the problem. Changing the word "gambling" to "gaming" is also a tactic to deflect criticism, as is the transformation of a casino into a total family entertainment complex. How can anyone criticize games and family fun?

The tobacco industry has stumbled badly in its inability to deflect criticism from its core products and now confronts an intractable problem. Scientific studies have now confirmed that *any* level of smoking is harmful to one's health—and to the health of those around the smoker. For sixty years, the tobacco firms have known about these health concerns and have attempted to hide them. Ever since the 1950s and 1960s, when the smoking and health problems first came to the public's attention, the firms have reduced the tar and nicotine content in many of their cigarettes but have been unwilling to remove all of it—to develop a "safe" cigarette—because smokers prefer the taste and the "lift" that the tars and nicotine provide.

The long run viability and legitimacy of the industry was sacrificed to meet quarterly and annual sales and profit goals.

Cure is Worse than the Disease

An alternative to the deflection strategy is to try to show that whatever social concerns are raised by the industry's products, they are less serious than the critics' proposed solutions. Marketers of pornography answer their critics by waving the First Amendment banner. Censorship, they proclaim, and the loss of freedom of speech is a far more serious threat to our society than pornographic magazines and videos that people, after all, can either buy or ignore as they choose.

The NRA also uses this approach, but its rallying cry is the Second Amendment. Whatever social ills gun critics complain about, whatever the level of violence in our society, however many deaths are the result of guns and their proliferation—as serious as these problems may be, they are not as serious as the threat to Americans of whittling away at the freedoms guaranteed by the Bill of Rights. When gun control advocates warn of violence and death resulting from handguns and assault weapons, the NRA and allied organizations warn of midnight searches of our homes and property by "jackbooted" federal agents.

This is also the thrust of the 1994–95 institutional ad campaigns sponsored by Philip Morris and Reynolds Tobacco. In response to the FDA's proposals for limiting the sale of cigarettes to minors, Reynolds ran full-page newspaper ads showing a smirking, corpulent, generally unattractive man over the headline, "WHO SHOULD BE RESPONSIBLE FOR YOUR CHILDREN, A BUREAUCRAT OR YOU?" The copy went on to read, "Right now, the Federal bureaucracy wants to tell you and your children how to behave." The ads called for "an informed debate" and ended with the tagline, "Together, we can work it out." Here again, the message is perfectly clear. As Reynolds framed the debate, whatever social problems are associated with tobacco, they are not nearly so dangerous as the proposed solution, which would mean more regulations, that is, more bureaucracy and less freedom of individual choice.

The Economics Card

If there is one thing that the five industries represented in this book have in common, it is that each of them, when confronted with criticism based on social concerns or moral values, responds with a justification based on economics. This fundamental struggle between personal, material well-being and moral principles is as old as Adam and Eve's fateful decision to taste the forbidden apple.

Every proposal for a new gambling enterprise—a riverboat for Indiana, a casino for Baltimore, a racetrack for Tennessee—promises more jobs and more tax revenues for the state. Never does the proposal try to convince us that gambling is a virtuous and healthy form of entertainment; the argument is that the economic benefits outweigh the social costs. How does a state government rationalize being in the business of owning and operating a gambling enterprise (i.e., a lottery)? Only by appealing to the economic necessities of the state and assuring the electorate that the social consequences will not be so bad.

What is the tobacco industry's response when the federal government proposes a stiff hike in the excise tax on cigarettes? The benefits to society would seem unassailable: reduced consumption, especially among teen-agers, and the resulting improvements in public health. Inevitably, the response comes in the form of warnings of economic chaos. Hundreds of thousands of jobs would be lost just in the convenience store industry. End U.S. government intervention to insure advertising of American cig-arettes in foreign countries? This would have a terrible effect on our bal-ance of payments. Restrict cigarette advertising in any of a dozen ways? The entire advertising industry joins the chorus warning of lost jobs and economic disruption.

Even in the business of pornography, adult videos are defended by explaining just how important they are to the profitable operation of most movie rental stores.

And so the debate is framed. With the exception of the firearms industry, or more specifically the NRA, the marketers of these socially unacceptable products do not try to convince us that the character of their products has been unfairly impugned. Alcoholic beverage and gambling proponents readily admit that their products are sometimes used to excess and, as noted, join with their critics in looking for solutions. Purveyors of por-nography recognize that their product should be purchased only by adults and are willing to join in the effort to keep it away from children. Even cigarette marketers now reluctantly admit that there are health risks as-sociated with their product. For all of these industry representatives, however, the economic justification is sufficient: jobs for workers and managers, taxes for governments, contracts for suppliers, and profits for shareholders.

Cynics may assume that economics always will win out over morality, but such is not the case. Questions of health and safety, and especially the protection of our children, are often enough to tip the balance in favor of social and moral values. Tobacco products are certainly still with us, but because of the now unassailable health concerns, significant restrictions have been imposed on how they are marketed. And the percentage of the adult population that smokes is now less than half what it was at its peak forty or fifty years ago. This is hardly a triumph for morality, especially not on the part of the tobacco industry; it is a victory for public health policy over the daunting economic arguments raised by the industry. Economic pressures, along with social preferences, may have rescued the alcoholic beverage industries from Prohibition, but when Mothers Against Drunk Driving framed the issue as the safety of our children, our society was willing to get tough on the problem of underage drinking. And the setbacks for gambling in the 1994 elections show that in some states and under some circumstances the electorate will give social and moral values the priority over economic arguments.

LEGITIMACY: LOST, MAINTAINED, REGAINED?

Finally, a review of these five industries and their marketing strategies must offer some insights regarding the question of legitimacy—for individual companies or for entire industries. Legitimacy itself is difficult enough just to define because it is dependant on the shifting sands of public opinion and social mores; it is all the more difficult to try to measure the legitimacy of a firm or an industry or to determine whether that legitimacy is waxing or waning.

Over the years, a number of scholars have developed approaches and models that can certainly help in this effort, even if they do not provide definitive or precise answers. For example, Charles Summer suggested that when firms find themselves in the "conflict stage" of their life cycle—and all of our five industries are in such a conflict situation—the question becomes whether the "zone of opposition" or the "zone of approval" will expand at the expense of the other.[1] In these terms, we can conclude that for the tobacco companies, their zone of opposition has without question been growing at the expense of their zone of approval. The gambling firms are experiencing just the opposite.

Ed Epstein and Dow Votaw have suggested three strategies by which firms can deal with challenges to their legitimacy: adapt to society's values, change society's values, or associate with other organizations that enjoy legitimacy.[2] The major brewers have taken some steps along the first of these paths, the tobacco firms and the NRA have chosen the second, and the gambling companies, to the extent they have allied themselves with the hospitality industry, have opted for the third.

Christine Oliver has created a framework, shown in a slightly adapted form in table 14.1, for classifying companies' responses to societal pressures.[3] The tobacco and firearms industries have been pursuing the manipulation and defiance strategies, alcoholic beverages and gambling have chosen avoidance and sometimes compromise, while pornography lies somewhere in between, choosing defiance on some occasions and avoidance on others.

Table 14.1
A Typology of Business Response to Social Pressures

Strategies	Tactics
Manipulate	Control Influence Co-opt
Defy	Attack Challenge Dismiss
Avoid	Escape Buffer Conceal
Compromise	Bargain Pacify Balance
Acquiesce	Comply Imitate Habit

Accommodation or Opposition

More is at stake here than simply marketing a product. We are discussing the marketing of the firm, or perhaps the entire industry—how that firm or industry will relate and respond to the society in which it is operating. But the different levels of marketing are inescapably linked. The decision of Reynolds Tobacco to continue the Joe Camel ad campaign for a year or more even after strong protests from critics is a part of the firm's, and the industry's, broader decision to choose a defiant stance against its detractors. The brewers' willingness to promote responsible drinking and similar messages are part of their choice of "compromise" and "pacify" as their corporate and industry marketing strategies.

Ultimately, the marketing of socially unacceptable products comes down to a choice of accommodation or opposition between a firm and the society in which it is embedded. Can the firm find a way to adapt its product and the way it promotes and distributes it, perhaps even shift its choice of target markets, to fit more comfortably within society's constraints? Or will it choose opposition and continue to fight a rearguard, minimize-our-losses kind of action?

The tobacco firms operated very profitably under the latter strategy for several decades, so one cannot simply dismiss that choice. It is carried out, however, at great cost to the firms and to society, and there is scant hope for anything but a continuously deteriorating situation. For tobacco, the current legal morass, the threat of billion-dollar jury penalties, and the specter of bankruptcy suggest that such an opposition strategy cannot prevail forever. For any kind of healthy, long-term relationship, however—if there is to be any hope for legitimacy—there must be a congruence between the operating decisions of the firm and the expectations of society. Achieving this relationship falls on the shoulders of the firm's managers and especially its marketers; it will depend on the decisions they make, the tactics they choose, and the strategies they develop.

NOTES

1. Charles Summer, *Strategic Behavior in Business and Government*, (Boston, MA: Little, Brown and Company, 1980), 18–26.

2. Edwin M. Epstein and Dow Votaw, eds., *Rationality, Legitimacy, Responsibility* (Santa Monica, CA: Goodyear Publishing Company, Inc., 1978).

3. Christine Oliver, "Strategic Responses to Institutional Processes," *Academy of Management Review* 16, no. 1 (1991): 145–79.

Index

About the Author

D. KIRK DAVIDSON is Associate Professor and Chair of the Department of Business, Accounting, and Economics at Mount Saint Mary's College in Emmitsburg, Maryland.

DATE DUE

OCT 3 1 2010			
DEC 2 2 2010			
GAYLORD			PRINTED IN U.S.A.